CURRICU ER

D1384298

Fluency and its Tec

MODERN LANGUAGES in PRACTICE

The Modern Languages in Practice Series provides publications on the theory and practice of modern foreign language teaching. The theoretical and practical discussions in the publications arise from, and are related to, research into the subject. *Practical* is defined as having pedagogic value. *Theoretical* is defined as illuminating and/or generating issues pertinent to the practical. Theory and practice are, however, understood as a continuum. The series includes books at three distinct points along this continuum: (1) Limited discussions of language learning issues. These publications provide an outlet for coverage of actual classroom activities and exercises. (2) Aspects of both theory and practice combined in broadly equal amounts. This is the *core of the series*, and books may appear in the form of collections bringing together writers from different fields. (3) More theoretical books examining key research ideas directly relevant to the teaching of modern languages.

Series Editor
Michael Grenfell, *Centre for Language in Education, University of Southampton*

Editorial Board
Do Coyle, *School of Education, University of Nottingham*
Simon Green, *Trinity & All Saints College, Leeds*

Editorial Consultant
Christopher Brumfit, *Centre for Language in Education, University of Southampton*

Other Books in the Series
Cric Crac! Teaching and Learning French through Story-telling
    ROY DUNNING
Effective Language Learning
    SUZANNE GRAHAM
The Elements of Foreign Language Teaching
    WALTER GRAUBERG
The Good Language Learner
    N. NAIMAN, M. FRÖHLICH, H.H. STERN and A. TODESCO
Inspiring Innovations in Language Teaching
    JUDITH HAMILTON
Le ou La? The Gender of French Nouns
    MARIE SURRIDGE
Switched on? Video Resources in Modern Language Settings
    STEVEN FAWKES
Target Language, Collaborative Learning and Autonomy
    ERNESTO MACARO
Training Teachers in Practice
    MICHAEL GRENFELL
Validation in Language Testing
    A. CUMMING and R. BERWICK (eds)

Please contact us for the latest book information:
Multilingual Matters, Frankfurt Lodge, Clevedon Hall
Victoria Road, Clevedon, BS21 7HH, England
http://www.multilingual-matters.com

MODERN LANGUAGES IN PRACTICE
Series Editor: Michael Grenfell

Fluency and its Teaching

Marie-Noëlle Guillot

MULTILINGUAL MATTERS LTD
Clevedon • Philadelphia • Toronto • Sydney

Library of Congress Cataloging in Publication Data

Guillot, Marie-Noëlle
Fluency and its Teaching/Marie-Noëlle Guillot
Modern Languages in Practice: 11
Includes bibliographical references and index
1. Language and languages–Study and teaching. 2. Oral communication–Study and teaching. I. Title. II. Series.
P53.6.G85   1999
418'.007–dc21   98-31864

British Library Cataloguing in Publication Data

A CIP catalogue record for this book is available from the British Library.

ISBN 1-85359-440-7 (hbk)
ISBN 1-85359-439-3 (pbk)

Multilingual Matters Ltd

UK: Frankfurt Lodge, Clevedon Hall, Victoria Road, Clevedon BS21 7HH.
USA: 325 Chestnut Street, Philadelphia, PA 19106, USA.
Canada: 5201 Dufferin Street, North York, Ontario M3H 5T8, Canada.
Australia: P.O. Box 586, Artamon, NSW, Australia.

Typeset by Archetype-IT Ltd (http://www.archetype-IT.com).
Printed and bound in Great Britain by WBC Book Manufacturers Ltd.

Contents

Preface

This book addresses a fundamental question: what kind of analysis of the spoken language is appropriate to the assessment and fostering of fluency at the various stages of a student's development?

Fluency is an elusive notion. It has a foot in almost every language-related discipline, without being the province of any one in particular, and crosses over boundaries in a way which has made it resistant to analysis and rationalisation, even within applied linguistics. Yet it is peculiarly available to all, language specialists and non-specialists, as a measure of oral performance, and is used with a confidence which hardly seems justified in view of the scarcity of accounts governed by anything other than intuition. Like the concept itself, the assumptions which underpin classroom approaches to fluency have remained mostly uninspected: practice may well make fluent, but is practice alone enough to enable students to locate themselves on the complicated map of fluency, and make optimal use of the various inputs to which they are exposed?

Fluency, in other words, is still beset by many questions, which this book sets out to revisit: it is both an enquiry into fluency, and an argument for doing it pedagogical justice. The first part deals with fluency in general terms, from different points of view, in different contexts, in order to map out appropriate pedagogic frameworks. The second part takes up the exploration with analyses of samples of speech focusing on key aspects and features of fluency, and doubles up as a methodological platform for promoting a more critical and informed approach to its teaching. Applications are targeted at advanced learners, of French specifically, but are handled generically, in the form of transferable principles which can be adapted to other levels and other languages.

While the pedagogic motives of the investigation and the material it covers make it particularly relevant to those involved with language learning (teachers, teacher trainers, applied linguists and their students), the issues it raises and the opportunities for the comparative study of languages it provides are equally pertinent to linguists.

Acknowledgements

My grateful thanks to all those, near and far, who gave me trust, support and momentum, or time away from them: Christopher Brumfit, Roger Fowler, Michael Grenfell, Clive Scott, my sister (for the samples of her and her pupils' speech), colleagues and friends, Clive, Sam and Tom. This book is dedicated to the memory of Betty and Denis.

Introduction

Fostering oral production, and fluency, has long had pride of place in FL teaching. It has been a cornerstone of communicative methodology: social intercourse is the immediate living function of language, and fluency the desideratum. But few proponents of communicative teaching, or indeed other approaches, have stopped to consider what a pedagogy of fluency is: while the close connection between aural reception and oral production is insisted upon, the teaching process turns out, by and large, to be the same as the objective — interpersonal exchange. Fluency, it seems, cannot be taught; it is largely left to emerge as a by-product of verbal involvement, and out of opportunities created for it to do so: situational dialogue, role-play, group discussion, debate, simulation. Not only that, but the concept of fluency itself remains mostly uninspected. Is speaking fluently the same as speaking with someone fluently? What features identify fluent speech? Is everyone fluent in the same way?

Even when applied linguists directly confront the issue of fluency, they often remain evasive or non-committal, when they do not sidestep it. In Hammerly's book *Fluency and Accuracy* (1991), for instance, fluency, despite its prominence in the title, is in the end dealt with directly in little more than a few footnotes and cursory remarks. Hammerly's motives are unambiguous. His central theme is this:

> balanced results in SL teaching are possible only when a beginning and intermediate emphasis on linguistic accuracy gradually shifts to an advanced emphasis on communicative fluency with accuracy (Hammerly, 1991: 55).

The thesis drives homes what the stress on '*and* accuracy' retrospectively makes clear enough: the book is essentially a reappraisal of accuracy and of systematic structural instruction in the classroom, based on a denunciation of the shortcomings of communicative approaches. What misgivings he has about what he describes as the trappings of 'ingrained classroom pidging' are reflected in the points he makes about fluency as an addendum to his first chapter:

1

Although the word "fluency" has long been used in everyday speech to mean speaking rapidly *and well*, in our field it has largely come to mean speaking rapidly and smoothly, not necessarily grammatically. This is the way the word will be used in this book, in contrast to "accuracy" (control of the code) (Hammerly, 1991: 12);

and again to his fourth chapter:

As the average English speaker understands it, fluency in an SL doesn't just mean speaking it rapidly and smoothly but also accurately. In our field however, "fluency" has come to emphasise rapidity, smoothness and "confidence" (often false confidence) in communication. It is this narrower usage of "fluency" in our field that is differentiated from "accuracy" in this book (p. 51).

The message about communicative laxity is plain, and no doubt reflects widely shared, and justifiable, concerns. But what is to be made of 'fluency'? Is there a consensus amongst native speakers, amongst applied linguists, on what speaking well means? Is rapidity a universal virtue in speech? What is the difference, or the relationship, between speaking well (NL) and speaking smoothly and accurately (SL)? What *is* accuracy in speech? Is fluency exclusively a speaker's attribute?

Other comments in Hammerly's text suggest that that there may be some ground for addressing these questions. How, for instance, is 'speaking well' to be interpreted, in its application to NS speech, when features like those referred to in the following proviso implicitly signal that it may need to be qualified?

We counted as errors only what no French speaker would say, discounting *colloquialisms, false starts, self-corrected errors, and so forth* (in studies of student oral production in Canadian French, [emphasis added]) (Hammerly: 4)

Or again, what is the part of the objective and the subjective in the listeners' assessment of the interlocutor's fluency if, as we are told:

Communication is most effective when it is grammatical, *when the attention of the listener is not drawn away from the message to linguistic errors.* (p. 44 [emphasis added])?

What hierarchy of criteria can be assumed to govern the listener's response? What is in fact the interlocutor's role in establishing what fluency is in a given exchange? And what are the implications of a statement like this:

While communicative feedback no doubt helps SL learners become more effective communicators, it rarely has a sufficiently linguistic focus to help improve control of specific SL structures (p. 80)

Could it begin to suggest, albeit indirectly, that fluency is negotiated?

Hammerly does not, in the end, engage with these issues. His understandable concern for greater linguistic discipline, and the resulting bias towards accuracy, relegates them to a background which takes much about fluency itself as read. Yet if fluency is to come into the equation at all, particularly at advanced stages, is it unreasonable to expect closer scrutiny of the concept, not least in its relation to accuracy?

This tendency to gloss over fluency is not uncharacteristic. On the whole, the notion has received comparatively little focused attention: while references to it in applied linguistics are frequent, attempts to circumscribe it and get to grips with what is involved are few, in a field otherwise so punctilious in defining its concepts. The term, like others in FL teaching (e.g. 'mistake' and 'error'), is borrowed from everyday language. Unlike them, however, its meaning has not undergone any significant adaptation, become tailored to the requirements of the field (see Corder's definitions of the above [1981]), or been the object of the kind of extensive discussions about interpretation generated by other recurrent concepts (e.g. learning/ acquisition, [communicative] competence/performance). Although the question of fluency is sometimes signalled as a problem area (see Faerch & Kasper's 1983 compilation of articles for example), its meaning on the whole tends to be simply assumed, taken for granted, or elusively defined — explicitly or implicitly — as something like 'ease of communication' or 'smoothness of expression', that is to say in ways reminiscent of general dictionary definitions.

Is this to say that 'fluency' should be understood in line with current dictionary definitions and uses? The *Oxford English Dictionary* (1933, reprinted 1961) defines *fluency*, in its language-related entries, as

> A smooth and easy flow; readiness, smoothness *esp.* with regard to speech (2.a.);
> Absence of rigidity; ease (2.b.);
> Readiness of utterance, flow of words (3.).

But to what features can these qualities be traced in speech? How does all this fit in with the fact that, as Goldman-Eisler points out, 'spontaneous speech is a highly fragmented and discontinuous activity' (Goldman-Eisler, 1968: 31), or with her observation that:

> When, even at its most fluent, two thirds of spoken language comes in chunks of less than six words, the attributes of flow and fluency must be judged an illusion (p. 31)?

There is, besides, the question of individual interpretation: Leeson reminds us that the word fluency 'appears to mean many things to many people and is bandied about with an ease and confidence which seems wholly unjustified when individuals are invited to define their terms even a little' (Leeson, 1975: 2); Brumfit acknowledges that 'even in common usage, "fluency" is difficult to define' (Brumfit, 1984: 53). How, then, can a term be "borrowed" from common usage and integrated in discussions as if its meaning were clear when it is apparently so difficult to make sense of?

Should it, on the other hand, be assumed that the meaning of fluency is somehow unequivocal in language teaching itself, that there is a consensus about the nature of its discourse and other features — to the extent that what it involves does not even need to be specified other than in very broad terms? Or is this want of clarification an invitation to treat the few studies dealing with fluency in applied linguistics as points of shared reference? Leeson, unhelpfully drawing on Chomsky's 1965 definition of linguistic competence to describe what is in fact a dimension of performance, defines fluency as:

> the ability of the speaker to produce indefinitely many sentences conforming to the phonological, syntactical and semantic exigencies of a given natural language on the basis of a finite exposure to a finite corpus of that language' (Leeson, 1975: 136).

For Brumfit, it is

> to be regarded as natural language use, whether or not it results in native-speaker-like language comprehension or production (Brumfit, 1984: 56), . . . seen as the maximally effective operation of the language system so far acquired by the student (p. 57).

There is a striking contrast in these accounts, between overall concern for conformity to rule-governed behaviour, albeit generative (in Leeson), and emphasis on natural language use over and above conformity (in Brumfit); nine years on, issues have changed (the case against habit-forma-tion/behaviourist approaches no longer needs to be made, the nature of communication and its relationship with language development have become a mainstay of theory and practice). But they have this in common: while both deal with what may be deemed to underlie fluency (ideational competence in Leeson, maximally effective exercise of transitional compe-tence in Brumfit), neither tells us very much about what it is, whether it is to be set against a norm or not (what, in any case, *is* the norm?). It is not their purpose: Leeson's ultimate concern is to uncover elements of a fundamental competence, and he concentrates essentially on features that can be described by linguists, at the expense of factors of performance which are part and parcel of fluency (e.g. temporal and sequential features); Brumfit deals with methodology, and is accordingly more involved with discussing conditions for promoting the emergence of fluency in the classroom than with investigating the end-phenomenon itself.

Fillmore (1979) is more explicit about the qualities associated with fluency, which he presents, though with acknowledged informality and cursoriness, and primarily with reference to production, as a set of (not necessarily mutually inclusive) abilities relating to flow and continuity, coherence and semantic density, context-sensitivity, and creativity in, and imaginative use of, language. His brief survey also draws attention to critical aspects of fluency generally — to its relative and interactive nature, to its variability and multidimensionality, and it is a pity, in the end, that he does not elaborate further. What he means, for instance, when he refers to one kind of fluency as 'the ability to talk at length with few pauses, the ability to fill time with talk' (Fillmore, 1979: 93), which he associates with people like disc jockeys and sports announcers, is easy to grasp. But how do these abilities apply to dialoguic speech, where the pressure of exchange exacerbates the likelihood of breaks of all kinds? Are they then measured primarily as a function of volubility and absence of hesitation phenomena? How justifiable is it in this case — bearing in mind Goldman-Eisler's observations about the fragmented, discontinuous nature of spontaneous speech — to equate 'fill time with talk' and 'talk at length with few pauses'? Or are pauses, and hesitation phenomena generally, somehow also part of fluency?

Dalton and Hardcastle suggest that they are. In a book about disorders of fluency generally and their effects on communication (Dalton & Hardcastle, 1977), they justify the dictionary definitions' emphasis on temporal and sequential features of speech, evidenced in the use of terms like 'smoothness' and 'readiness', by submitting that they must be deemed to cover a wide range of features, *including* breaks in the 'smooth flow of speech' such as pauses, interruptions, etc., as well indeed as repetitions of linguistic elements like sounds, syllables, words and phrases. More recent FL studies take the same view. Their technical handling of fluency essentially as a temporal phenomenon, whether to identify empirical correlates to use as objective indicators in assessing the speech of FL learners (Lennon, 1990; Möhle, 1984; Riggenbach, 1991), and/or to understand the psycholinguistic processes involved in its emergence (Schmidt, 1992; Towell, Hawkins & Bazergui, 1996), contrasts significantly with earlier work in this respect, and looks set to mark a turning point in approaches to the question. They, too, however, are concerned mostly with production, and leave aside, because they do not directly fit in with their purpose, aspects they otherwise identify as relevant to fluency in practice (e.g. interactional aspects). More importantly, their implications for a pedagogy of fluency are as yet not clear: being in a position to measure learners' fluency against quantifiable temporal variables, or to trace to what it can be ascribed, is an important step; but it is still one step away from assessing how to make use of this information in teaching to help students cope with what is involved on-line, including the interaction with other parameters of speech, and develop their fluency.

There is not enough, in the end, in these various studies, let alone in those which merely make passing use of the term, skim the surface of fluency (e.g. Nation, 1989) or review work about it (Chambers, 1997), to suggest that fluency has acquired a clearly specialised and identifiable status, at least in FL teaching. Unlike words like 'achievement' or 'proficiency', both firmly rooted in the teaching domain, 'fluency' is a term which remains peculiarly available to both language teachers and general users as a standard for the assessment of FL learners' abilities, and acts as a link between classroom language use and language use in native communities. It is indeed, willy-nilly, one of the main criteria by which the efficiency of language teaching institutions is judged in the outside world.

The enduring use of fluency as a yardstick for the general public is, in itself, enough of a justification for not dismissing its view as too elusive or unreliable to be of relevance to pedagogy, and for attempting, instead, to unravel where and how the various points of view on the question — lay people's, teachers', applied linguists' — converge, and how this may reflect on teaching: responses in the public at large may well be largely intuitive, but even intuitions, when embodied in a shared concept, must somehow be based on a common core. Overlooking them in any case passes over key issues, and leaves uncomfortable gaps between classroom practice and language at work outside.

Syllabuses and examinations guidelines advise teachers about what oral/aural skills they should promote in the classroom, and what criteria will be used in evaluating students' oral performance. Specifications for early stages, where fluency is not much of an issue yet, are not so controversial: now customarily expressed in terms of functions (e.g. ask for and provide personal information, or everyday goods etc., using appropriate forms of address), situations (e.g. shopping), topics (e.g. family, travel), they correspond by and large to objectively definable ends; there is, furthermore, a wide range of didactic materials on which to rely to implement objectives.

When it comes to more advanced stages, however, where fluency does become an issue, specifications become less tidy, more contentious, and more perplexing to apply, even when at their most detailed or technical. In the very thorough *Languages Lead Body National Language Standards* (1993, revised 1996), for example, which 'provide a nationally recognised framework for awarding bodies, lead bodies and training providers' (1993: 1) (albeit with a more vocational stance than standard examination board equivalents), the performance criteria for 'Speaking' at Level 5 (i.e. the most advanced level) include significant references to fluency in all aspects of performance covered — i.e. in the 1996 revised version: *Ask and provide highly specialised information and advice by speaking* [5S1.1] and *Present arguments and debate pros and cons by speaking* [5S1.2] under 5S1 (i.e. *Deal orally with complex and specialised tasks*), *Contribute to complex group discussions* [5S2.1] and *Deliver unscripted oral presentations* [5S2.2] under 5S2 (i.e. *Contribute orally to meetings*) (cf. excerpts in Table 1). How these references to fluency should be interpreted is to some extent clarified by the information given in the sets of criteria as a whole, or under other headings (e.g. under *Knowledge Evidence* in the 1996 edition), yet still prompts familiar questions:

- about the value to assign, generally, to qualifiers which are difficult to falsify, because impressionistic (cf. *sufficient, intended, clearly* in 5S1.1.5/S1.2.3 for example, or even *pace* [of delivery] [5S1.2.3]; or again *spontaneously, accurately, fluently, persuasively, required* [nuances], *optimum* [impact] in 5S1.2.1);
- about the value to assign to these qualifiers, in their applications to speech *specifically*, given that most are also used in parallel formulae in the criteria for writing at the same level (5W): under 5W1.3, for example, (i.e. *Present and debate arguments on complex matters in written form*), 5W1.3.1 (i.e. *language strategies are selected and used to present arguments and debate pros and cons accurately and persuasively with the required nuances and to achieve optimum impact* [LLB, 1996: 97]) is thus a direct echo of 5S1.2.1 under 5S1.2 (*Present arguments and debate pros and cons by speaking*); the only difference is the addition of *spontaneously* and *fluently* in the criteria for speaking (see 5S1.2.1 in Table 1), but what are its implications in practice?;
- about the relationship between fluency and accuracy in speech (cf. 5S1.1.2 and 5S1.2.1., where fluency and accuracy are placed on a par, and the frequent references to accuracy and appropriacy in the set of criteria);
- about the nature of accuracy in speech.

Similar observations would apply to the overview which prefaces each of the two units for Speaking at Level 5 (S1 and S2). On the other hand, the way these overview sections describe what can be expected orally from individuals at that level, i.e. as the ability to 'handle the most complex and demanding linguistic tasks, with a level of fluency approaching that of a native speaker' (*LLB*, 1996: 52 and 55; also 1993: 39), suggests that the

Table 1 Performance criteria for Unit 5S1 under Speaking at Level 5 (highest level) (*LLB: The revised National Language Standards*, 1996: 53–4) (emphasis added).

Speaking: Level 5
Unit 5S1: Deal orally with complex and specialised tasks

5S1.1	Ask for and provide highly specialised information and advice by speaking	5S1.2	Present arguments and debate pros and cons by speaking
Performance criteria		Performance criteria	
5S1.1.1	language strategies are selected and used which offer the greatest potential to achieve the purpose of the communication	5S1.2.1	language strategies are selected and used to present arguments and debate pros an cons spontaneously, accurately, fluently and persuasively with the required nuances and to achieve optimum impact
5S1.1.2	requests and responses are spontaneous, accurate and fluent		
5S1.1.3	nuance expressed is appropriate to the purpose of the communication	5S1.2.2	language, idiom and register are selected, adapted and used to communicate in ways appropriate to the communication task, the context and the emotive content of the occasion
5S1.1.4	language, idiom and register are selected, adapted and used to communicate in ways appropriate to the communication task, the context and the emotive content of the occasion		
		5S1.2.3	**fluency**, accent and the pace of delivery are sufficient to express the intended meaning clearly and to maintain the flow of the discussion
5S1.1.5	**fluency**, accent, and delivery are sufficient to express the intended meaning clearly and to maintain the flow of the discussion		
5S1.1.6	specialised and complex terms are used appropriately	5S1.2.4	specialised and complex terms are used appropriately
5S1.1.7	any necessary requests for clarification are made promptly, politely and sensitively	5S1.2.5	any necessary requests for clarification are made promptly, politely and sensitively
5S1.1.8	the meaning of complex points is expressed accurately, succinctly and without ambiguity	5S1.2.6	the meaning of complex points is expressed accurately and succintly
5S1.1.9	when it is apparent that others do not understand what is said, appropriate strategies are used to clarify meaning and confirm understanding	5S1.2.7	when it is apparent that others do not understand what is said, appropriate strategies are used to clarify meaning and confirm understanding

Excerpts reproduced with kind permission of Languages NTO.

equation fluency = native-like holds strong. But, when it comes to application, so do the questions it raises about comparability, stylistic normalcy, the relationship between fluency in production and receptive fluency, or simply about how to account for what may be adjudged 'fluent' or 'non-fluent' (Crystal, 1971: 47–72; see also Lennon, 1990: 392).

Equally significant is the issue of self-generated and continuous development which surfaces at the end of these introductory overviews:

> Performance at this level involves applying a significant range of language strategies selected from an extensive repertoire, which the individual *continuously updates to meet changing requirements.* (*LLB*, 1996: 52 and 55; also 1993: 39) [emphasis added].

The relevance of this issue at advanced level, where many FL students are expected to spend time abroad as part of their studies to refine their grasp of language and improve their overall fluency, is rapidly becoming even more central with funding bodies' growing insistence on cost-effectiveness and accountability (see Meikle, 1997 [*Guardian Higher Education*]). Yet whereas there is no shortage of materials and pedagogic advice to assist teachers looking after the early stages of FL learning, there is little in the way of guidance specifically adapted to cater for the evolving oral/aural needs of advanced students. Beyond pitching work at gradually higher levels and expanding its range, teachers are left with little other than to rely on the self-same diet of well-rehearsed activities — discussions, simulations, exposés of various kinds. These create useful opportunities for practice. But to what extent can the involvement they require, constrained as it is by context and the parameters of groups of learners with similar profiles, even begin to match the demands of interaction with native speakers of all ages and walks of life? And how effective are they in equipping students to capitalise on resources outside the classroom, at home and abroad, to achieve the fluency expected from and by them?

The idea behind this book is to revisit these questions, about fluency generally, and about its development from the classroom. It is an exploration, meant to kindle the debate on fluency from a teacher's point of view, and intended for those who find it perplexing still, are not altogether at ease with it, in their thinking or their practice, and who feel that there is more to promoting fluency than can be met by the usual repertoire of oral activities, in particular at advanced level. The questions it raises, the material it covers, are thus of direct relevance to teachers, teacher trainers, applied linguists and their respective students, yet also to linguists, for their research implications. The book should, in short, be of interest to anyone with a concern for language and learning, practical or academic.

It will, in the first instance, simply examine fluency, consider how it is projected, perceived or understood in various quarters, and try, in the process, to assess how the relationship between different outlooks on fluency may affect our approach to the question from a pedagogic point of view; and it will, as a corollary, suggest that for all its complexity, all its apparent elusiveness, fluency is a viable notion for the language classroom, can indeed, paradoxical as it may seem, be taught. Chapter 1 in this first part will use dictionary and general users' definitions as a platform for looking into fluency as it is experienced in practice, and compare its applications to NS and FL learner speech in differents contexts to highlight key issues (function of temporal and sequential variables as determinants of fluency, relationship with other features of speech, interlocutor's role) and aspects (relativity, variability, interactive nature). Chapter 2 will be more technical, and review these points against work in various domains (pausology, psycholinguistics, fluency itself) to gauge their impact and explore their implications in practice. Observations will be taken up in Chapter 3, where they will be harnessed more closely to the concerns of learners, integrated into a pedagogic framework bringing together the various ends of fluency under the two complementary notions of viability and efficiency, and so strengthen the argument for adopting a more discriminating approach to fluency in the classroom, based on the interplay between analysis of speech samples and informed practice.

The second part of the book will be practical. It will pursue the case for giving practice a more critical grounding by illustrating methodological possibilities for handling data with students, both to develop their awareness of what is involved in oral/aural fluency and to give a point of application to parallel activities. Each chapter will be devoted to a particular aspect or set of aspects (relativity and negotiation in Chapter 4, discourse/form features of verbal fluency in Chapters 5 (spontaneous speech) and 6 (planned speech), paralinguistic features in Chapter 7), and take advantage of the samples used as examples to continue the inquiry into factors and features of fluency generally.[1]

Analyses and applications will be targeted at advanced students, of French specifically, but will have implications for, and can be adapted to, other levels and other languages (see Chapters 3 and 4 for details on this point).

Note
1. The transcription conventions used for all samples of speech are detailed at the end of Chapter 3 (p. 65).

Chapter 1

Fluency and Dictionary Definitions:
A Stepping-Stone

Informal Accounts of Fluency and Dictionary Definitions

What do people mean by fluency? The small sample of informal accounts in Table 2 shows two noticeable poles of emphasis: fluidity/absence of (obvious) hesitation, ease (a, b, c, d) and coherence/effectiveness/ intelligibility (e, f, [g]). But it raises more questions than it answers. Is speaking fluently the same as speaking *with someone* fluently? Is fluency monologic, a feature of production alone (a, b, d, e) or does it make room for the interlocutor (f, g, [c])? Is it ultimately to do with fluidity and ease (a, b, c, d) or with intelligibility, effectiveness (e, f)? In any case, to what features can such qualities be traced? What is to be made of the interlocutor's perception (b)? Is the fact there is no specific reference to FL fluency in this small sample significant? Is it to say that it should be equated with NS fluency? Then again, what is the relationship between fluency as experienced by the general public and fluency as an educational desideratum? . . .

If a pedagogy of fluency is to be envisaged, these are questions which can scarcely be evaded. But where are answers to be found? The Table 2 sample is too limited in range to serve as a basis for analysis. Yet in view of the idiosyncratic and elusive nature of the responses one might expect from any survey on fluency (Brumfit, 1984; Leeson, 1975), we cannot be sure that a larger set would necessarily prove more revealing or reliable. Another option is simply to turn to the dictionary. Dictionary definitions are generalisations, and cannot begin to engage with the intricacies of what they describe. But they *are*, after all, syntheses of common perceptions, and as such stable points of reference. Indeed if the Table 2 sample can be claimed to be representative, it is so because of the striking extent to which the few accounts of fluency it provides cumulatively coincide with standard dictionary definitions (see Table 3), and thus validates using them as platform to launch the discussion.

Standard reference texts such as those cited in Table 3 — *Oxford English*

Table 2 Some on-the-spur-of-the-moment oral reponses to the question 'What do you understand by fluency'

Informal accounts of fluency
a) . . . Something that keeps going without pause, whether it's speech or anything else . . . without hesitation (Secretarial staff)
b) Fluency? . . . Person who can speak without hesitation, well, without *obvious* hesitation (Secretarial staff)
c) Fluency? being able to talk . . .without hesitation (Social services manager)
d) Words come out . . . words come out easily (FL lecturer)
e) Hurgh . . . something that I'm not . . . being able to speak coherently . . . and intelligibly . . . Certainly it's to do with speaking, fluency. . . . But of course it doesn't necessarily need to be, but it would be for me (Interior designer)
f) It's . . . the ability to communicate . . . effectively . . . with somebody to put your point across (Language lab technician)
g) . . . Is this a trick question? . . . Ability to understand, respond, express yourself spontaneously (Drama lecturer)

Note: The answers were collected on a casual basis from individuals encountered during a particular day. All were aware of my status as a foreigner and teacher of French, but did not, as I thought they perhaps had, interpret the question as referring specifically to FL fluency: it was subsequently made clear that the answers did not, in the first instance, discriminate between NS and FL fluency. Defining fluency was hardly straightforward: responses were very hesitant to begin with; once they gathered momentum however, it proved difficult to contain them to statements, and they rapidly spilled into exchanges involving me as a bouncing board (only the statements are reproduced here).

Dictionary [speech-related entries only], *Odhams Dictionary of the English Language, Collins English Dictionary, Longman Dictionary of Contemporary English* and *Penguin Wordmaster Dictionary* — are in fact, as we shall see, peculiarly effective as a lead-in for exposing the nature of fluency as the general public understands it, and for identifying features of relevance to a pedagogy of fluency. The sample would not be complete without reference to the *Collins Cobuild English Language Dictionary* (1987); its definitions, which are something of a special case, will, however, be treated separately.

What, then, do the dictionary definitions in Table 3 tell us about fluency? As with the informal accounts given in Table 2, all but the most

Table 3 Dictionary entries for *fluency* and/or *fluent*

Oxford English Dictionary (OED) (1933, reprinted 1961) [speech-related entries only]

Fluency 2.a.   A smooth and easy flow; readiness, smoothness esp. with regard to speech.

    b.   Absence of rigidity; ease. [+ *examples*]

    3.   Readiness of utterance, flow of words. [+ *examples*]

Fluent [*one entry devoted to expression*]:

    5.a.   Of speech, style, etc.: Flowing easily and readily from the tongue or pen [+ *examples*]

    b.   Of a speaker, etc.: Ready in the use of words, able to express oneself readily and easily in speech or writing.

Odhams Dictionary of the English Language (Smith & O'Loughlin, 1946)

Fluency [*defined by reference to the adjective, fluent*]

Fluent   having a ready command and flow of words;
voluble, glib;
spoken easily, rapidly and without hesitation;
flowing smoothly and continuous;
proceeding readily and naturally without effort.

Collins English Dictionary (1979 [third edition 1994])

Fluency   the quality of being fluent, esp. facility in speech and writing

Fluent 1.   able to speak or write a specified foreign language with facility

    2.   spoken or written with facility: his French is fluent

    3.   easy and graceful in motion or shape

    4.   flowing or able to flow freely

    [C16: from Latin: flowing, *fluere* to flow]

Longman Dictionary of Contemporary English (1987 edition)

Fluent 1.   (of a person) speaking, writing, or playing a musical instrument in an easy and smooth manner: *He is fluent in five languages.*

    2.   (of speech, writing, etc.) expressed readily and without pause: *She speaks fluent English.*

    [- ~ly *adv* -.ency n]

Penguin Wordmaster Dictionary (1987)

Fluent 1   (of a person) able to speak or write (a particular language) easily and smoothly.

    2   flowing easily and smoothly.

    [**fluency** n **fluent** *adv* < Latin *fluere* to flow.]

---

comprehensive definition — the *OED's* — define *fluency* primarily by reference to language, in particular to speech production, and pass over the more diverse uses of the term in the past (e.g. affluence, copiousness, abundance in entry (1) of the *OED*). One might suspect that the term is also gradually acquiring greater specialisation in its applications to FL expression. Yet only two of the entries in the sample — the *Collins'* and the *Longman's* — make explicit reference to foreign fluency, albeit through the definition of the adjective, *fluent*. This conspicuous lack of differentiation, also noticeable in the set of informal answers in Table 2, suggests that the discussion of fluency, before it turns to foreign speech, needs to be informed by native speech.

Fluency and Native Speech

Fluency as a rhetorical notion

Dictionary definitions describe fluency in speech essentially as a unified concept, as a single state encompassing all fluencies, irrespective of modulations that might be introduced to account for the diversity of its contexts. This may be to do with singleness of etymology (Latin *fluere* to flow). It may also be to do with the fact that definitions of this kind inevitably describe a norm, represent an abstract ideal which does not necessarily stand the test of practice.

All the same, the range of possibilities is difficult to accommodate. The features of the definitions — 'smoothness and connectedness', 'ease of flow', 'readiness of utterance', 'facility', absence of pause — may be appropriate to describe the kind of planned speech featured in speeches, lectures, radio or television commentaries exemplified in this extract from an academic lecture (see also Chapter 6):

> (..) /il y a ensuite un mot qui ressemble et qui s'appelle le . 'gaullisme/alors le gaullisme c'est déjà une notion plus . . plus floue/parce qu'au fond . c'est_un ensemble de 'principes/assez généraux d'ailleurs/qui ont . 'marqué/l'action du général de Gaulle/et qui . euh ont 'marqué aussi un certain nombre de gens/qui ont travaillé . avec lui/ (..)

Even then, the transcription reveals that the text is not free from breaks — mostly unfilled pauses [.] combined with stress ['] to achieve rhetorical effect, but also occasional hesitation features (e.g. repetition + unfilled pause (*plus . . plus*), filled pause (*euh*).

But spontaneous speech, as we hardly need to be reminded, seldom even closely matches the ideal embodied in the qualities of the definitions (Goldman-Eisler, 1968). How is it that something like the following extract, from an informal discussion recorded on the French radio (see also

Chapter 5), could, aurally speaking, be described as smooth, fluid, connected, continuous, etc. when it so clearly belies the fact on paper?

> (. . .) *bon alors y a euh/le journal Soixan-Soixante millions de consommateurs du numéro/le numéro de février qui vient de sortir/et qui a testé 'tous les_antivols . /pour les motos les scooters les vélos/euh ben y en_a pas un qui résiste hein heu en fait/alors y a trois marques hein/j'vais pas vous les citer/qui sont les fameux U hein euh/euh (. . .)*

The mismatch could be traced to the subjective nature of the features: speech may not be *objectively* fluent, but may be *perceived* as such. Accordingly, there is no reason why everyday speech which is in fact 'fragmented and discontinuous' (Goldman-Eisler, 1968: 31; Raupach, 1983) should not, within certain limits, give a global impression of fluency. Indeed if the pauses, hesitations, inaccuracies of all kinds, the vagueness and changes of mind which intersperse speech, pass undetected in a *perceptual* appreciation of fluency, they must be *part* of fluency, that is fluency in its actual manifestations, as opposed to fluency as a desideratum; conversely, too much accuracy, precision, planning, etc. in interactions in which they are not the norm might conceivably be regarded as suspicious, or pompous (see Brown & Yule, 1983: 21), if not inappropriate.

There is also another possibility. *Fluency*'s semantic range covers the closely allied notions of grace, facility and ease. It relates to production alone. The response it appears to seek is not one of participation, but of admiration for, or pleasure in, an individual's personal gifts. In this sense it has more to do with self-presentation than with communicative reciprocity, privileges the monologic at the expense of the dialogic/interactional. In this sense, *fluency* is perhaps really a rhetorical term, and does not relate to knowledge or linguistic competence so much as it relates to use, to delivery, is to do with persuasiveness, manipulation, ostentation even. If so, it may be that fluency only becomes an issue when it is in effect triggered as a criterion, when rhetorical effectiveness comes to the fore and speech is appraised on its own merits — with focus on the speaker alone. This would apply in situations in which speech *is* monologic — speeches, lectures (see earlier example), radio and television broadcasts, for example. It could also apply in situations where speech can be *treated* as monologic, that is to say where interactional factors come into play, but are disregarded because the focus is, from the outset, on the production of a particular individual — in verbal tests, teaching or examining situations, job interviews, for example. If this were so, fluency would have little relevance for normal everyday speech which is, on the whole, interactional in nature, and in which display and rhetorical effectiveness are not, generally speaking, a primary concern.

Fluency in spontaneous NS interactions

Could this mean that fluency is not an issue in everyday interactional speech? The term *fluency* is not, after all, particularly commonly used to qualify native speakers' everyday speech. On the other hand, there is nothing in the Table 2 sample of informal definitions to suggest that its application should be restricted to specific contexts or modes. And as for dictionary definitions, they ought, as general accounts, to cover all fluencies, *including* fluency in everyday native speech.

How, then, in interactional contexts, are we to accommodate the focus on production and rhetorical effectiveness of the dictionary definitions? When and why should *exchange-embedded* speech begin to stand out, take on, as it were, a monologic status, and its well-spokenness (or lack of it) become salient above and beyond its transactional/interactional functions? In the light of what precedes, we can only suppose that it is if, and when, speech begins to fall short of (or to exceed) the perceptual expectations of the interlocutor in terms of smoothness, connectedness, flow of words, readiness, facility. And this, given the actual fragmented and discontinuous nature of spontaneous speech, must be, as we know from intuition or experience, a highly relative matter, a matter, furthermore, which involves the interlocutor — through his/her perceptual reaction — as much as it does the speaker — through his/her actual verbal behaviour. But how? What features of speech foster the impression of fluency?

The qualities circumscribing *fluency* in the dictionary definitions relate essentially to the temporal and the sequential (Dalton & Hardcastle, 1977: 1), and are not, at least explicitly, connected with *linguistic* aspects of speech. There is no direct mention of such things as command of syntax, lexis, sociocultural rules, even though one knows that they must have a role to play. The *Odhams Dictionary* does mention 'a ready command and flow of words', yet the emphasis is as much on the temporal and sequential (cf. 'ready', 'flow') as it is on lexical variety and confidence. This comes as no surprise as far as planned speech is concerned: speech is prepared, linguistic aspects can, if need be, be monitored prior to production, and display features/rhetorical effectiveness come to the fore, both from the speaker's and the audience's point of view. Not so in spontaneous speech, where all relevant features, including the strictly linguistic, are intimately integrated during the actual process of speech production. Do the definitions then simply take it for granted that native speakers have a basic linguistic command of their language? The question hardly needs to be speculated about. For whether they do or not, we are still left with the fact that sequential and temporal features emerge as primary determinants governing the perception of fluency. And if they are, as it were, 'super-criteria' guiding the perception of fluency, they must be deemed to operate as a filter through which other features of speech — in particular strictly linguistic features — are processed.

This dominance, coupled with the interlocutor's role in assessing fluency, has important implications for FL fluency. But before we turn to FL fluency, we must briefly clear the question of those contexts, such as teaching or examining, in which fluency is, from the outset, activated as a criterion, with speech treated as monologic. One would suspect, in such cases, that the objective and the linguistic take precedence over the subjective and temporal/sequential in the assessment of a speaker's fluency. This, however, does not undermine the argument in principle. There is no reason to suppose that, in such situations, temporal and sequential features become irrelevant: the dictionary definitions themselves suggest that they do not; and they are, in any case, inherent features of speech and cannot but have a role to play both in its production and its reception. It would simply suggest that the perception of fluency is subject to shifts of emphasis, to permutations of its various features, and is context-dependent. And if these different outlooks are to be accommodated in a pedagogy of fluency, sequential and temporal features may well, as their one common denominator, prove to be a cornerstone for the discussion.

Fluency and Foreign Speech

As general accounts, dictionary definitions should cover not only fluency in everyday native speech, but also fluency in a foreign language. Yet when it comes to foreign speech, it is difficult to imagine that fluency could be restricted to rhetorical aspects: both *fluency* and the adjective *fluent are* commonly used to qualify the production of foreign speakers in interactional, everyday contexts. It is equally difficult to imagine that the definitions could take linguistic competencies for granted. Yet on the face of it, there is little evidence, in the set of entries and earlier comments, to confirm that NS fluency and FL fluency are not, in practice, approached in the same way. What little evidence there is, however, does have implications for the discussion.

To begin with, while only two of the Table 3 definitions — the *Collins'* [*CED*] and the *Longman's* [*LDCE*] — make room for FL fluency, either explicitly, or through examples referring to FL production, they are, significantly, amongst the most recent: 1979 (reprinted 1994 without change) and 1987 respectively (against 1933/1961 for the *OED*, and 1946 for the *Odhams*). The *Penguin Wordmaster Dictionary* [*PWD*] — also 1987 — is less forthright, but does accommodate FL production implicitly (cf. 'a particular language' in entry (1)). It was also noted that where a reference to FL expression is made, it is in the entries for the *adjective fluent*, cf. in the *CED*:

(1) able to speak or write a **specified foreign language** with facility
(2) spoken or written with facility: *his French is fluent* . . .
(see also entries (1) and (2) in the *LDCE*; (1) in the *PWD*)

The definition of the substantive, where given, remains a cover-all entry (see *CED*: 'the quality of being fluent, esp. facility in speech or writing').

This may suggest two things: that there has been a shift towards FL applications in the meanings assigned to *fluency* in modern usage; and that the adjective *fluent* is taking on a special function as a FL qualifier. The contrast between the substantive and the adjective is indeed revealing: it may well be that using *fluency* and *fluent* interchangeably obscures important distinctions.

The substantive *fluency* makes room for FL fluency implicitly, since it derives its meaning from the definition of *fluent*. But because it makes no explicit reference to FL expression, and covers the remaining entries for *fluent* (see *CED* (3). and (4). in Table 5), it is still sufficiently generic to cover *all* fluencies. And because it is a substantive, it tends to convey a single concept, an integrated and unified meaning, stable and circumscribable, and can, accordingly, operate as a (product-focused) criterion: criteria *are* part of a substantival way of thinking.

The adjective *fluent*, on the other hand, inasmuch as it describes a quality, has a breadth of application which makes it much more flexible, much more amenable to variation, in a sense more active, and also more polyvalent:

people can be fluent (*CED* (1); *LDCE* (1); *OED* (5.b))
speech can be fluent (*CED* (2); *LDCE* (2); *OED* (5.a))
actions can be fluent (*CED* (3)).

Its different syntactic positions are also significant. The predicative use of an adjective tends to imply a dominating or informing quality; whereas the attributive adjective is less absolute, more variable. Thus *fluent*, used as a predicate (e.g. 'this speaker is fluent'), assumes, despite its flexibility, a stasis which affiliates it to the substantive. Used attributively (e.g. 'a fluent speaker'), it becomes much less static, assumes flexibility in its full measure.

By virtue of its polyvalence, the adjective opens up possibilities which the substantive ignores. When it is associated with speech, as in *fluent speech*, *fluent* can still relate essentially to the verbal production of a particular individual. But when it is associated with speaker, as in *fluent speaker*, it begins to move beyond verbal production, can take in non-verbal means of expression. It can indeed begin to make room for the interactive: a fluent speaker is one whose resourcefulness makes him equal to any situation, who is able to adapt his production to the requirements of any situation, including the responses of his interlocutor(s) — which presupposes receptive and negotiative capacities. The adjective *fluent*, because of its potential for flexibility, thus allows for a more supple, less one-sided view of fluency. It is, in this sense, peculiarly suited to qualify interactive speech, and thus foreign speech: for in foreign speech, fluency *is* unquestionably an issue in everyday interactions, cannot be assumed to relate chiefly to rhetorical matters.

The most recent definitions, by locating foreign languages applications at the adjectival end of the fluency spectrum, may thus invite us to recognise foreign 'fluency' as a special case. Yet they give us little to build on. The 'facility', 'ease', 'smoothness', 'readiness' they associate with *fluent* and foreign languages fall within the category of features already discussed. They may well implicitly take in linguistic features, including the production of acceptable syntax, lexical variety, sociocultural appropriateness, etc., but it is not specified. They may also, by virtue of the adjectival flexibility of *fluent*, cater for a kind of general resourcefulness in adapting to the interactional demands of verbal exchanges. But the only ingredients explicitly identified in the entries remain bound in with sequentiality and temporality. As in native speech, temporal and sequential features thus emerge as primary determinants guiding the perception of the quality termed 'fluent'.

This dominance takes on particular significance in foreign languages: for if a speaker's contribution is perceived through the filter of temporal and sequential features, there is no reason why foreign expression which betrays weaknesses in terms of, say, syntax or lexis, should not be perceived as fluent, as long as the interlocutor's perception of its temporal and sequential flow is not disrupted. What factors may cause the flow to be disrupted thus becomes a key question in the enquiry; it will be addressed in the next chapter. In the meantime, however, the argument must still be put to the test with the *Collins Cobuild English Language Dictionary* (CCELD, first published 1987, see Table 4).

Fluency in the CCELD: A Special Case?

Much of what has been said about the entries of the more recent dictionaries — emphasis on production, recognition of the special status of FL applications, in particular — applies to the *CCELD*. What is striking about it, however, is its conspicuous and selective mention of accuracy — echoed in students' accounts of fluency (see Table 5a and comments to follow) — which apparently makes it difficult to uphold the argument

Table 4 Entries for *fluency* and *fluent* in the *CCELD*

	Collins Cobuild English Language Dictionary (1987)
Fluency	is the quality or the state of being fluent. EG *She could speak German with great fluency* . . . . . . *the clarity and fluency of his diction* . . . . . . *subjects that require fluency of the written word.*
Fluent 1	Someone who is *fluent* in a particular language, or who speaks *fluent* Spanish, French, Russian, etc can speak or write the language **easily** and **correctly**, with **no hesitation** or **inaccuracy**. EG *She was fluent in Spanish . . . It was hard to find people who spoke fluent Portuguese.*
2	Someone whose speech, reading or writing is *fluent* speaks, reads or writes **easily, smoothly** and **clearly** with **no hesitation** or **mistakes**. EG *Fluent readers rarely stop at an unknown word . . .* *Rage was making him fluent; the words came easily, in a rush.*

Table 5a French Honours first year university students' on-the-spur-of-the-moment *written* accounts of fluency (6 out of a sample of 24)

	Typical FL Students' Accounts of Fluency (and Breakdown of Features)
a)	Being able to speak and understand, without first having to pause to translate, etc. Ability to use correct tenses, etc. (+ *FL implicit*, + *production*, + *reception*, + *ease/facility/spontaneity*, [+ *absence of hesitation*], + *correctness*)
b)	Being able to do something accurately and with little hesitation. In language, being able to convey what you want to as quickly as you want to with being understood. (+ *production*, + *accuracy*, + *absence of hesitation*, + *speed*, + *intelligibility*)
c)	Being able to speak, write, read and understand a language without excessive hesitation and difficulty. (+ *production*, + *reception*, + *absence of hesitation*, + *ease/facility*)
d)	The ability to talk/speak another language without hesitation with your brain working in that language not translating it in your head. (+ *production*, + *absence of hesitation*, + *ease facility/ spontaneity*)
e)	Not only the ability to put a point across but to express a point of view clearly. (+ *production*, + *intelligibility*, + *articulateness*)
f)	When you can speak a language and converse with someone without having to stop and think too often about grammar and vocabulary. You can talk about a wide range of subjects. (+ *production*, + *interaction*, + *ease/facility/spontaneity*, + *range*)

about the dominance of temporal and sequential features in the perception of fluency generally.

Accuracy is referred to explicitly in the first *CCELD* entry for *fluent*, where it is, through its converse and along with correctness, placed on a par with temporality and sequentiality as a determinant of what being fluent is about, thus:

[speaking or writing] *easily* and *correctly*, with *no hesitation* or *inaccuracy*.

There is, however, a noticeable shift in the second entry, where *correctly* gives way to *clearly*, and *inaccuracy* to *no mistakes*. What implications this may have become apparent if we note first that entry (1), unlike entry (2), focuses more specifically on FL applications, then turn to applied linguistics to interpret the meaning of accuracy and mistakes.

In applied linguistics, accuracy calls forth associations with *errors*, in the sense of systematic errors indicative of the state of a learner's *transitional competence*; *mistakes*, in contrast, are described as unsystematic lapses incidental to *performance* (Corder, 1981). This would make an issue of competence in entry (1) — focused on FL applications — but not in entry (2), thus freed to cover NS (or NS assimilated) applications, and where it might be taken as read. The contrast, unique to the *CCELD*, would thus suggest that this particular dictionary, unlike the others quoted, recognises *in plain* that FL and NS fluency are not in practice considered in the same way. In providing distinct criteria for FL fluency by bringing accuracy and competence to the fore, it goes one step beyond them in signalling that the terms *fluency* and *fluent* are becoming more differentiated in their applications to FL expression. A similar concern for accuracy and correctness is manifest in the Table 5 (a/b) summary of students' accounts: most of the full accounts (see examples in Table 5a) are comparable in gist to those in Table 2, though with perhaps a greater emphasis on the relationship between absence of hesitation and ease/facility; in contrast, however, a conspicuous 8 in the full sample of 24 (directly or indirectly) include accuracy/objective features as determinants of fluency alongside subjective features, with some also referring to competence-related features (range [6], feel for language [1], grasp of language [3]) (see Table 5b).

How are we then to fit in this accuracy-related FL specialisation with the main observations made so far, i.e. that

(a) even though we may know intuitively or objectively that foreign language fluency and native language fluency are not approached in the same way, general dictionary definitions suggest that everyday perceptions treat them in a similar fashion;

Table 5b French Honours First-Year University students' on-the-spur-of-the-moment *written* accounts of fluency: breakdown of features for a sample of 24

Breakdown of Features for a Sample of 24 Student Accounts of Fluency			
FL (explicit or implicit)	10	Production	24
FL + NL explicit	1	Reception	6
Language unspecified	13	Interaction	4
Absence of hesitation	10	*Easelfacilityl*	
Continuity	1	*spontaneity*	14
Speed	1		
Range (e.g. lexical)	6	Articulateness	3
Feel for language	1	Intelligibility	4
Grasp of language	3		
Confidence	2	NS-like intonation	
Native-like	3	(but not accent [?])	1
		Good accent	1
Correctnesslaccuracy	8		

Note: this breakdown is only provided as a rough guide to the types of features given by students and to their frequency of occurrence; features, of course, never occur in isolation in the accounts, and depend for their value on the kind of sequence in which they combine (see Table 5a for examples).

(b) in both cases, temporal and sequential features play a dominant role in shaping everyday perceptions, act as a filter in the interplay between the characteristics of a speaker's production and the impressionistic reactions of the interlocutor?

The *CCELD* prides itself on basing its definitions on the modern usage of terms, selected according to their frequency in modern English. The prominence of references to foreign languages in the definitions of *fluent* and *fluency* (through the example) would thus confirm that the terms are increasingly associated with FL production. The explicit reference to accuracy could also indicate that accuracy is acquiring greater salience as a determinant of fluency in modern usages of the term as applied to foreign languages. The *CCELD* is, however, a special case: it is not a 'general' dictionary, but one which 'has been specially developed to help students and teachers of English' (front flap). As a learner's dictionary, indeed a foreign learner's dictionary (Jackson, 1988), it lays self-professed emphasis on precision and the grammatically and contextually accurate use of the words it defines: 'All students can now learn to use them [the most frequent

2000 words in English] naturally and accurately' (advertising comment on the cover front flap). This general bias may well account to some extent for a corresponding bias towards accuracy in the definition of *fluent* with respect to a foreign language: for the students for whom the dictionary is intended, accuracy is no doubt an important concern; it is also a tangible point of reference. This is indeed evidenced in the students' accounts (see Table 5), though not quite to the extent one might have been expected: 8 out of 24 mentions of accuracy is still only just over 30%.

There is perhaps, however, a more general and likely explanation. Foreign language development does not always take place in institutionalised contexts, nor does it necessarily entail systematic and rationalised learning. Yet 'foreign language', for the general public, arguably calls forth associations with learning and/or teaching in a way 'mother tongue' does not. By dint of such associations, foreign languages belong with viewpoints which privilege the foregrounding of objective features. Amongst these, accuracy remains traditionally a central point of reference in the general consciousness, even though it no longer is in quite the same way in applied linguistics, where its ins-and-outs in FL expression and learning has been, in recent years, the object of lively debate. The practical impact of this debate, reflected in the increased concern for the communicative functions of language in language teaching/learning, may well explain why accuracy does not figure more prominently in the students' accounts of fluency. All the same, it is not surprising that 'general public' comments on FL fluency should include reference to accuracy, at least from a criterion point of view.

That the 'objective' end of fluency should have become so conspicuous as to become explicitly integrated in the *CCELD* definition may thus perhaps be ascribed to the didactic function of this particular dictionary; on the other hand, it may simply reflect a general shift in the public's awareness, to do with the ever-increasing importance of foreign language learning/teaching in monolingual communities — in modern Europe in particular — and a concomitant strengthening of the associative tendencies noted above. In this sense, the *CCELD* would make it clear that there are indeed different outlooks on fluency in a foreign language, with different criteria given different weight depending on context; it may also reveal a gradual adulteration of the etymological meaning of the term under the influence of specialist viewpoints.

But these observations do not, in the end, invalidate earlier conclusions. For the fact that the general public may be objectively alerted to accuracy features in FL expression because of associations with learning/teaching does not necessarily affect their on-line overall perception of foreign speakers' performance in natural interactive contexts. In other words, there is no reason why perceptual responses should not be guided by the temporal and sequential, before, that is, objective features are activated as criteria. The enduring dominance of temporal and sequential features is borne out not only by their prominence and precedence in the *CCELD* definitions, but also by their continuing to act as a link between the entries for *fluent* in a foreign language (1) and *fluent* in a native language (2) — where the role of objective features is relativised to an even greater extent.

Fluency Revisited

Standard dictionary definitions, as general repositories of information, are notoriously difficult to make sense of: in aiming to account for all eventualities, they do not, in the end, give a focused picture of any, and leave much room for individual interpretation. They are, in this sense, a comment on the shifting nature and complexity of language, the medium for the expression of our equally shifting and complex perceptions. As the synthesis of our shared understanding, they are, however, a common stable point of reference, and provide useful insights into non-specialist under-standings of particular terms. The definitions of *fluency* and *fluent* are to a great extent as multiform and ambivalent as the actual phenomenon they describe. But their disussion has clarified issues.

The analysis has helped to make sense of the apparent paradox illustrated in Goldman-Eisler's statement about the illusory nature of fluency (see the Introduction and 'Fluency as a Rhetorical Notion', pp. 14–15), to be traced to discrepancies between fluency as a normative objectivised notion, and fluency as a global subjective experience which does not discriminate between the various criteria governing fluency objectively.

It has confirmed, as one might expect from experience or intuition, that foreign languages and mother tongue command different responses in practice. Yet even though recent definitions of fluency are becoming more forthright in acknowledging these differences, they still suggest that everyday reactions operate along similar lines in both cases, with a perceptual foregrounding of temporal and sequential aspects of expression, at least in the first instance. Hence perhaps the customary though problematic equation 'fluency = native like' (see Crystal, 1971: 47–52 and Introduction). Hence also the need to pay closer attention (a) to the interlocutor's role in assessing and shaping fluency, and (b) to the relationship between various ingredients of fluency in practice, if we are to integrate the views and perceptions current outside educational institu-tions in a pedagogy of fluency.

Thus if sequential and temporal features are key determinants in everyday global perceptions of FL fluency, then other relevant features — such as accuracy-related features — need to be approached through the screen of temporal and sequential aspects rather than as direct determinants. In other words, the function and impact of such objectively-magnified features, however important they may be in other respects — not least for teaching purposes — need, as far as fluency is concerned, to be relativised.

In concentrating on the interplay between the substantive *fluency* and the adjective *fluent*, the discussion has also intimated that our view of fluency will need to be supplemented. *Fluency* as a normative notion is a useful notion: it sheds light on general criteria informing perceptions of fluency, is a platform for defining pedagogic objectives. But it fails to capture interactive aspects of fluency, better embodied in the adjective *fluent*, which are equally relevant to a pedagogy of fluency. While *fluency* as a criterion may apply essentially to the speech production of an individual, it does not in practice manifest itself in a contextual vacuum, nor is it connected solely with speech characteristics. Rather it results from a global experience of verbal exchange as *exchange*, and requires from individuals not just the ability to produce speech, but equally the ability to operate interactionally, both verbally and non-verbally, to exercise a general resourcefulness in adapting to the demands created by exchange context and participants. And clearly both the interactive dimension of fluency — attested, revealingly enough, in only 4 of the students' accounts (see Table 5b) — and what it means for individuals, will need to be integrated into our study. For fluency is also infinitely variable in its actual manifestations: any judgement of fluency is necessarily affected by a perception essentially unique to any specific exchange. Our notion of fluency will accordingly need to be harnessed to the particularities and demands of different contexts of exchange, including those imposed by the participants' differing and evolving level of linguistic capacity; as the notion of accuracy itself, it will thus need to be relativised (see Chapter 2).

What all this amounts to is a shift of focus. The discussion has helped to provide guidelines against which to explore the phenomenon of fluency in greater detail. But it has also, concomitantly, helped to specify its nature. It has directed attention away from the stasis of a normative notion towards a notion which calls for greater flexibility, indeed asks, by virtue of its relativity, to be envisaged in such a way as to allow for the dynamic of both (interactive) verbal (and non-verbal) communication and language development. And if there is a relationship between fluency and language development (see Chapter 3), if fluency is more than a desirable end-product and more than a by-product of interpersonal exchange, then clearly it deserves a pedagogy in its own right, based on more than an implicit but elusive consensus.

These general lines of enquiry find an echo in the specialist *Longman*

Dictionary of Applied Linguistics definition (Richards, Platt & Weber, 1985). As in general-purpose dictionaries, the umbrella entry for fluency and fluent is characterised by a foregrounding of temporal and sequential features, with the terms jointly defined as:

> the features which give speech the qualities of being natural and normal, including native-like use of *pausing, rhythm, intonation, stress,* rate of speaking, and use of interjections and interruptions.

From a foreign language teaching point of view, fluency is said to describe 'a level of proficiency in communication' which includes:-

(a) the ability to produce written and/or spoken language with ease;
(b) the ability to speak with a good but not necessarily perfect command of intonation, vocabulary, and grammar;
(c) the ability to communicate ideas effectively;
(d) the ability to produce continuous speech without causing comprehension difficulties or a breakdown of communication (pp. 107–8).

And it is not be confused with accuracy, which 'may not include the ability to speak or write fluently' (p. 108).

The definition thus integrates aspects of fluency which have emerged as central to our purpose when considering general dictionary accounts: prominence of temporal and sequential features, interactivity, relativity. Yet, like all others, it begs basic questions. Terms such as 'natural', 'normal', 'native-like', 'ease', 'good', 'effectively', 'continuous', 'comprehension difficulties', call for external value judgements, remain largely open to individual interpretation. Individual language teachers may well have a fair idea of what such qualities entail from their point of view, just as individual native interlocutors may do from theirs. All the same, the inherent variability of subjectively perceived qualities ultimately negates their explanatory power within a definition; and any notion in which they have a role to play is, in this sense, ultimately undefinable.

Such is the paradox of fluency, which, as an intrinsically impressionistic and plural notion, defies all attempts at neat and succinct categorisation. But this is not to say that it cannot, should not, be explored: its frequency of occurrence as a qualifier of foreign expression in all quarters is sufficiently compelling as a motivation. And if the key to its intractability lies in its impressionistic nature, then questions about what governs its perception, what is entailed in being considered, and becoming, a 'fluent' FL speaker, cannot be avoided.

Chapter 2

Interlocutors' Perception of Fluency: Aspects and Interactional Impact

What, then, does it take to be considered a fluent FL speaker? Once fluency is triggered as a criterion and measured against more or less objective yardsticks, the various characteristics of the speaker's output take on normative salience. But dealing with fluency normatively is dealing with it in a way which distances it from its exchange contexts, that is to say in a way which, as we have just seen, overlooks some of the very aspects which give it shape in the first place:

- it does not take into account the interlocutor's on-line response, which is, in the first instance, primarily subjective, and guided by temporal and sequential factors which are likely to play a significant role in modulating the impact of other characteristics — including linguistic characteristics;
- nor does it take into account the interactional dimension of fluency, or its situational variability, which call for linguistic abilities to be supplemented, not least by a general (verbal and non-verbal) resourcefulness and readiness to adapt to exchanges.

Yet these observations raise important questions about how fluency is projected in the first place: what *is* the relationship between, on the one hand, the interlocutor's perceptual response, its temporal/sequential and related aspects, and interactional aspects of fluency, which integrate speaker and context? What does it mean for the speaker as speaker? And what does it mean for the learner, and for a pedagogy of fluency?

Temporal/Sequential Flow and Perception of Fluency

The production and reception of speech inescapably proceed along a temporal axis. This makes temporal and sequential features of speech (see Grosjean & Deschamps, 1975; also Crystal & Quirk, 1964; Lhote, 1995; Matter, 1989; Wioland, 1991; Wioland & Wenk, 1983) as inseparable a part

27

of speech production and reception as the utterance and aural perception of sounds and words themselves. As was mentioned earlier, their relationship to fluency has recently been brought into sharper focus by studies concentrating on monologue-type production (Lennon, 1990; Towell *et al.*, 1996), or production in exchange (Riggenbach, 1991). But their relevance to the argument at this point goes beyond their function in speech production and reception as will be briefly summarised below. It is more specifically to do with their impact on the decoding process in terms of *perception*. The theme of interlocutors' perception does come up in work on fluency: Lennon (1990) in particular refers to it repeatedly (see also Schmidt, 1992). But it remains peripheral, given over to matters of production. Yet in the end, it is probably the key to the interlocutor's response to the performance of other exchange participants, and the key to some of the elusive facets of fluency.

Temporal/sequential variables in speech production/reception: Overview

The importance of temporal/sequential variables in speech *production* and their matching effect in *reception* is fairly well documented, as far as can be observed. It covers a number of interrelated functions, ranging from the expressive — stylistic, grammatical, pragmatic, strategic — to the cognitive.

Thus pauses and/or hesitations or drawls, fluctuations in speech or articulation rate, pitch and tempo for instance, can result from a deliberate intention on the part of speakers to achieve rhetorical/stylistic effect, particularly in planned speech — political speeches, lectures, etc. (Darot & Lebre-Peytard, 1983; Fillmore, 1979; Duez, 1982) (see Table 6). They can operate as devices for signalling or recognising discourse units, syntactic boundaries (intra- or inter-clausal boundaries), pragmatic intentions, or again provide contextualisation cues (Callamand, 1987; Chafe, 1980; Handel, 1989; Kerbrat-Orecchioni, 1990; Lhote, 1995; Local, 1992; Matasci-Galazzi & Pedoya-Guimbretière, 1987; McCarthy & Carter, 1994; Selting, 1992; Schwitalla, 1992; Uhmann, 1992) (see Table 6; also Chapter 5). They also play a significant role in the management of interactions: hesitations, pauses, repetitions, changes in pitch and tempo have been shown to be instrumental in keeping, surrendering or taking control of the conversational ball, amongst other things (Beattie, 1977, 1983; Kerbrat-Orecchioni, 1990; Langford, 1994; Local, 1992; Maclay & Osgood, 1959; McLaughlin, 1984; Tannen, 1989; Stenström, 1994; see also Couper-Kuhlen, 1992 on the function of prosody, especially rhythm, in interactive repair) (Table 6; also Chapters 4 and 5).

The use of such features is not always intentional. It has also been shown,

Table 6 Examples of functions of temporal/sequential features

Pausing and stress to serve rhetorical/stylistic purposes — here to draw attention to the subject of an academic lecture (i.e. [De Gaulle's presidency 1958–69]: important transitional period for France), introduced after a long preamble (see Chapter VI):

c'est aussi une période qui est intéressante/parce que/à 'beaucoup 'd'égards/elle apparaîtra/je crois/comme une période . 'importante . de . 'transition/dans . la vie . française/et . c'est . 'sur ce point . que . je voudrais . essayer . de vous donner .. un certain nombre . 'd'indications/ . . .

Change of tempo/pitch to introduce parenthetical matter (signal of intra-clausal boundaries, using lowered pitch (↓) and acceleration (→) on *moi j'vais . . . combine'*) (extract from an informal discussion on the radio; see Chapter V):

l'antivol/↓→ moi j'vais l'donner puisque j'connais la combine[-]/c'est exactement comme la serrure fichée dans les immeubles . . .

Hesitations, repetitions, drawls, overlaps to keep/take control of the conversational ball (extract from *Apostrophes* [book review programme presented by Bernard Pivot. TV5 Europe, 1987):

X   *oui parc'que c'est-c'est du pur Français du seizième siècle/ . c'est {en en//*
Y   *{pas du seizième*
siècle/c'est du Français du . 'quatorzième siècle/ 'juste avant le seizième/cette langue là {est du moyen
X   *{c'est du p-c'est d//*
                Français/
X   *c'est-c'est du pur Rabelais/e c'est c'est-c'est du c'est-c'est du pur Rabelais/il . il sort en . en di-en disant une phrase de Rabelais . . .*

Filled pauses, hesitations, drawls, repetitions as time-gaining devices while verbal planning is taking place; see also changes of mind (extract from an informal discussion on the radio; see Chapter V):

bon/heu alors le le la l'antivol/j'trouve que/une minute huit secondes pour ouvrir/alors Libé/pisque que c'est dans Libé qu'j'lis euh cet article/dit/une solution . . .

Hesitation/repetition for post-articulatory monitoring (extract from an informal discussion on the radio; see Chapter V):

[la serrure fichée] . . . tout l'monde/enfin tous les cambrioleurs savent l'ouvrir/simplement si y a deux fi-deux serrures/ . . .

in L1 as in L2 research, to result from the demandingness of the task of production, to reveal the cognitive activity of the speaker, particularly in unplanned speech (Darot & Lebre-Peytard, 1983; Dechert, 1980, 1984 [FL]; Goldman-Eisler, 1968; Pawley & Hodgetts Syder, 1983; Raupach, 1983 [FL]; Temple, 1985). Hesitations, pauses, false starts, repetitions can act as a time-gaining device while thoughts are gathered, occur at points where verbal planning and selection is taking place (Darot & Lebre-Peytard, 1983;

Faerch & Kasper, 1983 [FL]; Möhle, 1984 [FL]; Temple, 1985; Wagner, 1983 [FL]) (see Table 6; also Chapters 4 and 5). They operate as devices permitting error correction in utterances not yet, or already, vocalised, i.e. as devices for pre- or post- articulatory monitoring (Hieke, 1981; Morrison & Low, 1983 [FL]; Wagner, 1983 [FL]), and generally point to 'the speaker's struggle to achieve control over planning, processing, production, and post-articulatory editing' (Hieke, 1981: 148) (see Table 6; also Chapters 4 and 5).

The more one is confronted with encoding difficulties, the more likely is the occurrence of features which facilitate the encoding operation (Dechert, 1984 [FL]; Goldman-Eisler, 1964; Lennon, 1984 [NL/FL]; Wiese, 1984), and the more time is likely to be needed. Dechert thus submits, with particular reference to FL productions, that the deteriorations resulting from what he calls 'task stress', cause an increase in the time needed for planning, correcting, etc., and that assessing temporal variables, along with error phenomena, represents an important methodology in second language processing research (Dechert, 1984: 224). What temporal variables can indirectly reveal about the psycholinguistic processes of speech planning, hence about FL acquisition, has indeed been the main drive behind their study in FL speech production (Dechert *et al.*, 1984; Möhle & Raupach, 1989; see also Towell, 1987; Towell & Hawkins, 1994; Towell *et al.*, 1996).

In keeping with this, Möhle (1984) suggested using temporal variables — speech rate, length and positioning of silent pauses, length of fluent speech runs between pauses, frequency and distribution of filled pauses, frequency of repetitions and self-corrections — as a possible measure of fluency. The idea is taken up by Lennon (1990) in his exploratory investigation of performance features that might function as objective indicators of oral fluency: his small-scale study of (German) NNS samples of narrative — elicited with picture story sequences at the beginning and end of a six-months' residence in Britain and rated for fluency by NS judges — found statistically significant improvement on three of the 12 variables assessed: faster speech rate, fewer filled pauses per t-unit (i.e. one main clause and its attendant subordinate clauses and non-clausal units), and fewer t-units followed by pause. Towell *et al.* (1996), beyond measuring progress in (French) NNS fluency against temporal variables in similarly elicited narratives (retelling of the story of a 7mn 27s film), were concerned to discover to what improvement could be attributed, and traced it mainly to increases in the degree of proceduralisation of knowledge: the increase in mean length of run (number of syllables produced in utterances between pauses of 0.28 seconds and above), which they identified as the most important of the temporal variables contributing to fluency development after a period of residence abroad, is explained by an increase in 'the rapidity with which syntactic and discourse knowledge can be accessed for on-line speech production' (Towell *et al.*, 1996: 113). Riggenbach's cross-sectional work on a small sample of NS/NNS *conversation* data also highlighted the relationship between judgements of fluency and temporal variables (speech rate and unfilled pauses). It is, however, different in essence: both her concern for the *identification* of features of fluency and the nature of her data mean that her study, though it still focuses mainly on productions, takes in interactive phenomena which, although they are not temporal variables as such, have an effect on the temporal flow of exchange (e.g. backchannelling, echoes, latching, overlapping, etc. (Riggenbach, 1991: 429–430) and are, for design reasons, left aside in the other two.

The results of these studies clearly demonstrate the productivity of more technical approaches to fluency. But because they deal with fluency under very specific conditions and, in the end, concentrate chiefly on the speaker — the first two (Lennon; Towell *et al.*) in particular — their relevance to the argument at this stage is only limited.

For one thing, what matters, in the heat of exchange, is not what these various phenomema subsumed under temporal variables may ultimately reveal about a speaker's fluency, but simply that they are *produced*. Whether intentional or not, native-like or not, they are part of the make-up of exchange, combine with other aspects of verbal communication to modulate its dynamic, and affect its fluency in relation to both speaker and listener/interlocutor; this is something to which we will return when dealing with learner issues (see Chapter 3).

In any case, what needs to be looked into for the moment, to get a better sense of how fluency is projected, is the activity of the *listener*, particularly in spontaneous interactions. Because of 'task stress', incoming speech is typically fragmented and discontinuous (Goldman-Eisler, 1968), hence potentially difficult to reconstruct into meaningful messages. So how do listeners cope? Part of the answer, it seems, lies with those very features that make the speakers' task easier, though it can make their messages characteristically bitty. As Tannen puts it, 'just as the speaker benefits from relatively dead space while thinking of the next thing to say, the hearer benefits from the same dead space and from redundancy [from repetitions] while absorbing what is said' (Tannen, 1989: 49). In other words, the temporal breaks/hesitation features produced by speakers to create time for planning and encoding, not least under 'task stress', also provide listeners with time for decoding, and make *their* task easier.

The facilitating function of pause phenomena in comprehension is, according to Griffith (1991), well established in L1 pausological research, at least as in so far as they provide processing time, and no doubt warrants the advice about pausing and articulation rate given to would-be public speakers in specialised manuals (e.g. Fluharty & Ross, 1981): speeches can, by virtue of their being planned/rehearsed, proceed at a high rate of delivery and with few hesitations and breaks, making the listening task extremely demanding; hence the desirability for speakers to ensure they provide their audience with sufficient processing time to digest what they have just heard. Advice also includes using pause phenomena to break continuous utterances into clearly related thought groups. Griffith reports, however, that while pauses can indeed be regarded as reliable segmentation markers assisting comprehension in *oral reading*, evidence is less conclusive for spontaneous speech (Griffith, 1991) (though this does not mean that they do not have a syntactic function). L2 studies are producing similar observations (see Chaudron's 1988 review of classroom-based studies), but work in this area is, again according to Griffith, yet to be as thorough and reliable as it is in L1 pausological research.

There are, in any case, questions attached to the claim that the broken and discontinuous nature of spontaneous utterances makes the interlocutor's task easier. How broken and discontinous can utterances get before requiring too much perceived or unperceived effort for decoding to proceed comfortably? And how does this claim relate to fluency?

Temporal/sequential aspects of the interlocutor's perception of fluency

With these questions, the discussion is shifting to somewhat different ground. What we are talking about now is not so much the temporal/sequential flow of speech production and its effect on the listener, as the temporal/sequential flow of the listening process itself: we have moved from the speaker's point of view to the *listener*'s point of view. And with this substitution, we are refocusing on the true object of the discussion: fluent speech, we must recall, is not necessarily smooth, continuous, uttered readily, but rather *experienced* as such, albeit when fluency is not activated as a criterion. The temporal/sequential aspects of fluency discernible in dictionary definitions are, one suspects, detachable facets of production alone, and relate to speakers as performers and monologists; this is also how they are ultimately projected in the studies of Lennon and Towell *et al.*, with their focus on production. Whereas the temporality and sequentiality of speakers' speech as perceived by exchange interlocutors are more likely to be an indistinguishable part of the interlocutors' (perceptual) decoding and processing operations.

Thus if exchange-embedded fluency is interactional, it is so on several counts. It is interactional in the sense that it requires the speaker as speaker to adapt to the demands of each exchange, whether imposed by context or participants, as we have seen. But it is interactional also in the sense that, inasmuch as it engages the interlocutor's response, the onus in setting

fluency parameters rests with *both* interlocutor and speaker: what constitutes 'fluency' in any exchange emerges as a cooperative venture whereby
the speaker's production and the listener's receptive tolerance can be
matched, can converge in some kind of reciprocity, and in which both share
responsibility (see Grice's co-operative principle, 1975, of which this is
reminiscent). But what makes for 'smooth', 'continuous' receptive processing of verbal strings which are *not* smooth and continuous? What is the
relationship between temporality and sequentiality — now addressed from
the listener's point of view — and receptive tolerance? And what are its
implications for fluency within the interactional framework of its exchange-
embedded manifestations?

Unlike the temporality and sequentiality of speech production, which is
observable and quantifiable, the temporality and sequentiality of receptive
processing is necessarily — by definition and because it is intimately
connected with perception — internal and qualitative: while temporal
speech phenomena can be observed, precision-measured with instruments
(as they are in the studies of Lennon and Towell *et al.*), the resulting
information does not, as Callamand points out, always correspond with the
way it is perceived (Callamand, 1987: 51; see also Mackay, 1987). This point,
and the questions it raises, can perhaps be made clearer using Bergson's
generic polarisation of chronometric time and *durée*, the one a rational and
external measure of time, the other internalised and purely experiential
(Bergson, 1959).

Chronometric time, insamuch as it is external to the individual, and can
be measured and organised objectively, e.g. by clocks, in calendars, is
shared by all individuals on the same grounds; it is quantitative and
homogeneous (all units of time, seconds, minutes, etc., have the same
duration); and it is discontinuous, because connected with spatiality (i.e.
divided into units). In contrast, *durée* corresponds to an internal perception
perceived by each individual in a unique fashion; it is properly temporal
and qualitative, as well as heterogeneous (i.e. hours can seem to go in a
flash, minutes can seem to go on for hours: each of an individual's moments
can be experienced differently), and continuous (Bergson, 1959). If the
subjective and idiosyncratic nature of the listener's perception is paralleled
with the subjective and idiosyncratic nature of *durée* — which makes *durée*
infinitely fluctuating — then the fluctuating nature of the listener's
perception becomes only too evident. As does its resistance to analysis.

In view of this resistance, it may seem hardly justifiable to dwell on the
temporal/sequential ins-and-outs of how decoding is perceived to proceed: it is not, after all, directly relevant to the purpose of this study, which
is to explore how to do pedagogical justice to fluency; and it is likely to
remain highly speculative. But it is important for our understanding of the

mechanics of fluency, and requires at least some attention, if only to outline issues.

Of particular interest in this respect are the possible factors likely to disrupt the decoding and reconstruction processes involved in the listening task: when and why do they cease to be experienced as smooth and continuous? What are the limits of interlocutors' receptive tolerance?

Receptive tolerance to temporal/sequential disruptions

By and large, interlocutors cope and respond to spontaneous speech with relative ease. It must thus be part of their ability to process apparently discontinuous and fragmented verbal strings, utterances, or stretches of discourse throughout a conversational exchange without overtly deliberate effort (Halliday, 1987; Taylor & Cameron, 1987: 133; Van Dijk & Kintsch, 1983). Equally, it is part of their ability to process language which does not necessarily conform to an idealised norm, at least to the extent that they are able to produce a response, in whatever form: even native spontaneous speech is not error/mistake free, syntactically, lexically or socioculturally accurate, homogeneous or even phonologically homogeneous (cf. dialects), let alone planned and formally cohesive — as is evidenced in the following extract (see also Chapter 5):

(. . .) [*l'antivol*] (. . .) /*c'est exactement comme la serrure fichée dans les immeubles/. tout l'monde/enfin tous les cambrioleurs savent l'ouvrir/simplement si y a deux fi-deux serrures/celle-ci est plus dure que l'autre/i suffit de s'mettre à côté d'un scooter plus facile à voler que l'sien/ (. . .)*

As was noted earlier, those temporal and sequential variables which facilitate the production of speech are also deemed, at least within certain limits, to facilitate the process of reception, e.g. by providing processing time, or acting as segmentation markers. It seems reasonable to assume that the same applies to other features of spontaneous speech. Brown and Yule (1983) note that it is rare, in spontaneous spoken language — where processing time is limited and consciousness can focus only on a limited amount of material at one time —, to find the kind of 'heavily premodified noun phrases with accompanying post-modification, heavy adverbial modification and complex subordinating syntax' which can occur in the written language or in planned speech (Brown & Yule, 1983: 7; also Chafe, 1982; Chafe & Danielewicz, 1987; Pawley & Hodgetts Syder, 1983) (see the above extract, which, with its mostly paratactic syntax, is typical in this respect). Spontaneous speech, then, tends to be comparatively simpler, to give the general impression that 'information is packed very much less densely' (Brown & Yule, 1983: 6), and thus is 'a great deal easier to understand . . . than "written language spoken aloud"' (p. 7), hence presumably easier to decode as well as less demanding to produce.

There is a fair degree of agreement about this, but it is not unanimous. Halliday (1987) for one contends that this simplicity may be deceptive. He agrees that (English) speech is indeed lexically sparse compared with writing, and, in this sense at least, simpler. But its build-up of interdependent sequences, he argues, often adds up to quite extensive and intricate clause complexes, and the dynamic mobility of the spoken language, whereby 'each figure provides a context for the next one, not only defining its point of departure but also setting the conventions by reference to which it is to be interpreted' (Halliday, 1987: 67) makes for complexity. On the other hand, he also describes it as spun out, oriented towards events (doing, happening, sensing, saying, being), process-like, with meanings related serially (see also Brazil, 1995; Blanche-Benveniste, 1995, for application to French). Because of its immediacy of delivery and purpose, its forward momentum, its step-by-step build-up, it can thus hardly allow for the degree of planning, classification, embedding, and thus density, possible in writing (as needs to be borne in mind when dealing with learner productions/fluency; see Chapter 3).

All the same, loosely organised syntax, lack of cohesion and coherence, lack of precision at word or phrase level (vagueness of expression, hedging, word coinage) — another feature of informal speech (Brown & Yule, 1983; Chafe & Danielewicz, 1987; Crystal, 1981; Crystal & Davy, 1975) — overabundance of hesitation phenomena and inaccuracies, together with the strain of keeping with the dynamic flow of incoming messages, may well, in the end, make testing demands on receptive processing. Without venturing into the complexities of the process of language understanding, its many unknown quantities and controversies (De Beaugrande, 1985; Flores D'Arcais & Schreuder, 1983; Horowitz & Samuels, 1987; Brown, Malmkjaer, Pollit & Williams, 1994), it seems plausible to assume that while the listener has a certain level of tolerance to the effort required, there must come a point when the processing operations become too demanding for the time available, and begin to be perceived as infringing normal processing rhythms (see p. 37 for individual variations).

Thus a listener may be able to accommodate syntactic mistakes/errors in a speaker's productions without perceiving undue disruption in the process of decoding and reconstruction, which may well, in any case, proceed on the basis of 'only a partial, approximate analysis' (De Beaugrande, 1985: 162). Indeed syntactic errors/mistakes do not necessarily make great decoding demands when it comes to making sense of a message. In the following string (from a student exchange analysed in Chapter 3):

'*[les petits déjeuners]* . . . *c'est dégoûtant*',

c'est is incorrect in terms of agreement (with '*les petits déjeuners*') and confuses *ce/il*; yet as the referent is never in doubt because of its proximity, it seems unlikely that the time required to process this string would much exceed the time required to process a well-formed equivalent (c.f. notion of 'error domain', i.e. the amount of (linguistic or non-linguistic) context needed by hearers to recognize an error, in Lennon (1991)). But this is not always the case. In

'*qu'est-ce que c'est (qui) c'est comme de l'huile*' (same transcript),

there is a confusion of construction — resulting in redundancies — which is likely to make the sequence comparatively more demanding and time-consuming to process than equivalent acceptable strings such as '*qu'est-ce qui est comme de l'huile*' or '*c'est quoi qui est comme de l'huile?*' (see also Burt & Kiparsky (1972) on the impact of global errors vs. local errors on the comprehension process).

This may apply to other kinds of errors/mistakes, including those connected with lexical vagueness, inappropriacies, mishandling of conversational conventions, and pronunciation for instance, whether in combination, or as isolated occurrences, or both: the time and sequence of the process of reconstruction may be hindered simply by an overabundance, throughout the incoming message, of effort-costing elements which, on their own, would not necessarily affect it (see Lennon (1991) on the cumulative effect of infelicities on acceptability judgements). It may, on the other hand, or concurrently, be seriously affected by a particular problem. An offensive conversational overture — e.g. *salut m'sieur, ça va?* from a job interviewee to a potential employer — is for instance likely, because it puts pressure on contextual relevance (Wilson, 1994), to create something of a processing hitch for the recipient, if only to decide what kind of response might be called for: e.g. is this interviewee being deliberately offensive and should he be instantly dismissed, are there reasons which might justify such behaviour and should he be given a second chance, is this a foreigner who does not know any better?

This rather crude example is significant on other grounds, particularly when it comes to foreign speakers: 'effort-costing' elements may immediately alert the listener to the status of the speaker, and thus to the kind of production he may come to expect (and one would expect pronunciation and the handling of conversational openings to act as determinant factors in this respect (see Lennon (1990) [quoting Shiro — personal communication] and the next section for comments on this point).

In the worst cases, the individual or combined presence of production features which put strain on the overall process of reception may result in a partial or complete breakdown of this process. But it may have less dramatic effects: it may simply create an awareness that what is being produced exhibits certain idiosyncrasies (e.g. in terms of speech variety), or does not conform to standard norms (e.g. syntactic, lexical, pragmatic, sociolinguistic) or to the expectations associated with both context and speaker, at which point fluency may become an issue.

In other words, the perceived smoothness and continuity of the process of decoding/reconstruction may well, all things being equal, be a function of its demandingness in the mind of individual listeners (see section on individual variations in the perception of fluency). And what this would mean is that the more 'difficulty' incoming messages are perceived to create, the less a speaker is likely to be considered 'fluent'.

But this assumption raises as many questions as it answers. For the notion of time-related difficulty itself is not an absolute: it, too, is subject to individual variations, which need to be addressed against the background of general aspects of receptive processing.

Individual Variations in the Perception of Fluency

What is involved in comprehending verbal messages? How do we respond to auditory signals and how do they combine with other kinds of signals? When, how, and to what extent is (phonological, semantic, syntactic, pragmatic . . .) information processed? What kinds of constraints are imposed by memory or resource limitations? . . .

It is perhaps hardly necessary to reiterate just how complex the issue of language processing is, or how contentious it remains within and across concerned theoretical disciplines. Reactions against the idealised sentence-based structural analyses performed by linguists (see De Beaugrande's 1985 critical review), coupled with input from other sources, not least cognitive psychology (Anderson, 1983, 1985; McLaughlin, 1987 [SLA]; Rumelhart & Norman, 1978; etc.), have, however, promoted a broader approach to language comprehension. The full presentation of the different views about it goes beyond present requirements. Their significance for the argument lies in the implication that there is more to comprehension than the processing of actual messages: it is generally regarded as an interactive process, involving the interplay of various kinds of pre-established knowledge (linguistic, conceptual, knowledge of the world), actual stimulus information and context in the production of a meaningful representation of messages (Brown *et al.*, 1994; Flores d'Arcais & Schreuder, 1983; Garman, 1990; Van Dijk, 1987; Van Dijk & Kintsch, 1983; see also interplay between top-down processing and bottom-up processing in O'Malley & Chamot, 1990; also McLaughlin, Rossman & McLeod, 1983).

What concerns us, for the moment, is the relationship between, on the one hand, what listeners bring with them in the comprehension process, and, on the other, processing effort and individual listeners' perception of fluency.

Impact of expectations on the perception of fluency

Listeners do not come to their task empty-headed. Prior conceptual knowledge, or knowledge of the world, supports the comprehension process itself, yet listeners are thereby also allowed to make inferences about the processing task in relation to context and participants, to build up expectations about the task on the basis of what they know, do not know or can discover/guess prior to the verbal exchange (e.g. sociocultural characteristics of the situation, of the interlocutor/s). They may thus approach the task with a number of expectations about what it might involve, about, in particular, the amount of effort that will be required.

Expectations are, for instance, likely to be different if the speaker is a child or an adult, a native speaker or a foreign speaker, if the context is formal or informal. They may not be confirmed (they may prove too high or too low), and may need to be adjusted when the exchange gets under way, as for instance when a child turns out to be more articulate, a speaker less formal, than anticipated, or, more to the point here, when a speaker betrays by his production that he is a foreign speaker.

But if listeners do approach their task with a notion, however approximate and liable to change it may be, of the kind of effort that will be required from them, then, equally, they may approach the task with an intuitively predetermined level of perceptual tolerance to the effort required. In other words, the temporal and sequential allowances they will intuitively be willing to make may well vary with the kind of expectations they bring with them: the willingness to make allowances may, for instance, be greater for a task that is expected to be difficult, such as listening to an academic lecture, or is in some way special, such as the decoding of the idiosyncratic speech of a child or of a foreign speaker.

Thus, if the perception of fluency is sensitive to disruptions of the temporal/sequential flow of receptive processing, and if tolerance of disruptions is intuitively pre-set by expectations, then the perception of fluency too is bound to be a function of individual expectations: the extent to which a speaker is sensed to be fluent, must, at least to some extent, be relative to the expectations of his interlocutor.

Other factors affecting the perception of fluency

Just as expectations are not the only factor influencing perception in general (Malim, 1994), they are not, one suspects, the only factor affecting individual interlocutors' threshold of perceptual tolerance in their response to speakers' productions. It may also depend on their processing capacity and experience (which may in turn affect expectations): an adult may thus have a greater tolerance to the effort required than a child. It may depend on their individual qualities, e.g. greater or lesser tolerance of approximations in general, greater or lesser empathy, and on the relevance of messages to their interests or concerns: the more relevant the message, the more effort they may covertly tolerate. Or again it may be a function of their particular physical and psychological state at the moment of processing — greater or lesser fatigue, anxiety etc. — and/or external conditions — background noise, etc. And their response may change, too, as they adapt to the speech characteristics of a particular speaker: while, for instance, parents, close relatives or friends usually have no trouble in coping with a small child's idiosyncratic/developing speech, it is often more difficult for those not familiar with it: but with time and exposure, they are likely to find it increasingly easy. Similarly, one may get so used to the features of a foreigner's output that these features, which may initially have disrupted the flow of processing, no longer do so, or not to the same extent: one may for example get used to a foreign accent to the point of no longer noticing it.

If perceptual tolerance to effort is thus so individual and liable to change, and if there is a connection between individual thresholds and perception of fluency, it is difficult to imagine that fluency itself should not be infinitely variable in the way it is experienced, whatever the actual characteristics of incoming messages: not only is the response likely to be different in different exchanges, but it is also likely to change during exchanges themselves in line with perceptual adaptations. These changes may become indiscriminately assimilated into the listener's global impression of a speaker's production; but their occurrence and influence, and what they mean for the learner, need to be integrated in a pedagogy of fluency.

Compensatory factors in the perception of fluency

A full discussion of the question of receptive processing/understanding would require looking at other issues which, though high on the psycho-linguistics research agenda, are, by all accounts, still far from being resolved (see Caron, 1989; Clifton, Frazier & Rayner, 1994; Flores d'Arcais & Schreuder, 1983; Garman, 1990; Kess, 1992 for a cross-section of textbooks on the subject). It would need to include reference to the relative importance of the various features of messages in the process of comprehension, and to the interaction (or lack of interaction) between levels of processing: is lexical processing, or syntactic processing, for instance, carried out independently, or continuously interrelated with other subprocesses? Are the various levels of processing activated serially or in parallel, or a combination of both? And if comprehension is a multidimensional process involving interaction of stimulus and conceptual information, or interaction among levels of processing (eg. syntactic and semantic) and organisation (Flores d'Arcais & Schreuder, 1983: 11), how, at what level of processing, and when, does interaction take place? Interactive views suggest that listeners can use evidence from any level of processing to proceed with their task, that 'the processor may choose to use whatever information is more useful, be it phonological, syntactic, semantic, or pragmatic' (Flores d'Arcais & Schreuder, 1983: 10; Moore, 1982; Garman, 1990).

Compensatory phenomena, whereby listeners can make up for deficiencies in some areas by relying on other available information (including non-verbal information), would explain further why foreign speakers whose production displays observable weaknesses can nonetheless be perceived as fluent, that is within the limits of receptive tolerance to effort. But it raises a further question: is there a hierarchy in the extent to which types of errors/mistakes affect the comprehension process? Are listeners more tolerant of some than of others? And conversely, is there a hierarchy in the extent to which certain features (e.g. non-verbal behaviour, expressive use of hesitation phenomena, etc.) facilitate the process of comprehension of fragmented, discontinuous and not necessarily accurate speech?

There are no definitive answers to these questions. And if they remain matters of controversy in studies of the comprehension process and of speech perception (see Cole, 1980; Frauenfelder & Tyler, 1987), one suspects that approaching them through the added filter of temporality/sequentiality is likely to prove all the more frustrating.

But if there is one conclusion to be drawn from these observations, tentative and fragmentary though they are, it is that, whatever the actual characteristics of a speaker's verbal production, the degree to which he is in practice regarded as fluent is highly relative. And if the interlocutor's expectations, his processing capacities and tolerance do have a role to play in the setting of fluency parameters, what does it mean for the speaker as speaker and for the speaker as learner?

Negotiation of Fluency and the Learner

Aspects of negotiation

Unlike fluency as a *concept*, which conveys the image of an essentially unified and stable yardstick applicable *in abstracto*, fluency as it is experienced in practice is, then, intimately connected with the notions of interaction and interactivity. It is interactive because it is inseparable from the business of exchange. It is interactive because the degree of fluency of a speaker is a measure not only of his capacities for production, but equally of his capacities for 'live' reception: fluency is about producing messages, but it is also about tuning in and responding to messages without jeopardising the flow of exchange. And it is interactive, too, because, as we have just seen, it is a measure of the interlocutor's own processing capacities, expectations and tolerance, all of which modulate his perception of, and response to, speakers' messages. But in what ways does this affect our pedagogical thinking about fluency and FL oral development?

One might, in view of earlier remarks, readily concur with Lennon's statement that fluency 'is an impression on the listener's part that the psycholinguistic processes of speech planning and speech production are functioning easily and efficiently' and 'reflects [to some extent] the speaker's ability to focus the listener's attention on his or her message by presenting a finished product rather than inviting the listener to focus on the working of the production mechanisms' (Lennon, 1990: 391–2). It validates his pedagogically-orientated preoccupation with the identification of quantifiable (sequential and temporal) variables in fluent speech to assess progress. But measuring progress in *production* against empirical correlates, or investigating to what progress can be traced (see Towell *et al.*, 1996), is one thing. Bringing it on is another. Towell *et al.* have little to say about this — it is not what their study is about. Lennon suggests, in his concluding comments, that it might eventually become possible for teachers to identify learners' fluency strengths and weaknesses in terms of specific performance features, and make them the focus of remedial work. Yet building in such features of performance into the teaching of fluency goes beyond their quantification, diagnosis and correction in production alone: as in the study of fluency itself (Riggenbach, 1991), it also calls for a more holistic and qualitative approach.

For it must again be stressed that fluency, if we look at it in context, is far from being a one-sided speaker-related notion. It has emerged as the product of a (largely intuitive) fine tuning between participants in an exchange according to the parameters of the exchange, as a process of negotiation. What projecting oneself as a fluent speaker involves, then, in this reciprocal sense, is taking an active part in negotiating the fluency contract in context: taking the measure of one's interlocutor, of his expectations and tolerance, and adapting to them to sustain the temporal/ sequential flow of his processing response, i.e. understanding what interaction is about.

The fact that verbal interactions are a cooperative venture, jointly constructed by those who take part in them, is nothing new: it is a recurrent theme in studies on the subject. Nor is the idea of 'negotiation' new either, whether as a feature of verbal interactions in general, or in what it can do to assist FL learning (see Pica (1994) for a review, and below). But looking at exchange from the point of view of fluency, and thus more specifically through the filter of temporal/sequential aspects of exchange, has brought into sharper focus the functional significance of aspects and features of [FL] verbal communication which either have been awkward to accommodate in teaching, or have received little attention.

Concentrating on the interlocutor's perceptual response and its temporal ins-and-outs has highlighted how important it is for speakers to be able to adapt to their interlocutors and to the parameters of exchange, a necessary condition for the negotiation of the fluency contract, for the process of converging with the interlocutor. It has also simply confirmed how relative the impact of the various ingredients of speech production is in exchange. Linguistic accuracy, an uneasy issue in its relationship with fluency, stands out in this respect. It is a legitimate teaching objective, not least from a fluency point of view: errors and infelicities, whether of grammar, lexicon or appropriateness, put a strain on processing, disrupt its temporal flow, and affect the way a speaker's fluency is experienced. And once fluency turns into an issue in its own right, such inaccuracies become, as we know, all the more salient: one of the subjects in Riggenbach's study was, for instance, not rated as a fluent speaker on account, as some of the raters' comments later bore out, of the conspicuous agrammaticality of her speech, even though it was comparable in quantity, speed and 'pause profile' to the speech of speakers rated as fluent (Riggenbach, 1991). Nonetheless, there are a number of closely related points which we should bear in mind as far as on-line fluency and teaching are concerned, and which we will need to pursue in subsequent chapters.

There is first the ubiquitous question of the nature of accuracy in verbal expression, which, in one way or another, bears upon all that is to follow. Some errors are distinctively FL learner errors — problems with gender in French, for example — and cannot be brushed under the carpet. All the same, learners are not alone in producing infelicities or even errors in speech. Nor are they alone in being vague, hesitating, repeating themselves, producing redundancies, changing their minds, repairing utterances, etc., — as the few examples in this chapter testify. We know very well that spoken messages are, as a result of temporal constraints and task stress, often a far cry from neatly edited written versions. But how distinctive does this make spoken language, and how much room do we make for this distinctiveness in teaching/learning — not only in production, but also in comprehension and interaction? What indeed is the status of accuracy in *exchange*, and how does it affect its relationship with fluency?

What we also need to remember, to get back to the question of relativity, is that the extent to which errors and infelicities affect the interlocutor's response is a matter of degree. What matters, in actual exchange, is not the effect of errors and infelicities *per se*, or *post-hoc*, but how they interact with other features in the construction of exchange: accuracy is not an absolute, and weaknesses can be compensated for, either linguistically (e.g. weak syntax can be compensated by linguistic variety, cf. Fillmore, 1979) or by other means (use of body language, of performance features such as pauses or repetitions, or of communication strategies (see Chapters 4, 5 and 7)). Compensatory measures are not, however, a mere remedial *pis-aller* to keep conversation going, important though this is to increase opportunitities for practice, and learning (see Chapter 3). They involve an interplay of available resources which is part and parcel of verbal exchange (for learners as for native speakers), yet is only selectively incorporated into teaching.

Little is made, in particular, of those temporal/sequential parameters, including hesitation phenomena and related interactive features — filled/unfilled pauses, repetitions, repairs or echoes, for instance — which have been a central concern in this chapter. Ill-served by their unfortunate label, hesitation phenomena are still too often treated merely as an undesirable by-product of the effort to communicate, particularly exacerbated in learners, or as foolhardily flaunted proofs of illusory confidence. As an ex-colleague of mine disparagingly liked to note about the performance of students after their year abroad: 'you don't need to teach students to *'heu'* and *'eh ben'*, they manage it quite well on their own'. Either way, it is missing an important point, and betraying an ill-advised impermeability to the findings of pausological research: whatever prompts the occurrence of performance features, they fulfil functions in verbal expression which are as relevant to FL learners as they are to native speakers, and are not restricted to production.

Coping with performance features, for learners, is a multi-faceted activity. It is to do with monitoring their own, whether native-like or not. It is also to do with recognising the impact they have on interlocutors, and on exchange. On the negative side, Harder warns against the undesirable social effects that can result from an excessive reliance on what he presents as trouble-shooting procedures: the picture that emerges from a (hypothetical) learner 'assiduously saying *huh* whenever there's a pause, always repeating bits of the previous utterance, blocking out interruptions by saying *uh-uh* ... (etc)', he observes, is that of an 'utter pest' (Harder, 1980: 269). This remark, or comments about students using pause phenomena as confidence-boosters, should not be taken as a reason to be dismissive, but rather as an incentive to help learners temper the use of performance features with an awareness of their consequences, in their different aspects.

Though lacking in social control, Harder's hypothetical learner would at least demonstrate a by and large atypical grasp of the interactive value of performance features, albeit still too one-sided. For coping with performance features is to do, too, with responding to the performance clues of other speakers, as features of *their* productions and as features of exchange: it is both a matter of comprehension and a linchpin of negotiation.

Similar remarks extend to other aspects of verbal expression, including kinesics, which will be dealt with in Chapter 7. But there is perhaps no need to take this particular side of the discussion further at this stage, except to reaffirm its implications. Taking the measure of fluency amounts to little less than a reassessment of the relative value and function of the ingredients of verbal expression at large: whatever quantifiable criteria may ultimately become available for evaluating fluency, fostering its development entails doing justice to the interplay of all those resources which can create a 'sense' of fluency and sustain the on-going negotiation of the fluency contract. What is at stake for the learner is communicating. The real challenge, however, is control, and learning — test-themes for championing a pedagogy of fluency. Both will be central in subsequent chapters, but may already be put in context by a few brief indications of some of the restrictive aspects of the fluency contract.

Limits of negotiation

To be generally in tune with the interlocutor may be sufficient to ensure the continuability of the exchange on the mutual grounds established by its protagonists. It is thus desirable from the point of view of communication. But it can have mixed effects. If the interlocutor's expectations affect his/her perception of a speaker's output, they can equally affect his/her own, cause him/her to adapt his/her speech to the speaker's perceived potentialities (c.f. caretaker speech (Ferguson, 1977), foreigner talk (Ferguson, 1971); see also teacher talk/classroom language (Chaudron, 1988)). He/she may for instance provide all the answers to his/her own questions: this is something people often do when speaking with my children in French (their second language), thereby leaving them little room for anything other than minimal acknowledgements; needless to say, they are always very impressed with their fluency and ability to sustain a conversation . . . . Thus if an interlocutor's expectations are too low, he/she may come to modify his/her talk to the extent, or in a way, that it is no longer a challenge for the exchange partner, whether as listener or speaker. Rather it may encourage a kind of fossilisation at the level set by expectations. While speech adaptations may make it easier to fulfil communicative aims in FL learners'/native speakers' exchanges, they may well then, in reducing the learners' scope for receptive and productive involvement, have a limited value for their linguistic development (see Chapter 3 for further comments).

Foreign accents, in immediately alerting the interlocutor to the status of the speaker, are a liability in this respect. It is not unusual for even the most experienced and proficient foreign speakers to be addressed at a level set far below their actual capacities simply because their accent betrays their foreignness, at least during the initial conversational moves (and vice versa when no accent is detected). Nor is it unusual for them to be drawn time and again into what can, in the end, become just derivative chatter: the 'so where are you from', 'I went there X years ago' or 'how do you like it here' likely to be prompted by *any* sign of foreignness may have conversational appeal to begin with; they can soon become less than welcome, and every bit as restrictive, in their topic-narrowness, as other forms of speech adaptations — unless one is able, or willing, to take counter initiatives.

In other words, capitalising on fluency for learning may involve rather more than adapting and responding to the expectations of interlocutors: it may equally require learners to become effectively involved in negotiating the fluency contract at a level and on a plane likely to challenge their potentialities, i.e. to engage with language and interaction critically.

Adjustments may occur spontaneously to some extent: the interlocutor's perception, hence his expectations, can, as we have seen, be the object of on-line variations in response to the speaker's production. More importantly, there is evidence to suggest that learners do in fact play an active role in the negotiation of interactions, and do not, on the whole, behave as passive recipients (see Long, 1983a, b). Negotiation itself, in addition to serving as a means of bridging perceived or actual gaps in communication, is credited with assisting language learning in a number of ways: by making input comprehensible to learners, but also by helping them to modify their own output and by providing them with opportunities to access L2 form and meaning (see Pica's 1994 review of research on NS/NNS negotiation). Just how much they do build on these various opportunities is, as Pica reports in her concluding comments, as yet not very clear. Nor is it very clear how to integrate these findings into pedagogy, and engage learners in making the most of the learning opportunities offered by negotiation.

Fluency is plagued by similar questions. In view of all that precedes, however, it is not unreasonable to suggest that for learners to be aware of what being experienced as 'fluent' entails in all respects, to have the opportunity to reflect on matters of fluency and engage with them, could enhance the educational function of fluency in practice: it could highlight, if not minimise, the danger of complacency connected with a view which considers fluency merely as the ability to carry out communicative tasks successfully, and the development of fluency as a function of communicative involvement.

Hammerly's condemnation of what he presents as a misguided emphasis on communication in FL development may be somewhat extreme. But he is not alone in pointing to the limits of the pragmatic use of language for communicative effect in FL learning. Widdowson, in particular, demonstrates that 'the conditions favourable for establishing external relations necessary for effective use are different from the conditions necessary for effective learning' (Widdowson, 1990: 162), and thus contends that for the different aspects of FL development to be catered for, the external synthesis called for by the process of communication needs to be supplemented with an internal analysis of the language itself.

The adoption in the classroom of an analytical stance directed at something as complex as fluency may seem pedagogically overambitious. This may be true for the early stages of language teaching/learning where both teachers and learners have many other challenges to confront. But it is not unreasonable for students who already possess a degree of control over the foreign language studied, and/or students who expect to develop this control to a high level of sophistication within and beyond the bounds of the classroom (students in tertiary education in particular). As Widdowson reminds us, the whole point of pedagogy is that it 'can make arrangements for learning to happen more easily and more efficiently than it does in "natural surroundings"' (Widdowson, 1990: 162), that it can rationalise learning. In this sense, encouraging students to acquire a meta-awareness of what fluency is about may be conceived as a way to equip them with the necessary critical wherewithal to make the most of their resources and to maximise linguistic and cultural opportunities, wherever and whenever present. In other words, it could play a role in developing this potential for exploiting resources and creating meaning in response to change which Widdowson associates with 'capacity' (Widdowson, 1983), could be considered as a means of bridging the gap between in-class time-bound FL development and the realities of continuing development beyond institutional learning.

But how is this aim to be achieved? Clearly there is more to fluency than meets the eye for FL learners. It is on FL learners specifically that the next chapter will focus, with particular reference to verbal fluency in French, to its characteristics, its variability, its relationship with accuracy, and with learning.

Chapter 3

Factors of Fluency: A Framework for Teaching/Learning

The immediate task is to find a middle ground between common sense views, represented by dictionary and informal definitions in Chapter 1, and the kind of academic discussion to which they led in Chapter 2. Fluency is variable, multi-faceted: each point of view from which it is considered — native speaker fluency, foreign speaker fluency, fluency in a teaching perspective, fluency in a non-teaching perspective, fluency as a product-related criterion, fluency as an interactive and relative process — is likely to generate its own set of parameters. This does not mean that these 'fluencies' have nothing in common, as we have seen. But if a case is to be made for a pedagogy of fluency, and if the relationship between those different viewpoints is to be more properly assessed, the balance of argument needs to be redressed, and more attention paid to foreign speaker fluency in a teaching perspective.

How, in particular, can the shared underlying attributes of fluency in these different contexts be integrated into a framework for teaching/learning taking in the specific concerns of learners? How does fluency, within this framework, fit in with learning? And how can it translate into pedagogy?

Towards a Framework for FL Fluency: Viability and Efficiency in Interpersonal Performance

Fluency is a matter of performance, in the sense the term has been widely used, in contrast with internalised competence, to refer to actual language use, which perhaps explains its comparative neglect. Yet for all the competence model itself has done, in its various forms, to advance research generally and our understanding and teaching of language as, and for, communication, it does have grey areas in relation to performance. Thus no matter what components are deemed to make up individuals' competence (linguistic, sociocultural/pragmatic, discourse, strategic), with

47

reference not only to knowledge but to ability for use (see Hymes, 1972; Canale & Swain, 1980; Canale, 1983 amongst others), what is involved in the transition to actual (interpersonal) performance is not clear (Spolsky, 1989). As the construct of analysts, competence accounts essentially for what can be rationalised by reference to a system, and cannot, strictly speaking, but leave aside all that is not in conformity with the 'representation' of language knowledge to which it corresponds, yet is attested in language use (Widdowson, 1983); and although incorporating 'ability for use' in competence makes room for individual differences, of a non-cognitive nature in particular, the differences to be allowed for are so numerous and wide-ranging that to account for them is, in practice, impossible (Widdowson, 1989: 134). While (communicative) competence in this sense may find a correlate in a normative, ideal-bound and speaker-related kind of fluency — objectively measured by reference to accuracy, albeit in a wide sense —, it caters less readily for its no less representative flexible, relative and interactively negotiated end.

As far as conversational exchanges are concerned, the inadequacy of conformity to rule-governed behaviour to satisfy the requirements of a theory of performance is exacerbated by its 'written language bias' (Taylor & Cameron, 1987; Horowitz & Samuels, 1987): thus, to edit utterances into sentences assimilable to the operation of a system requires more than the strict applications of rules, supposes a knowledge of editing rules which, paradoxically, cannot be formulated without reliance on the prior understanding of utterances; this at any rate is what Taylor and Cameron demonstrate with reference to elliptical and discontinuous utterances (Taylor & Cameron, 1987). According to them, the assumption of a rule-governed relationship between conversational utterances and sentences 'leads to the assumption that the differences spoken language style exhibits, in contrast to written language style, are obstacles to spoken communication' (p. 154).

These kinds of problems are well documented (see for instance Kerbrat-Orecchioni, 1990: 29–54 for French). Interest in spoken discourse and interpersonal performance themselves, whether native speaker or FL learner performance, within psycholinguistics, conversation analysis, sociological, ethnomethodological or other traditions, is now buoyant. What is still difficult to foresee, however, is how their contributions will converge and filter down to FL teaching level in applicable form. In the meantime, there is some justification in concentrating, as a first step in refocusing on fluency and teaching, precisely on the function of features which are peculiar to spoken communication.

Aspects of fluency as performance

Features which set verbal and written expression apart have been highlighted for the benefit of FL teachers and learners in a few dedicated studies, explicitly or implicitly (see for instance Brown & Yule, 1983; Crystal, 1981; Crystal & Davy, 1975; Carter & McCarthy, 1997 for English but with implications for other languages; studies for French remain more technical: Kerbrat-Orecchioni, 1990; see also Blanche-Benveniste, 1997; Traverso, 1996). They cover a range of aspects: qualitative differences at the level of phonology (such as the changes sounds undergo in connected speech), at the level of lexis (e.g. lack of precision, word coinage, etc.), at the level of syntax (e.g. types of connectivity: juxtaposition/addition vs. subordination) for instance; also, differences resulting from the occurrence of features associated with performance, and for this reason left aside in systematic accounts of language — hesitations, pauses, false starts, changes of mind, slips of the tongue, etc. — not to mention features of physical projection — facial expression, body gesture (see for instance Hurley, 1992; Kellerman, 1992; Pennycook, 1985). But it only takes a few examples of FL learners' and native speakers' speech to be reminded of just how awkward all this is to accommodate in teaching, and reminded, too, of what is at stake in pedagogy: bringing together ends which, as the short extracts in Table 7 illustrate, are as conspicuous for what they share as for what sets them apart (see transcription notations at the end of this chapter).

Linguistic features of learners' speech

Even without being told what the various extracts are, it would not take long to sort the learner's exchange (Extract 1) from the rest, and to pinpoint in it what, in linguistic terms, could be described as weaknesses:

- discrepancies in level, reflecting an inadequate grasp of appropriateness:

  cf. for example A's formal opening with *monsieur . . . vous* vs. the subsequent conversational *qu'est-ce que c'est votre opinion* [1] (which also exemplifies a transfer from the English 'what is your opinion of') (compare with 'que pensez-vous des . . . '); or again B's *dégoûtant* [2], later reformulated and intensified in the very colloquial *dégueulasse* (though without accentual emphasis) [4, 10], both of which breach the level of formality set by A;

- errors of syntax and grammar:

  cf. for example B's confusion of *ce/il* and disregard of the plural referent in *les petits déjeuners c'est* [2, 6, 9] (cf. also *je ne l'aime pas* [9]); or again A's *qu'est-ce que c'est (qui) c'est comme de l'huile* [7] which

Table 7 Examples of FL learners and NS exchanges

Extract 1: FL learner exchange (1st Year University students; beginning of the year)
1 A   *monsieur Constance/ . qu'est-ce que c'est votre opinion des . petits déjeuners/*
2 B   *oh mais c'est . 'dégoûtant/*
3 A   *vraiment/*
4 B   *oui c'est 'vraiment dégueulasse/*(laughs)
5 A   *et pourquoi ça/*
6 B   *parc'que/ parc'que/ . c'est comme de l'huile/*
7 A   *de l'huile/ {qu'est-ce que c'est (qui) c'est comme de l'huile/*
8 B   {ouais/
9 B   *parc'que/je ne l'aime pas et c'est/ . c'est trop/ c'est trop/c'est . trop ..*
10   *dégueulasse/*   (laughs)

Extract 2: NS exchange (TV interview with a young boy; see Chapter 4)
1 A   *et comment les gens ont réagi en vous voyant/*
2 B   *ben au début i-i(l)s ont regardé parc'que/i trouvaient pas ça euh/pas tellement*
3   *normal/on aurait dit que c'était un/un truc(que) pour euh/pour euh/soi-disant qu'on*
4   *.. voulait se rendre intéressant/quoi euh/qu'on apporte une . remarque sur nous/dans*
5   *les journaux tout ça/mais c'est pas du tout ça/c'est notre rôle de la nettoyer/nous/*
6   *et de la nettoyer quoi/de la sauver quoi/*
7 A   *est-ce que vous sentez une certaine solidarité autour de vous quand vous prenez une*
8   *telle initiative/est-ce que vous vous r'trouvez avec plein d'gens/qui sont du même*
9   *avis/et qui ont envie d'vous aider/*
10B   *ben oui/un p'tit peu/*
11A   *un p'tit peu/c't'-à-dire/*
12B   *c't'-à-dire que les gens euh/quand ils quand ils voyent ça/ça leur fait quelque*
13   *chose/mais du moment que euh/du moment qu'i qu'i sont pas contraints/et ben/i s'en*
14   *foutent/*

Extract 3: NS exchange (ad-lib radio talk on France Inter; see Chapter 5)
1 A   *j'ai connu/et ça n'est pas d'la blague/j'ai connu un collectionneur*
2   *d'antivols/c'est-à-dire un voleur d'antivols/il ne volait que d'ça/il laissait*
3   *les/[rires] oui oui absolument/il il mettait un point d'honneur à ne voler que*
4   *l'antivol/il laissait l'vélo et il avait une très jolie collection/une bonne*
5   *centaine/*
6 B   *il est dans votr'livre/il est dans l'livre des Bizar{res/*
7 A   {non c'était_
8   *après euh c'était_après la publication de la dernière euh édition du livre des*
9   *Bizarres/*
10C   *mais dans les années 68 euh/justement {y avait eu un scan-un un scandale avec les sa-*
11B   {ouais/mais c'est_assez joli {hein/
12A   {oui c'est joli/
13C   *les sa- les fameux sabots d'Denver/Jean Yanne avait réussi à euh ouvrir un un sabot*
14   *d'Denver/à défaire un sabot d'Denver/avec une épingle à ch'veux d'une dame qu'avait*
15   *traîné dans sa voiture/*
16A   *c'était vous/*
17C   *non/et pis quoi encore/et tant d'autres(?)/*

becomes entangled in itself (compare with *'qu'est-ce que c'est qui est comme de l'huile'* and *'qu'est-ce qui est comme de l'huile'*);

- vagueness:

  cf. for example B's ambiguous *c'est comme de l'huile* [6] — does it refer to taste, to colour, to consistency?; or again his constant recourse to purely adjectival opinions;

- argument:

  B's evasive and minimalist statements, his failure to break out of the pattern he has created, by, for instance introducing new lexis or illustrating his assertions, confine the argument to a circularity which, in the end, makes it non-viable and compels A to bring the exchange to a close by turning to another interlocutor.

On the other hand, it does not take long to pinpoint how assessing the learners' performance along these lines, and equating fluency with linguistic accuracy, lexical variety, syntactic complexity, appropriateness, in some respects fails to do them justice, just as it would, too, fail to do justice to the NS speakers in the other extracts in the Table (cf. B [2] in Extract 2 [young boy/interviewer exchange]), for example, whose speech, like B's in Extract 1 [learner exchange], is characterised by vagueness, changes of mind and lexical infelicities). It does not engage with the performative and interactive features which, as in the other examples, modulate the exchange, and it gives no credit to strategies which do sustain it in a relativised situation in which, again as in the other examples, the degree of fluency is ultimately a measure internal to the participants themselves. More particularly, it is wanting on two counts: it does not recognise that what it identifies as shortcomings may have a positive value, and it does not measure the effectiveness of what is correct but linguistically unnoteworthy.

Positive value of linguistic weaknesses

The problems identified in the learners' exchange thus have mitigating features. Mixing levels may well infringe on appropriacy. But it may also be a tacitly agreed tactic whereby speakers, including native speakers, avail themselves of a wider range of lexical and syntactic resources, a wider range of responses, and promote spontaneity and flow (see B's lapses into the colloquial with, for instance, *truc* [3] and *i s'en foutent* [13–14] in Extract 2 [young boy/interviewer], or geniality (see *une dame qu'avait traîné dans sa voiture* [14–15] in Extract 3 [ad-lib radio talk] for instance). Students themselves may well not make appropriate discriminations: thus the fact that B in Extract 1 [learner exchange] gives no accentual emphasis to *'dégueulasse'* [4, 10] may suggest that he sees the word simply as a stronger synonym of *'dégoûtant'*. It is also likely that the classroom, which is after all no less valid, as a determinant of fluency parameters, than any other setting, peculiarly minimises differentiation of levels. But students know well enough that they are engaged in the study of a foreign language at all of its levels, and can be justified in assuming that oral practice is an opportunity to exercise production also at all levels, in an exploratory play mode leading to finer discriminations.

B's grammatically incorrect *'c'est'* in the learner exchange can be similarly qualified. First, its referent is never in doubt, there is no danger of incomprehension. It is also a construction which FL learners affiliate, along with other items (e.g. *'quelque chose comme ça'*, *'ça'*, *'bon'*, *'mais'*, *'et'*, *'il y a'*, *'il faut (que)'*, *'je pense (que)'*, *'je veux dire (que)'*), and with some justification (see Towell *et al.*, 1996), to the spoken language. So that their use of it is a marker of their desire to engage in oral performance in the spirit of the language, and an invitation, too, for others in the group to operate in that lingua franca of learners of French in which these kinds of items are important: they may not always be appropriate, but they act as useful ready-made platforms providing time and impetus to proceed with the construction of messages, as they do, too, for native speakers (see examples in all three extracts).

Again, vagueness, or the repetition of a certain restricted lexis, may betray lexical weakness. It may, on the other hand, be a way of authenticating the speech of the interlocutor, become part of an agreement between speakers to use one word as the most satisfactory to their purpose, and a guarantee of continuability in the terms they have set for the exchange (cf. *c'est comme de l'huile* [6, 7] in Extract 1 [learner exchange], and the repetition of *joli* [11, 12] in Extract 3 [ad-lib radio talk]). To the extent that it invites question or elaboration, it can also have turn-offering functions. This is perhaps not what B had in mind when he introduced his *c'est comme de l'huile* simile [6] (Extract 1 [learner exchange]), but this does not make it any less provocative. Simile itself, as a figure which appeals to common knowledge and is a way of sharing experience, has, quite apart from introducing a new lexical set, an important communicative value. This can also be true of minimalist or evasive argument: it is inappropriate in the learners' exchange, which it dooms to a premature end, but may, in other contexts, work as a kind of exchange-nurturing conversational irritant (see examples in Chapter 4).

Linguistically inconspicuous features

Equally relevant are those features which, though correct and linguistically inconspicuous, play an active role in the management of exchange, in its engineering: B's *mais* for instance, in *oh mais c'est . dégoûtant* [2] (Extract 1 [learner exchange]) which has no adversative function, yet not only combines with *oh, c'est* and the silent pause to provide time, but also has a coordinating function, makes exchange fluid and continuous (compare with '*c'est dégoûtant* on its own), and builds into this function a note of mild outrage then authorised by the choice of a suitably negative adjective; or again A's *vraiment*, which, while exposing some dissatisfaction with B's unsupported claim, also, by its economy and concessive overtone, acts as an encouragement: it both acknowledges B's utterance and obliquely requests further explanation, at once expresses interest and asks a question (all of which is unfortunately lost on B, who takes this '*vraiment*' as an invitation to reaffirm his statement and borrows it as an intensifier; cf. *oui c'est 'vraiment dégueulasse* [4]); A's subsequent *et* in *et pourquoi ça* [5], see the question she is then compelled to put more directly to elicit an explanation, is equally tactful: it is as though B's *vraiment* had been a satisfactory response and she was now moving on to the next step; a '*mais*', in contrast, with its intimation that no progress had been made, would have made her question more impatient and hostile. A's linguistic clumsiness is, in other words, compensated by an interactional finesse akin to [interviewer] A's in the NS Extract 2 [young boy/interviewer exchange], whose *un p'tit peu/c't-à-dire/* [11] to elicit further information from the young boy after a minimal answer (*ben oui/un p'tit peu/* [10]) is similarly supportive (see use of repetition as a softening device; compare with '*c't-à-dire*' on its own; see also his use of '*et*' in the first question [1]).

Performative features

There is perhaps no need to spend too long here on performative features such as hesitations, filled and unfilled pauses, repetitions, vocalisations etc., whose functions (time-gaining and interaction management devices, syntactic markers, etc.) were already introduced in the previous chapter, and will be taken up again later, except to confirm two things: their frequent occurrence and multifunctionality in native speech itself, whatever the context; and their redeeming effects in learners' speech. Thus the first pause in A's opening utterance in Extract 1 (i.e. after *monsieur Constance* . [1]) has a touch of deliberateness which helps settle into the discussion and ensure attention; it is a formality feature as well — a sign of polite respect for the interlocutor. B's time-gaining pauses and repetitions take on a rhetorical force which gives his statements finality and authority and excuses him (almost) from elaborating (see *oh mais c'est* . *dégoûtant* [2], *parc'que/parc'que/* . *c'est comme de l'huile/* [6]), becomes, at the end of the exchange, a way of toying with his listeners: see *et c'est/* . *c'est trop/c'est trop/c'est* . *trop* .. *dégueulasse* [9–10] in which what is a latent weakness is converted into an expressive and manipulative feature, made to work to his advantage.

What even a cursory review confirms, in other words, is that those very features of the spoken language which make exchange linguistically less demanding are equally integral components not just of conversation, but of conversational *engineering*. And thus, even though they may not, in the non-confident FL learner, have strategic motives, may derive simply from a lack, they do have strategic implications, both for his own production and for the interlocutor's perception of it (see previous chapter), which he needs to understand: a learner may hesitate because he is momentarily at a loss for words, but that hesitation has, willy-nilly, an expressive range/effectiveness, which, whatever its motives, must be integrated into the exchange. On the other hand, responding to such characteristics is a prerequisite for dealing with the speech of other speakers, who may start in one direction and proceed in another, produce utterances which are so discontinuous that the reconstruction process and the search for coherence become very complex; it is part and parcel of receptive fluency, and vital for keeping exchanges on track.

Yet it would be inadequate to equate the high incidence of these features with fluency. Fluency lies in the performative embedding of these features, in the linguistic strategies and psychological/behavioural moves which make interactional and transactional exchange *viable* and optimally *efficient* (with 'interactional' referring to the maintenance of social relationships and 'transactional' to the conveying of information (Brown & Yule, 1983: 11)). For, as the previous chapters made clear, the notion of exchange, and those factors which promote, facilitate or simply sustain it, are, in the end, central to the question of fluency. How, then, can the notions of viability and efficiency be defined to fit in with this view?

Viability and efficiency

The idea of *viability* presents an image of an exchange in which the speakers meet on grounds of *assumed* or *constructed* equality (see Grice, 1975) so that the continuability of the exchange is more or less guaranteed. To establish this play of equality, certain communicative competences are obviously highly desirable for the foreign language learner — defined in terms of pronunciation, intonation, syntax, lexis, level and appropriateness. But just as important is a feeling for those strategies and behavioural moves which can actively equalise conversation as it occurs, which can reduce inequities: a primary responsibility of those taking part in a conversation is to make other participants feel at home in it, to constantly share possession of that conversation. In other words, viability views exchange as a sequence of linguistic and behavioural negotiations designed to support, maintain and facilitate the transmission of meaning, and likely to contribute to the smoothness, continuity and facility of the exchange.

The examples in Table 7 give a taste of some of the kinds of resources on which language learners can draw to maintain viability. The point is to understand how they work and to make strategic use of their complementary functions: to capitalise on the interactional and syntactic value of what are also task stress features, including filled pauses (e.g. *'euh'*, *'ben'*, *'et ben'*, *'bon'*, *'hein'*, *'alors'*, etc.), of phatic fillers and discourse markers (*'tu sais'*/*'vous savez'*, *'tu vois'*/*'vous voyez'*; *'je veux dire'*, *'je pense'*, *'c'est-à-dire'* etc.), of pitch, rhythm and intonation; to build on more properly 'linguistic' features, such as pre-packaged formulae or again the resources made available by the interlocutor (e.g. lexical items or syntactic constructions, reformulations and prompting), coordinating devices (coherence markers yet also agents of smoothness and continuity, e.g. *'et'*, *'mais'*), simile or other figures of speech, which, while eloquent in expressing meaning, are also, inasmuch as they appeal to common knowledge, a way of sharing experience; and, generally, to build up a repertoire of communication strategies (Faerch & Kasper, 1983; Ellis, 1985; Tarone, 1980; etc.) and draw on them not merely as remedial *pis-aller*, but as vehicles for promoting more constructive verbal involvement and exchange. It would, concurrently, involve use of non-verbal features (facial expression, gestures, body projection) which only play a very small part in the learner Extract [1], and, not unusually in the classroom, remain rather constrained: their function is essentially limited to role definition (e.g. use, by A, of an imaginary microphone to assert her role as discussion leader and interviewer), with neither speaker making much at all of their expressive and interactional potential.

For languages as close as, say, French and English, processes of negotiation, including those involved in sustaining viability, may not be very different. According to Brown and Yule, this is particularly true in interactional speech, where what a student knows of his own language can be transferred to the foreign language. But, as they also note, 'it may be necessary to bring to his [the student's] attention what happens in his native language, since our "knowledge" of . . . communicative matters is usually held well below the level of consciousness' (Brown & Yule, 1983: 23; see also O'Malley & Chamot, 1990). Since this process of transference does not, then, necessarily occur spontaneously in learners, not least perhaps because of the psychological pressures they experience (lack of confidence, feeling of inadequacy, maintenance of classroom roles), it seems important that while they should become aware of what differences there are, they should equally be helped to assess and exploit what is already at their disposal, and in particular rationalise its use in different contexts. What is perhaps even more crucial, because it often tends to be neglected in teaching, is that they should be able to take in, and respond to, the various signals given by viability features, that they should, in other words, be able to understand their relevance to receptive and interactional fluency. These various points will be taken up in greater detail in subsequent chapters.

Viability is a prerequisite for efficiency, inasmuch as all exchange, whatever its immediate function, is made more efficient by its value as socialisation. While viability establishes and maintains the framework of exchange, speech *efficiency*, which more narrowly depends on the exercise of linguistic abilities (i.e. on the implementation of what are described as production strategies — see Ellis, 1985; Faerch & Kasper, 1983; Tarone, 1980, etc.), relates to the expression of meaning proper and capitalises upon the framework to achieve objectives (transfer of information, expression of feeling, opinion, etc.). But optimal efficiency is not an absolute: each speech situation defines its own level of optimal efficiency, where equations between the needs and competences of each participant, and what each participant can be expected to derive from, and contribute to, the competences and needs of the other(s), should be taken into account. Unlike accuracy, which is ultimately speaker- and norm-related (and bound with individual competence), the notion of efficiency is context-determined, varies with each exchange situation, and is a function of the interaction of the speakers' individual competences even though it relates to the exploitation of the speakers' own resources; it is, as it were, an interactive correlate of accuracy. As such the notion of optimal efficiency needs to be relativised, just as does the notion of fluency itself. In each exchange situation, it is the speakers involved who, through the strategies of viability, through a kind of linguistic and paralinguistic barter, establish what constitutes fluency in that situation. Once the level of fluency has been set, then each speaker can exploit it *more or less efficiently* in relation to his own capacities. In other words a speaker cannot be more fluent, or indeed less fluent, than the parameters of the particular exchange situation permit; but he can use the given fluency *more or less efficiently*. More fluency (in the sense of a higher degree of carefully articulated 'educated' speech), could in many exchange situations lead to a much lower efficiency if it involved a breaking of the viability contract. A child speaking with his mother can operate with the same degree of efficiency within *his* given, though perhaps more limited, parameters, as a politician speaking with another politician within *his* parameters; and in this sense, a small child may be as fluent as a politician.

The interviewer/young boy TV exchange in Table 7 (Extract 2) is interesting in these respects. It is really a three-way exchange, involving not just the two protagonists, but also the public for whom it is intended. What the interviewer does, accordingly, is negotiate viability, and the interplay between viability and efficiency, on two different planes, corresponding to different parameters and expectations: those he associates with the audience (as evidenced in the linguistically more sophisticated first part of his second question in [7–8]), and those he associates with the young boy (see subsequent more conversational reformulation [8–9]). The boy's speech is equally revealing: his efforts to increase his efficiency in a context which clearly makes heavy demands on his linguistic abilities, including his reliance on viability features, are a reminder of just how relative efficiency is, even for native speakers, depending on age, linguistic experience, setting, and a reminder, too, of just how closely interrelated efficiency and viability are in practice. These points will be taken up in Chapter 4.

In the meantime, what can be confirmed *a fortiori* is that the concept of a target language, with its attendant notion of conformity, is itself a relative notion: the foreign language is not a ready-formed entity which exists beyond the student, towards which he is always struggling and which he will never reach (since it is implicitly defined as a totality); it is something always available for use, potentially efficient in all its transitional stages (as one's native language is), as long as speakers are prepared to interact with the proper viability moves. And in this sense, the oral target for the foreign language learner in any exchange is not a language beyond the exchange, but rather the maximal use of all his own present resources (linguistic and non-linguistic) (see the fluency end in Brumfit's fluency/accuracy methodological continuum (Brumfit, 1984)), yet also its *critical* use and the absorption of the resources of the interlocutor for now and for later, when they can serve as a platform for ever more intricately negotiated interactions.

Fluency and Language Learning

What, then, would constitute an increase in, or development of, fluency in these conditions? Not just the ability to speak *better*, if that merely meant in a linguistically more sophisticated fashion; nor indeed the abiltiy to speak *more*, or *more easily*, if that merely meant stringing words together indiscriminately. Rather it would mean three things: the ability to communicate more efficiently in a given exchange situation, which involves, as we have seen the ability to understand, and operate with suitable, viability moves, the ability to cope with an ever larger variety of exchange situations discriminatingly, and thirdly, the ability to capitalise on both in a dynamic fashion to expand and refine language capacities.

Extensive exposure to native speakers will in many cases produce an increase in the viability/communicative efficiency of FL learners. But this is not always so (see Schuman's (1976) pidginisation hypothesis for example). In any case, cannot, indeed should not, the process be speeded up and rationalised by helping learners to develop self-monitoring mechanisms in the classroom beforehand? The classroom, which gathers together a stable group of individuals in controlled conditions, is, in fact, an ideal context in which to identify and measure efficiency, understand its relation with viability, and invest existing knowledge at reduced risk, whatever drawbacks it may have otherwise. Yet involvement in communicative activities — the main medium to improve fluency in the classroom — is not necessarily sufficient to achieve this: if such activities merely create the situational and psychological/motivational *conditions* for learners to activate their communicative competence through interpersonal exchange, without ostensible reference to those features which actively promote it, or indeed simply make it what it is, they are in effect little more than a contrived — if less daunting — substitute for (some forms of) natural exposure, and can hardly prove more efficient and economical. Furthermore, as was previously noted, the external synthesis involved in the communication process, whether in the classroom or in a native setting, cannot guarantee that necessary differentiations and rationalisations will be made (see Widdowson, 1990): thus even though students abroad undoubtedly find themselves in many different exchange situations, they seem unable to perceive, in many cases, the viability coefficient peculiar to each situation. For many university students returning from a year abroad, in France in this instance, conversational French means a French of idiom, slang and contraction, regardless of what specific situations demand in terms of appropriacy, acceptability, etc.; and this cannot but raise questions about the extent to which they actually take notice of, and receptively and interactionally integrate, the viability and efficiency features characteristic of the verbal behaviour of the (native) speakers which whom they interact.

Fostering the development of fluency in and beyond the classroom, may, then, mean more, in particular for more advanced students, than making methodological provision for (communication-based) fluency activities alongside (communication-based) accuracy activities (see Brumfit, 1984) — the better scenario; as to equating it with tightly controlled practice subordinated to the building-up of (primarily linguistic) competence and accuracy (Hammerly, 1991), it is at best naive, if not ill-informed and misguided. If taken seriously, helping students on the road to fluency is also to do with empowering them to identify, and assess the value and function of, fluency parameters, in both production and reception, thus enabling them not only to cope with the ever-fluctuating nature of fluency in practice, but also to assimilate it critically. And if fluency is a legitimate aim for FL pedagogy, to neglect the opportunities offered by the classroom to help students develop a meta-awareness of what it entails and to promote it other than as a by-product of exchange is to lay the virtues of pedagogy to waste.

The role of actual verbal involvement itself in language development cannot, of course, be minimised: the familiar 'practice makes fluent' of popular wisdom has long been given theoretical credence with the widespread acknowledgement that communication is conducive to learning: this at least is not a bone of contention in language learning research, however inconclusive or polemical it may be in other respects, and whatever directions it may now take, under, in particular, the influence of cognitive psychology. First of all, it is a source of data, whose role in learning is axiomatic, even though the effect on acquisition of the nature of the input to which a learner is exposed — and its value as intake — *has been* a matter of controversy (see Krashen's monitor theory and notion of comprehensible input (1977, 1981, 1982, 1985) and critical reviews thereof (Gregg, 1984; McLaughlin, 1978, 1987); see also Hatch, 1983). If, however, the tailoring of input to the requirements of participants in any particular exchange is a function of the interactional negotiation of meaning to achieve communication (Hatch, 1983; Long, 1983 a, b), then for students not only to engage in meaning negotiations, but equally to develop an *awareness* of what this involves, to understand the function of viability features, may help them not only to elicit input, but to elicit input likely to challenge their potentialities: as a shared activity, the negotiation of meaning engages the responsibility of all participants in exchanges, not least that of the learner, whose feedback 'affects the nature of subsequent input from the native speaker' (Ellis, 1985: 138; see also Chapter 2). And, secondly, communication is practice and the opportunity to activate cognitive processes involved in learning — directly through learning strategies (hypothesis formation, hypothesis testing and, crucially, automatisation; c.f. for instance Ellis, 1985; McLaughlin, 1987; also Schmidt, 1992; Towell *et al.*, 1996 for an update with reference to fluency specifically), or indirectly through strategies of use (production and communication strategies; see Ellis, 1985, 1990; Faerch & Kasper, 1983; Tarone, 1980, 1983).

However, with the increased convergence of work on strategies in second language acquisition research and cognitive psychology, and the surge of interest in the relationship between language and cognition generally, evidence is also building up in support of the assumption of a relationship between learner reflective empowerment and language learning and language use: despite variations in both theoretical and empirical justifications and pedagogical proposals, there is a growing consensus that a meta-awareness of what is involved in communicating and learning can assist learners in extending and challenging their mastery of language (Bialystok, 1990; Ellis, 1990; Johnson, 1996; McLaughlin, 1987; O'Malley &

Chamot, 1990; Skehan, 1989; Widdowson, 1983, 1990). The theme is also recurrent in the literature on learner independence and autonomy, where the importance of learners' informed cognitive participation for language learning and language use, including self-monitoring of progress, is an underlying premise (see for instance Benson & Voller, 1997), as it is indeed in applied linguistics generally, where the idea of viewing and treating learners as active agents in their own learning is rapidly gaining ground (see for instance Grenfell & Harris, 1993; Oxford, 1989).

As far as developing interactional verbal fluency is concerned, the case for combining practice with an analytic and reflective approach to language learning and use is all the more compelling as some of its aspects defy systematic description, and cannot be, or have not been, encapsulated as stable teaching or learning points in the traditional sense. Amongst those whose value can be assessed, some clearly have a point of reference in (communicative) competence, and are an essential norm-related investment for fluency. Others, features of the spoken medium which tend to be neglected in teaching as performance factors, are far less incidental, in some of their manifestations, than their 'performance' status makes them out to be: the use of hesitation phenomena and temporal and sequential features as discourse markers within utterances, is, for instance, as was indicated in Chapter 2 and will be confirmed by analyses of NS speech in Chapters 5 and 6, noticeably regular; it is, in particular a frequently occuring means of introducing the kind of lateral information normally contained in subordinate clauses in the written mode. The impact of this for the learner as hearer or interlocutor, for receptive fluency, cannot be underestimated: processing native speaker verbal output is notoriously troublesome for FL learners, however advanced, not least because they find it so difficult to identify discourse boundaries, assess the status of the information within stretches of utterance and cope with the form of spoken language generally.

Contrary to Hammerly's conviction, to cater for fluency *and* accuracy in the classroom is not, even on these lines alone, just a matter, then, of refocusing on language structure, with fluency subordinated to the classroom-bound imparting of (essentially linguistic) competence. 'Pushing' learners into the production of precise, coherent and appropriate messages *is* — as Swain (1985, 1995) demonstrates — essential to systematise syntactic processing in production, and has, accordingly, an important role to play in verbal development (hence the peculiar relevance of planned speech to students' concerns; see Chapter 6). But to reconcile fluency and accuracy also supposes that we should come to terms, and help students to come to terms, with the very nature of verbal accuracy and with what is involved in fluency above and beyond accuracy.

To do justice to fluency is all the more justifiable as fluency is also, and perhaps first and foremost, *creative* performance, re-invents and re-invests itself with each new exchange and within each exchange, enriches itself with all that it makes available to itself at any one point, ceaselessly plays on, challenges even, its linguistic foundations, is an individual but constantly negotiable paradigm, is, in short, a dynamic of language use. In this sense, pedagogical approaches to fluency can only be data-driven, inductive in nature. But inductive capacities are not necessarily a given. And it is also to these inductive capacities that students must consciously devote their energies to come to grips with their own and other people's fluency, and to these inductive capacities, and inductive analysis, that the teaching of fluency must, too, be directed. That is the central assumption behind the methodological procedures and applications to be illustrated in the next few chapters, and the central assumption behind their underpinning motif — the mutually supporting interplay between study of data and practical activities.

Teaching Fluency

There are practical as well as academic reasons for making the study of spoken data — native speaker and learner data — an integral ingredient of a pedagogy of fluency:

- it makes for an integrated approach to the mechanisms of verbal performance as a whole, inclusive of aspects which transcend conformity to rule-governed behaviour;
- it is a means of equipping learners with the critical wherewithal to build on exposure to resources within and beyond the classroom more discriminatingly;
- it can facilitate the emergence of individual paradigms of fluency, enable students to identify the features and strategies of greatest relevance to them as learners and communicators, and, concurrently, help them to exploit both their strengths and weaknesses more efficiently;
- it can encourage them to take greater responsibility for their learning, to create their own objectives, individually or as a group;
- it can give them the diachronic opportunity to see where progress has been made despite the persistence of, say, linguistic errors — thus increase their confidence and motivation through sense of success (O'Malley & Chamot 1990: 161; Savignon, 1972).

By the same token, it creates opportunities for giving focus to practice itself, and a meta-cognitive edge to exercises, including, with adaptations, the wide range available from communicative methodology (cf. however,

Nolasco & Arthur (1987), whose exercises are particularly interesting for their awareness-raising functions). In other words, it provides a teaching and learning framework for approaching fluency more critically, can be used as a platform for helping learners to negotiate the shift from communicative ease to communicative control and sophistication, and project the developement of their fluency beyond the confines of formal settings to transcend their inescapable limits — time and restricted exposure to resources. To teach fluency, in this sense, fits in with what Grenfell and Harris describe as returning 'ownership' of the language to learners (Grenfell & Harris, 1993). What is also at stake is returning to them ownership of their learning.

That leaves the question of classroom implementation. What the next few chapters will set out to do is harness these general observations to classroom practice, show how the analysis of data, and the interplay between analysis and informed practice, can be handled to teach fluency along the lines outlined here, using viability and efficiency as a backdrop. Each will focus on one of the main questions identified so far, from the complementary ends of production and reception: aspects of relativity and negotiation, relationship between the form/discourse features of speech and fluency in different modes (i.e. unplanned speech and planned speech) and paralinguistic behaviour. There are, however, still a few practical points to clear by way of general introduction, and by way, too, of pre-empting possible objections.

About overall content, rationale and applicability

All chapters in this second part by and large follow a similar pattern: all hinge on one or several samples of spoken data in transcription, sometimes set against other kinds of texts (e.g. written passage in Chapter 6), and build on their study, handled from the point of view of teachers and learners (see 'level and approach' below), to (a) draw out implications and (b) give a point of application to exercises or prompt other enquiries (some described in full, other more briefly outlined). There are, all the same, variations or different emphases in each (Chapter 4 for instance grows directly out of the study of data, Chapters 5 and 6 use exercises as a grounding platform), so as to diversify teaching options and illustrate a wider range of possibilities, that is to say *methodological* possibilities.

What must be made clear from the start is that the studies of samples and exercises in the pages to follow are not meant to be applied to the letter in the very same way, in the same sequence, or exhaustively. Rather they are intended to work as a general guide, exemplifying techniques for inducing analysis, eliciting observations about different facets of fluency, devising supporting applications or harnessing existing exercises to the objectives pursued (see rationale at the end of Chapter 4). They are, in short, to be read at the level of principles, generically, and adapted to suit available materials and particular classroom conditions or groups of students.

Because the studies of extracts, beyond giving examples of ways to handle analysis with students, are also designed to corroborate and expand what has been said so far about fluency, they are, in any case, far more detailed in their coverage than would be called for in the classroom, where time available and students' response regulate their depth and range as a matter of course, and where selectivity needs to apply.

About the choice of samples

There is little point in making teaching suggestions for approaching fluency through data if the kind of materials to which they are meant to apply are difficult to come by. The main criterion in the choice of extracts was, accordingly, ready availability. With one exception (an exchange recorded in a French nursery school in Chapter 4), all come from widely accessible sources (radio, TV5). In all but this instance, they were in fact simply selected from existing tape library stock on the basis of general characteristics (e.g. kinds of interaction, types of individuals involved, type of speech) likely to generate forms of comparison consonant with the objectives of individual chapters, rather than because they were particularly suited to make specific points: given the nature of fluency, any extract is as fitting as any other, within its own contextual attributes, to prompt comments about aspects and parameters reviewed so far, or still to be reviewed.

The downside of this is that everyday conversational interactions are not very well represented. Recordings of bona fide everyday exchanges (i.e. recorded under conditions safeguarding their authenticity) are still, by and large, difficult to come by: the corpora of spoken language collected in various quarters (e.g. for research) are not yet not readily available for classroom use, or adapted to it, with some rare exceptions (for instance Carter and McCarthy's (1997) corpus of conversational interactions for English). Once they are, they will open up exciting didactic possibilities: electronic databases in particular, used in conjunction with concordancing software look set to have a major impact in this respect.

In the meantime, what materials *are* available, in the form of radio and TV debates, ad-lib discussions, interviews, etc., as well as film or other forms of acted out dialogues (a useful counterpoint to real-life examples), samples of planned speech (e.g. news items or speeches — equally relevant, in their own way, to students' concerns) and video-recordings of learners' own exchanges, are, as we shall see, ample for prompting students to get to grips with what is involved in verbal communication in different contexts and types of exchanges.

About level and approach

The work proposed has been developed for, and for the most part used with, undergraduate students about to spend a year abroad in France, for whom being prepared to optimise exposure to resources is particularly important. It is, in other words, targeted at advanced learners. But this does not restrict its application exclusively to them: as was previously made clear, it can be adapted, and in particular toned down and graded to work at less advanced levels, in several different ways, if only by dealing with fewer, shorter and simpler extracts, and restricting observations to a subset of points — the most conspicuous, or the most relevant to learners' immediate concerns (see practical tips for handling analysis at the end of Chapter 4).

All the same, it could still be argued that engaging students in analysing verbal behaviour is perhaps expecting too much: after all, specialised research itself bears witness to its complexities. The point, however, is not to emulate state-of-the-art studies in discourse or conversational analysis so much as to harness their approach to the concerns of fluency development: to give students the initiative and confidence to reflect, at their level, on the ins-and-outs of verbal behaviour and, in so doing, place them in a position to develop a better working grasp of what is, after all, the mainstay of their learning activities; and to give ourselves, their teachers, the means of guiding them in achieving these ends. This does not, in the first instance, require much more than common sense and some basic points of reference — such as those discussed in this and earlier chapters. What matters is to root the work in what students already know, and to gradually build up their capacity to handle enquiry and make insights their own. That is the underlying principle behind the approach adopted for handling data in the next few chapters.

Analyses, while drawing on conversational and discourse analysis, are accordingly conducted from the point of view of students and teachers, with their particular concerns in mind: samples of text are explored inductively in a gradual guided discovery mode with a dual function — eliciting observations and making sense of them step-by-step, while simultaneously giving students a framework to rationalise and build on what they already know, and teachers a framework in which to integrate what they may already be working with. There are shortcuts, to cut down on extended question/answer sequences or convoluted explanations, and, for the same reason, shifts from fairly standard to more technical terminology. All the same, writing and cross-referencing have the inevitable consequence of projecting the processes described as longer, and more complex, than they are in practice: the pace at which they are handled orally in a group is, in my experience, far brisker, and the motions of discovery far less tangled.

About the transcriptions

The transcriptions of the extracts used are very simple: they were produced using a standard tape recorder, that is to say without the specialist's expertise or high-tech equipment to decide unreservedly where breaks between tonal groups fall, or accurately to measure rate of speech, length of pauses or changes in pitch — an exacting task at the best of times, let alone when working by ear alone; it is indeed a measure of the subjectivity of perception, and of the perception of fluency itself, that it should be so absorbing to locate where pauses, repetitions, drawls or hesitation fillers occur, and in what sequence (see Blanche-Benveniste & Jeanjean (1987) about transcription problems). The transcriptions are nonetheless as scrupulous as they can be under the circumstances, yet confined to what it is in the power of teachers to produce under the kinds of pressure to which they are subjected, or to what students themselves can be asked to produce. Notations are kept to the minimum necessary to support the argument about particular stretches of discourse, and, in some cases, are provided only in the examples quoted rather than included in the full text given in accompanying tables. They include the following:

/	break between tonal groups
/ /	interruption by another speaker
{	overlaps
x_x	liaison
<u>x</u>	articulated vowel (e.g. articulated 'e')
.	silent pause (. . , . . . for longer silent pauses)
'xxx	stressed word
<u>xx</u>	drawl
???	inaudible matter
[↑].[-]	faster speech rate in framed sequence
[↓].[-]	slower speech rate in framed sequence.

Chapter 4

Relativity and Negotiation in Verbal Interactions

One way for language learners to approach fluency is to observe it in the speech of those for whom it is assumed to be a given — native speakers themselves, of different maturity, in different contexts: how do *they* manage, what can be learned from them?

These questions will be applied to four extracts of NS interactions in transcription (see Tables 8–11), about which no contextualising information is initially given. Making out what verbal exchanges are from their transcriptions alone, and without knowing anything about them at all, is an unnatural challenge. Because clues are limited, or elusive, interpretation is bound to be speculative, even when it comes to basic details (e.g. setting, status and age of participants, specific topic). But the unravelling process is an incentive to be more inquisitive, to look for clues which would perhaps otherwise pass unnoticed; and it prompts comparison, the methodological platform needed to shift the discussion to its intended grounds.

The purpose of comparison in this case is to draw students' attention to the relative nature of fluency and to the way it is negotiated in different interactive set-ups, with analysis proceeding in three stages, to: (a) contextualise the four extracts, (b) trace aspects of relativity and negotiation in the extracts, concentrating initially, by way of introduction and sensitisation, on the sections in bold, and (c) diversify findings by taking in their wider context. The next section considers the implications of the analyses for learners, before observations are taken up in a sample of empirical activities with related purposes, but with the angle of approach shifted to first-hand experience. The chapter concludes with practical considerations on handling analyses in the classroom.

Investigating Data: Comparison of Extracts
Setting the extracts in context

What basic contextual information can, to begin with, be inferred from the four extracts in Tables 8–11, what first textual clues do they provide?

Table 8 Extract 1

(.)	
1 A	*mais vous savez qu'c'est fini la fête là/d'hier/hein/. la fête c'est terminé/*
2 B	*moi à la fête foraine/et ben j'ai vomi/parce que . /y avait des grands manèges/*
	[ctd 6]
4 C	*moi j'ai ???*
. . .	[indistinct overlaps]
5 A	*comment/*
6 [B]	*j'ai eu peur des manèges/j'ai vomi moi/*
7 A	<u>ah</u>/toi tu as eu peur/[B oui]/ben c'est vrai qu'y a des grands manèges hein/oui
8	<u>Sanah</u>/
9 D	*ben moi j'ai fait des grands manèges hein/*
10 E	*moi maîtresse/j'ai fait la roulotte en glace/*
11 A	<u>ah</u>/oui/la galerie des glaces/c'est rigolo ça/hein/
12 F	*moi aussi . . .*
. . .	[indistinct overlaps]
13 A	*faut pas t'gratter Kevin/{parc'que sinon tu vas passer la varicelle {aux autres/*
14 E	{quand {quand/quand
15 "	*j'étais <u>euh</u>/au manège/ben j'étais allée . dans/dans la maison de de glaces/et pis*
16	*j'a-j'arrive là/j'avais même pas vu qu'y avait une glace/j'me 'cogne d'un coup/*
17 A	*'aïe aïe {aïe/*
18 G	{c'est normal/faut faut mettre les mains pour que/pour que ???//
19 A	*faut mettre les mains devant/pour pas s'cogner/.. {ah ouais*
. . .	[indistinct overlaps]
20 H	*eh ben moi/j'ai fait des voitures tamponneuses/* [indistinct overlaps]
21 A	*oh <u>là</u>/toute seule/des petites . /ou des grandes/*
22 H	*des petites/*
23 A	*ah ouais/* [indistinct overlaps]
24 I	{y a des petites et des grandes/
25 K	{moi maîtresse j'suis restée deux minutes coincée là-bas/
26 A	*deux minutes coincée là-bas/* [indistinct overlaps]
27 J	*???/les grandes tu peux pas ça/*
28 A	*mais pourquoi on peut pas les grandes/*
29 G	*et ben Guillaume/il est y allé/mais il est encore plus p'tit qu'eux/.. il est y*
30 "	*allé hein/[sic]*
31 A	*c'est-à-dire qu'y a des enfants qui montent dans les grandes avec leurs parents/ ..*
32	*c'est ça/*
(.)	

Table 9 Extract 2

```
 1 A   (.)/tout l'monde sait 'bien/(que ce n'est pas la publicité/qui fait fumer/ici/j'ai
 2 B                        (?...............?
 3 [A]  en face de moi des tas d'jeunes/ici i peuvent "tous me dire/c'est/qu'est-ce qui
 4      les_a fait 'fumer leur première paquet de cigarettes/ce n'est pas (. si vous
 5      voulez de la publici-//
 6 B                                                            (ah non/on n'a
 7      jamais dit (ça//
 8 A              (mais/ce n'est (pas de la publicité//      (tout le monde//
 9 B                            (c'est vrai/non mais la pub(licité doit
10      entretenir/doit entretenir le le (le//
11 A                           (non la publicité est_un_'instrument de
12      compétition 'commerciale entre les marques/c'est ça q'nous_oublions (aujourd'hui//
13 B                                                            (si demain
14      c'est 'vraiment 'totalement 'interdit 'partout/est-ce que . vous mettez la clé
15      sous la porte/ [short silence]
16 C    'oui/(je je crois que c'est vraiment leur inquiétude/(c'est_effecti(vement leur
17 A    (j'ai pas/j'ai pas/non-on oh//             (je crois pas//(oui mais/vous
18 C    plus grosse inquiétude/
19 A    vous m'prêtez/vous m'p(rêtez/des points de vue qui (n'en sont pas/
20 ?                 (Monsieur//                (Mon(sieur Fernandez//
21 B                                                    (j'vois pas l'intérêt
22      d'faire de la pub si ça fait pas vendre . quand même//
23 A    mais . cela fait vendre/mes 'produits . /ici on est quand même dans_un
24      (marché d'économie//
25 B    (oui mais vous dites ça fait pas ça fait pas ach'ter un paquet d'Marlboro la-de
26      Marlboro la pub (sur euh//
27 A                  (ça fait/ça ne fait pas fumer un non-fumeur/c'est_un 'instrument
28      de compétition 'commerciale/dans_un marché concurrentiel/qui est_un marché
29      (comme le p-tabac/ 'éminemment concurrentiel/
30 B    (alors vous nous dites que les médecins/ . vous vous dites des choses un peu
31      (dures/vous dites que/attendez/attendez/attendez/
32 D    (bon ??? y a un certain nombre d'erreurs qui ont été dites là/y a quand même deux
33      profondes_erreurs/la première c'est que/vous l'savez comme moi/le tabac est
34      justement 'un des produits que la population modifie le 'moins/dans ses
35      comportements/c'est-à-dire que/on change très très peu de marque/(seuls 2%//
36 A                                                            (c'est pas vrai/
37      c'est (faux/
38[D]   (se(uls//
39 A          (c'est faux/plus d'50% [non non] des (des fumeurs change de marque/
40 D                                    (seuls 2% (d'la population change/
41 A                                              (écoutez c'est 'mon
42      (métier//
43 D    (oui mais c'est aussi 'mon travail de l'(savoir/hein//
44 A                                          (écou// non mais si vous
45      voulez mon (métier c'est d'vendre des cigarettes tous les jours/mon métier c'est
46 D               (j'vais un tout p'tit peu plus loin/
47[A]   d'connaître les ci-les les . les consommateurs/votre métier/c'est la santé/je le
```

48	*respecte/respectez mon métier si vous voulez/je suis un honnête homme/je me 'pose*
49	*un certain nombre de questions/quand je vois ce jeune . l'fumer dans la rue/vous*
50	*croyez pas qu'j'me pose des questions/(???) et la question qu'je me pose/je me*
51	*dis/mais pourquoi i fume/*
52 B	*mais pourquoi i fume pas des Phillip Morris/*
53 A	*ouais/ . . éventuellement/* (audience clap) (.)

Table 10 Extract 3

(.)	
1 A	*et comment les gens ont réagi en vous voyant/*
2 B	*ben au début i-i(l)s ont regardé parc'que/i trouvaient pas ça euh/pas tellement*
3	*normal/on aurait dit que c'était un/un truc(que) pour euh/pour euh/soi-disant*
4	*qu'on .. voulait se rendre intéressant/quoi euh/qu'on apporte une . remarque sur*
5	*nous/dans les journaux tout ça/mais c'est pas du tout ça/c'est notre rôle de la*
6	*nettoyer/nous/et de la nettoyer quoi/de la sauver quoi/*
7 A	*est-ce que vous sentez une certaine solidarité autour de vous quand vous prenez*
8	*une telle initiative/est-ce que vous vous r'trouvez avec plein d'gens/qui sont du*
9	*même avis/et qui ont envie d'vous aider/*
10 B	*ben oui/un p'tit peu/*
11 A	*un p'tit peu/c't'-à-dire/*
12 B	*c't-à-dire que les gens euh/quand ils quand ils voyent ça/ça leur fait quelque*
13	*chose/mais du moment que euh/du moment qu'i qu'i sont pas contraints/et ben/i s'en*
14	*foutent/*
15 A	*et vous avez des ambitions d'aménagement/par exemple/*
16 B	*oh là là ouais/on avait parlé avec le maire de Roquevert/pour euh/'emmenager [sic]*
17	*cette rivière/mettre des bancs/des poubelles/ des sentiers de promenade/.. euh*
18	*mettre des euh/des canards aussi/on avait/parc'que/en mettant les canards/les*
19	*gens/i voient qu'i y a de la faune/alors i-z osent pas y toucher/*
20 A	*et la bataille pour la protection d'l'environnement/elle commence ici/*
21 B	*ouais/et elle s'arrêtera pas/* [From outdoor sequence to TV studio]
22 C	*et précisément Emmanuel/nous sommes là pour qu'tu puisses 'témoigner du fait que*
23	*./il y a beaucoup d'gens qui sont 'de ton avis/qui sont sensibilisés à ça d'façon*
24	*à c'que cette bataille/comme tu l'dis si bien/ne s'arrête pas/*
	. . . [Introduction of guests]
25 C	*j'rappelle que tu as treize ans/euh j'voudrais savoir si parmi les copains qui*
26	*sont avec toi/tous ceux qui font soit partie de l'association ou qui t'ont aidé*
27	*dans tes différentes actions/il y a euh une limite d'âge/est-ce que ça va de sept*
28	*à soixante dix sept ans/ou ou n'y a-t-i/ou n'y a-t-il pas d'frontière/*
29 B	*ben y a les gens de euh/les jeunes/les le les tout p'tits jeunes/h//*
30 C	*ça commence à quel âge/*
31 B	*oh ben j'sais pas moi/[C les tout p'tits jeunes]/six ans/à peu près [C ouais]/et*
32	*ça s'arrête à soixante ans/parc'que les les personnes âgées elles peuvent pas/*
33	*descendre les pentes/tout ça//*
34 C	*elles peuvent vous soutenir/mais elles sont/moins actives/disons/[B voilà]/et et*
35	*tu penses que dès six-sept ans/on peut 'commencer malgré cet âge/comme tu l'disais*
36	*euh/un p'tit peu jeune/commencer à être sensibilisé aux problèmes d'environnement*
37	*enfin de propreté d'la nature [B ouais]/tu discutes un p'tit peu avec eux toi/ (.)*

Table 11 Extract 4

1 A	*(.)/est-ce qu'il vous_'arrive d'avoir comme ça des craintes/qui peuvent euh presque*
2	*vous dominer euh/crainte de la gaffe euh euh crainte euh du stress extrême/*
3 B	*euh/d'abord je n'suis sous_aucune influence/[chuckle]/c'est c'est_important à*
4	*dire/et que le non c'est le la la seule drogue euh que je prenne/c'est peut-être*
5	*un cachet d'aspirine avant d'aller à l'antenne quand/par hasard/euh j'ai la*
6	*migraine/c'qui arrive quelquefois le dimanche après un week-end de de travail un*
7	*peu dense/eh non/c'que je crains c'est la fatigue/en direct/vous savez la*
8	*fatigue/qui fait que de temps_en_temps peut-être euh euh/on n'est pas complètement*
9	*attentif à c'que vient d'dire la personne qu'est en face de vous/on pense_à aut'e*
10	*chose/moi ça m'arrive de . euh me dire euh/de r'garder les les les pieds du du*
11	*cadreur/qui est_en face de moi/par exemple là en c'moment/euh ou de voir un une*
12	*poussière sur la table/et pis de décrocher/vous savez/deux trois secondes/deux*
13	*trois secondes et pis tout_à coup on reprend contact avec la réalité/on dit/zut/*
14	*mais qu'est-ce qu'i vient de dire/c'est_épouvantable/j'ai pas écouté/et avoir à*
15	*rebondir derrière c'est quelquefois prendre le risque de dire écoutez j'vous en*
16	*prie madame/je j'viens d'vous l'dire/vous êtes complètement gâteuse/ou vous_avez*
17	*euh vous_écoutez rien/euh et 'là c'est la la vraie panique/c'est la panique de se*
18	*dire/j'ai absolument 'rien écouté d'sa réponse/je suis obligée de 'relancer et je*
19	*me 'lance à l'eau/et et je vais me faire 'ramasser/non c'est c'est pt'ête la seule*
20	*crainte/c'est parfois un peu d'fatigue qui fait que euh/l'attention dans_une*
21	*émission elle est forcément 'énorme/et la concentration est très forte/c'pour ça*
22	*qu'on sort d'une émission/vous l'savez bien/une émission d'télévision on_en sort .*
23	*'vidé/on_en sort . 'mort/on pourrait 's'allonger par terre dans l'studio et*
24	*dormir/parce que c'est une_'dépense nerveuse extraordinaire/c't' un effort de*
25	*concentration/alors vous l'faites d'autant mieux que vous êtes_reposé/et d'autant*
26	*plus plus mal que vous êtes_un peu fatigué/*
(...)	
27 A	*et pourtant . euh/je pense qu'un jour on vous_a posé la question/voudriez-vous .*
28	*euh inviter . 'Saddam Hussein/vlà un personnage euh qui quand même présente de*
29	*'l'intérêt objectivement/pas 'moralement mais objectivement/'et . votre réponse*
30	*est venue très sèche/vous_avez dit 'non/alors je m' suis dit/tiens il faut .*
31	*qu'elle ait quand même euh/qu'elle 'éprouve quelque chose en 'faveur de l'invité/*
32	*sinon elle peut pas/ou elle veut pas/*
33 B	*oui là c'est_un peu différent/c'est_un peu différent/c'est que je pense*
34	*que/c'était_à une époque où le le monde occidental était euh/était quasiment en*
35	*'guerre/contre Saddam Hussein/et là je pense . qu'on n'a pas d'fascination à avoir*
36	*. pour des gens contre lesquels . on_est 'en tant que citoyen engagé dans_un*
37	*combat/[↓]euh y a euh/moi je n'ai/je je pense que y a une sorte de euh euh/comment*
38	*dire/là un réflexe de 'citoyen/qui vient euh à la rescousse/et qui est de dire/*
39	*euh/surtout Saddam Hussein qui utilisait si complaisamment euh les média/euh et*
40	*les réseaux de télévision euh étrangère/il n'y a pas for-forcément . 'lieu de*
41	*'mettre au service de ben d'une . puissance totalitaire/euh [↑]les moyens*
42	*d'information dont_on dispose/tout simplement pour faire des taux d'audience et*
43	*des taux d'écoute[-]/alors là si vous voulez c'est_un p'tit peu particulier/euh*
44	*c'est pas que c'est-c'est pas mon jugement 'personnel sur Saddam Hussein/dont*
45	*finalement per-tout l'monde se fiche/mais c'est simplement ne pas 'permettre . [↑]*

46	*à quelqu'un qui se situe aux 'marges de la démocracie[-]/et là . aux marges de-e*
47	*la démocracie mondiale/telle qu'elle était_envisagée à l'époque/de d'utiliser <u>euh</u>*
48	*simplement les les canaux d'information/[↑]pour que soi-même on fasse des gros*
49	*taux d'écoute[-]/alors ça c'est un peu contraire à à ma déontologie/ (.)*

[↓] ... [-]/[↑] ... [-] *very conspicuous slowing down/acceleration on framed sequences*

Extract 1
(Table 8) is fairly staightforward in its main particulars:

- the exchange is set in a classroom (cf. *maîtresse* [10], the term of address used for (A), and involves a woman teacher (cf. gender of *maîtresse*) and a group of pupils talking about the fun fair (see *fête* [1], *fête foraine* [2], *manèges* [2] ...) ('maîtresse' of course occurs in other contexts, but the evidence overall rules them out);
- the topic of the discussion and the term of address used for the teacher further suggest that the pupils are probably quite young, of nursery or primary school age (secondary level teachers are addressed as *'monsieur'*, *'madame'* or *'mademoiselle'* and referred to as *'professeurs'*).

The children are in fact four- and five-year-olds, and this is the early stage of a warm up session (there is no evidence of structured teaching as such in the exchange)[1].

Extract 2
(Table 9) is less transparent:

- as in Extract 1, the exchange involves a number of participants talking about something to do with advertising and smoking (*ce n'est pas la publicité/qui fait fumer/* [1], see also [4], [5], etc.];
- the discussion seems fairly heated: there are many (often inaudible) overlaps, interruptions [8, 10, 12, ...], tussles to hold the floor [18, 21, ...], and disagreements — as is evidenced in the number of adversatives alone (e.g. *non, mais, mais non,* etc.); *j'ai en face de moi des tas d'jeunes/ici/* [1–3] signals the presence of a fairly large audience;
- the use of *'vous'* throughout the extract and the form of address in [20] (*Monsieur . . . Monsieur Fernandez*) rule out a conversation amongst close friends; the reference to *'jeunes'* (see above) suggests that the participants include at least some adults, one of whom has professional connections with the tobacco or the advertising market (cf. *cela fait vendre/mes 'produits* [23] and subsequent reference to Marlboro) . . .

Evidence seems to point in the direction of some public discussion between mature individuals, professionals perhaps. As it happens, it is a clip from half-way through a 45-minute television debate on the pros and cons of anti-smoking campaigns, with a TV host (B) and assistant, various opinionated professionals (a general practioner (C), a physician, the general manager of Phillip Morris-France, a journalist, a publicist (A)) and representatives of different associations (tobacco sellers, anti-smoking lobby)[2].

Unlike 1 and 2, Extracts 3 (Table 10) and 4 (Table 11) each involve two participants only, interacting in a regular (A)/(B) question/answer pattern (cf. beginning of (A) turns: *et comment . . .* [1], *est-ce que . . .* [7], *. . . c't'-à-dire* [11] in Extract 3, and *est-ce que . . .* [1] in Extract 4). They are in fact televised interviews (cf. the reference, in Extract 4, to the presence of a cameraman in *ça m'arrive . . . de r'garder les les les pieds du du cadreur/qui est en face de moi/par exemple là en c'moment/* [10–11]; evidence in Extract 3 is less obvious, though there is a clue in the formulation of (A)'s second question [7–9], as we shall see. Here again, however, the interlocutors differ in age (and experience): the interviewers are adult men in each case, the guest is a boy in his teens in Extract 3, but an adult woman in 4.

Extract 3

This extract is not altogether explicit, at least in the section in bold:

- *c'est notre rôle de la nettoyer/ . . . de la sauver quoi/* [5–6], and (A)'s reference to people's reactions, to some kind of venture and to public help/support in the section in bold may suggest that the interview is to do with something environmental worthy of public interest; both the teenager's age (13) and the topic of the exchange become clear with the wider context of the interview, which was prompted by the teenager's setting up of a project to clean up his local river (the first part of the extract is in fact filmed on site, the second in a TV studio with a different journalist (C))[3].

Extract 4

In contrast Extract 4 swarms with clues:

- (B), the woman (*madame, gâteuse* [16]), is a TV personality interviewed about her own role as a TV interviewer (*aller à l'antenne* [5], *en direct* [7], *on n'est pas complètement attentif à c'que vient de dire la personne qu'est en face de vous* [8–9], *une émission d'télévision on en sort . 'vidé* [22–3];
- (A), the host, is someone with similar professional activities (cf. the appeal to shared experience in *c'pour ça qu'on sort d'une émission/vous l'savez bien/ . . . 'vidé/* [21–22])[4].

Even on the basis of the available textual evidence alone, there are enough first indications in the extracts to signal that they consist of two multi-participant structured interactions and two interviews, involving in each case individuals of different ages and status. Closer inspection of parallel texts, however, brings out contrasts which confirm the degree of maturity and status of the participants in each, and also sets the scene for reflecting on the relative characteristics of their performance. All speakers in the extracts are native speakers, and can be postulated, for the sake of discussion, to have a competence commensurate with their experience. But how does this manifest itself in practice: are they all 'fluent' in the same way? And how do they manage with what they have, in the situation they are in? How do they respond to one another? With these questions in mind, we can perhaps begin by comparing like with like, starting with Extracts 1 and 2.

Tracing aspects of relativity in Extracts 1 and 2

It is not surprising that clues in these two passages should suggest that the children's contributions in Extract 1 contrast with the contributions of the adults in Extract 2 in three main respects:

Life experience

The children's ability to relate to the world around them is, in Extract 1 (section in bold), confined to their own limited physical or emotional responses. They only talk about what they have experienced first-hand (e.g. fair, [size of] merry-go-rounds, sickness), from their own point of view: their turns consist of stand-alone statements in the affirmative, factual in content, and expressed in the first person (*je*) (with the exception of *y avait* [2]) (e.g. . . . *j'ai vomi/* [2], *ben moi j'ai fait des grands manèges hein/* [9]; they are short, with no expression of opinion, of complex sensations, no reference to other peoples' experience or reactions . . .

The adults in 2, on the other hand, can rely on their extended knowledge of the world, their personal or professional experience to:

- make generalisations (*tout l'monde sait 'bien/que ce n'est pas la pub-licité/qui fait fumer/* [1]) or authoritative statements (*la publicité est_un 'instrument de compétition 'commerciale entre les marques* [11–12]);
- express opinions (*j'vois pas l'intérêt d'faire de la pub si ça fait pas vendre . . .* [21–22]);
- expose bad faith (*'oui/je je crois que c'est vraiment leur inquiétude/* [16], i.e. a main fear of cigarette manufacturers is the banning of advertising).

There is, accordingly, a constant interplay in 2 between the first and the third person, between the personal and the general, the concrete and the abstract, and routine cross-referencing.

Experience of language

The syntax in the children's utterances is by and large simple (mostly basic VPs; the one audible complex string [2, continued in 6] is built mostly paratactically (*moi à la fête foraine/et ben j'ai vomi/parce que . /y avait des grands manèges/j'ai eu peur des manèges/j'ai vomi moi/*, where '*y avait des grands manèges*' does not follow on from '*parce que*', but is marked out as a new start by both the pause and a change in intonation) (but is paratactic utterance construction children-specific? — see Chapter 5). The lexis, too, is simple — *passe-partout* words ('*faire*', '*avoir*') and common topic-related items ('*fête*', '*fête foraine*', '*manèges*'), with few qualifiers or modifiers; less routine words are difficult to recover, but are nonetheless given a try (c.f. *roulotte en glace* [10] vs. *galerie des glaces* [teacher repair in 11].

The adults' utterances in Extract 2 contrast in both respects. They, for instance, feature multiclausal strings and embeddings (e.g. *tout l'monde sait 'bien/que ce n'est pas la publicité/qui fait fumer/ . . .* [1]), including conditional clauses (*si demain c'est 'vraiment 'totalement 'interdit . . .* [13–14], *si ça fait pas vendre . . .* [22]), and a conspicuoulsy large number of negative and adversative constructions [1, 4, 6, 8 . . .]; their syntax is not, however, particularly dense (see Chapter 5 on this point), and does display evidence of task stress:

> /j'ai en face de moi des tas d'jeunes/ici i peuvent "tous me dire/c'est/qu'est-ce qui les_a fait 'fumer leur première [sic] paquet d'cigarettes/ . . . [3–4])

is for instance conspicuous by its avoidance of subordination, its change of mind after *c'est*, its shift to direct speech and its gender slip on '*première*'. The lexis encompasses different registers — the everyday and the professional, the formal and the informal (cf. for instance /est-ce que . vous mettez la clé sous la porte/ [14–15] vs. /la publicité est_un_'instrument de compétition 'commerciale entre les marques/ [11–12], covers a wide range of word classes, shifts between the abstract and the concrete, all this in a mix which, as we shall see, has significant strategic functions for fluency.

Interactional experience

The children in Extract 1 rely on one main strategy for turn-taking: the use of the disjunctive pronoun *moi* (in all contributions); but it is also a platform for the construction of utterance, and possibly a means of sharing the exchange through a sharing of tactic. This sharing is perhaps also manifest in the repetition of platforms such as *j'ai, j'ai fait*, or lexical items (*manège, grands manèges*). Other interactional features include the occasional use of turn-surrendering devices — *hein* at the end of turn 11, and *moi* at the end of turn 6 (continued from 2), which otherwise stands out by its persistence, its step-by-step build-up supported by repetition and the use of *'et'* and the filler *'ben'* to sustain its flow (*moi à la fête foraine/et ben j'ai vomi/parce que . /y avait des grands manèges/*[2] *j'ai eu peur des manèges/j'ai vomi moi/* [6]); *ben* in 9 has an adversative function which provides evidence of turns building up from one another. Even though the majority of turns are mostly disconnected, with everyone dipping in, sometimes simultaneously, without much reference to what is said by anyone else (save by the teacher, whose turns regulate the exchange — see below), this example and the features identified above nonetheless provide evidence of cooperative build up, of viability at work.

Extract 2 is more sophisticated in these respects. The range of interactional strategies the adults rely on is a token of their underpinning role in the engineering of debate. Keeping and taking turns, asserting oneself and one's ideas are major activities, achieved more or less successfully by a variety of combined means, which double up as platforms for the articulation of utterance and time-gaining devices, and include:

- headstrong use of adversatives and negative forms; 2/3 of the turns are for instance initiated, and often sustained, in this way;
- repetitions:
  - within turns (. . . *mais la publicité doit entretenir/doit entretenir le le le//* [9–10]), *alors vous nous dites que les médecins/ . vous vous dites des choses un peu dures/vous dites que/attendez/attendez/ attendez/* [30–31];
  - across turns, using items borrowed from a previous speaker (. . . *si ça fait pas vendre . . .* [22] and . . . *mais . cela fait vendre . . .* [23], . . . *ça fait pas ça fait pas ach'ter . . .* [25] and *ça fait/ça ne fait pas fumer . . .* [27]), or reiterating one's own statements (cf. (B)'s . . . *la publicité est/c'est un 'instrument de compétition 'commerciale . . .* in 11–2 and 27–28);
  - with intensifiying paraphrase (. . . *c'est vraiment leur inquiétude/ c'est effectivement leur plus grosse inquiétude/* [16–18]
- appeals for acknowlegment (*si vous voulez* [4]), or for attention (*Monsieur Monsieur Fernandez* [20]);
- latchings on to turns, sometimes taking advantage of pauses or tonal breaks (note for instance how (C) takes advantage of the short silence at the end of 15 to break into the (A)/(B) two-way exchange), mostly just elbowing one's way in by initiating an overlap; only two turns in fact come to an end without being latched on to in this way [13–15 and 21–22];
- use of paralinguistic features, indissociable from the others though they do not appear on the transcript (except for the most prominent word stresses) — stress, changes of pitch and tempo (on repetitions in particular), and hand and body movement (in 27–28, for instance,

stressed words are punctuated by downwards motions of the hand
with fingers gathered on the thumb on stressed words) (see Chapters
5 and 7 on these points).

The whole exchange is permeated by an interactional aggressivity
seldom observed in English equivalents. But it is far from unusual in
discussions amongst French people, and is difficult for English speakers to
emulate. It is not there in Extract 1, however, partly for want of know-how,
partly because of the exchange set-up (children are quite capable of being
verbally aggressive, too, in some situations). We must in any case remember
that Extract 1 comes early in a warm-up session, Extract 2 in the middle of
a discussion. And like 1, 2 begins with a round of sedate statements, elicited
by the host in a perfectly civil manner. Extract 1 itself grows animated to
the point of becoming impossible to transcribe (and Extract 2 to the point
of breakdown — it has to be rescued by the host).

The participants' verbal behaviour in these extracts is, in other words,
modulated by a range of factors: it is relative to their experience of life,
language and interaction, to the nature and context of exchange, as might
be expected, and relative, too, to the phases through which exchanges proceed.
These observations, however, need to be qualified, related more closely, in
particular, to the conditions of exchange and patterns of negotiation.

Tracing aspects of negotiation in Extracts 1 and 2

What we have yet to look at are exchange features attributable to
differences in status and capabilities within each extract, and the resulting
verbal and negotiative adaptations. How, in particular, does the teacher relate
to the children in Extract 1? Her turns are a little longer on the whole, and
a little more complex syntactically. Yet while they do feature subordination
within tonal groups [1, 7], they otherwise build up in short paratactic spurts
(e.g. *ah/toi tu as eu peur/ben c'est vrai qu'y a des grands manèges hein/oui Sanah/*
[7–8]) and are far less diverse in form than the adults' turns in Extract 2).
Like her syntax, her lexis is harnessed to the children's needs: the words
she uses are words they could use, and do share in the exchange. But it
is the diversity of their functions that marks them out, and the additional
evidence they provide about the role she plays in managing the exchange,
responding to individuals yet also drawing in the group at large, adapting to
the capacities of her pupils yet also challenging them, through various means:

- factual input (*mais vous savez qu'c'est fini la fête là/d'hier/*) in 1,
  rebounding in a reformulation removed from the more complex
  syntactic context of the beginning (*la fête c'est terminé*) — and thus
  easier to process;

- factual acknowledgement of individual turns, subsequently taken up and lifted from individual to shared experience:
  — after (B)'s (persistent) turn in 6 (continued from 2): cf. *ah/toi tu as eu peur*, taken up and authorised in */ben c'est vrai qu'y a des grands manèges hein/* by the shift to a general truth statement based on*/y avait des grands manèges* [2] and handed out to the group with *hein* [7–8];
  — after (E)'s turn in 10: cf. *ah/oui/la galerie des glaces/*, which expands into a general qualitative statement, again offered to the group for response, with *c'est rigolo ça/hein/* [11];
- appeals for group acknowledgement: cf. *hein* in 1, 7, and 11 where it doubles up as turn offering;
- individual turn offering: cf. *oui Sanah* [7–8];
- repairs: cf. *la galerie des glaces* [11], reformulated from *roulotte en glace* [10].

The exchange, in other words, is a fittingly negotiated cooperative exercise, modulated by the teacher's expectations of her pupils and her role as teacher, and finely tuned to their needs by an interplay of linguistic and interactive means. To put it another way, when there is a perceived gap, there is help at hand.

Negotiation of the role and experience gap in Extract 2 takes a different form, illustrated by the tension between (A), the publicist, and (B), the TV host. Whenever (A) is challenged in his statements, he displays a tendency to switch registers, to resort to the authoritative language and experience of the expert to defend his ground — cf. for instance the contrast between his first turn, when he emphatically bends to the audience, linguistically and factually, with

> *tout l'monde sait 'bien/que ce n'est pas la publicité/qui fait fumer/ici/j'ai en face de moi des tas d'jeunes/ici i peuvent "tous me dire/c'est/qu'est-ce qui les a fait fait 'fumer leur première paquet de cigarettes/ce n'est pas . si vous voulez de la publici-//* [1–5],

and subsequent turns, following on from rebuttals, where the professional takes over at the first opportunity:

> *non la publicité est_un_'instrument de compétition 'commerciale entre les marques/* . . . [11–12] (following on from (B)'s *ah non/on n'a jamais dit ça* . . . *c'est vrai/non mais la publicité doit entretenir* . . . [6, 9–10])

> *mais . cela fait vendre/mes 'produits . /ici on_est quand même dans_un marché d'économie//* [23–24] (after (B)'s *j'vois pas l'intérêt d'faire de la pub si ça fait pas vendre . quand même* [21–22], and again after (B)'s interruption

(oui mais vous dites ça fait pas ça fait pas ach'ter un paquet d'Marlboro la-de Marlboro la pub sur euh// [25–26]) ça ne fait pas fumer un non-fumeur/ c'est un 'instrument de compétition 'commerciale/dans un marché concurrentiel/qui est un marché comme le p-tabac/éminemment concurrentiel/ [27–29].

The host does not fail to grasp the strategic function of (A)'s shifts and reiterations, and, perhaps out of irritation, or because of his responsibility to the public, or both, makes it his business to undermine them — by making himself the devil's advocate and the public's voice, and appealing to common sense rather than theory, but also by relocating language in a layman's register (see citations in bold above; also [30–1] on the transcript). This is not to say that the exchange is not a cooperative venture. What it means, rather, is that it is negotiated using different sets of rules, dictated by its function as debate and the responsibilities of its protagonists: as they are all no doubt aware, a TV debate is a confrontation of views for the benefit of a public represented by the host, and more often than not, in a French context, relies on conflicts of interest to air issues. Tension is its mode of engineering, is what sustains its viability: convergence amongst the protagonists derives from the understanding that the exchange is a battle of wits, to be survived by the fittest. If none emerges, the exchange breaks down, the ship is abandoned, and it is up to the host to find a raft. But one thing is clear: making oneself heard in an exchange, let alone breaking into it, in this as in other kinds of discussions — private, amongst peers, with friends or strangers — means having appropriate linguistic and interactional strategies at one's fingertips.

Relativity and negotiation in Extracts 3 and 4

Extracts 3 and 4 illustrate other kinds of differences, other aspects of relativity and negotiation, and other strategies. The most striking physical contrast between them is in the length of the guests' turns: the TV personality in 3 hardly needs prodding to launch into an extended turn (24 lines on the page); the teenager in 4, on the other hand, seems to require constant prompting (on 3 occasions in the section in bold) to produce rather shorter answers (five lines, five words and two lines). But to say what? How does volume relate to content, and how does it relate to form?

The TV personality's answer to her guest's question about the anxieties connected with her job boils down to a very simple answer — tiredness, to which she refers *directly* on two occasions: /c'que j'crains c'est la fatigue/ [7]; . . . la seule crainte/c'est parfois un peu d'fatigue [20] (where tiredness is, interestingly enough, now played down). The main thrust of the teenager's answers about people's response to the venture and their degree of cooperation can be summed up as follows: people initially assumed that the project was a public relations exercise, when it was in fact motivated by a sense of duty; people are not concerned unless they are compelled to be. If anything, then, the teenager in 3 actually says more, in bare terms, than the TV personality in 4. So what accounts for the difference in volume?

The answer seems to lie in what Fillmore (1979) describes as 'filling time with talk', which (B) in Extract 4 does, after a preamble [3–7] referring back to earlier comments by (A) on famous TV hosts' problem with drugs (also a handy platform to gather her thoughts), in two main ways:

- factual padding:
  with an account of the effects of tiredness (*la fatigue/qui fait que . . . on pense à aut'e chose/* [7–10] and a long anecdotal illustration (*ça m'arrive . . . de r'garder les les les pieds du du cadreur . . . et pis de décrocher . . . je vais me faire 'ramasser* [10–19] after the first mention of fatigue; and, after the second [20], with an account, again interspersed with illustrative material, of the pressures TV shows impose on hosts (*l'attention dans_une émission . . . concentration* [20–25]), before a final summing up (*alors vous l'faites . . . un peu fatigué* [25–26]) (explaining why tiredness is a liability for them);
- language padding, doubling up as a planning device to thrust utterance on:
  — with reformulations and shifts from the general to the particular (e.g. *on n'est pas complètement attentif . . . on pense à aut'e chose* [8–10], *. . . on reprend contact avec la réalité/on dit/zut/mais qu'est-ce qu'i vient d' dire* [13–14]);
  — with more or less functional repetitions (e.g. *deux trois secondes/deux trois secondes* [12–13], *. . . /euh et 'là c'est la la vraie panique/c'est la panique de se dire* [17–18]); *la la la* [4], *les les les* [10];
  — with recycled formulaic platforms (*. . . la fatigue/qui fait que* [8] and *. . . un peu d'fatigue qui fait que* [20])
  — with numerous adverbs and adverbial qualifiers (*peut-être, quelquefois, un peu, de temps en temps, complètement,* etc.), which, like little linking items such as *'et', 'eh non', 'non'*, create continuity, yet also soften the impact of an aplomb which could otherwise be perceived as verging on arrogance.

The diversity of her strategies gives her answer a vitality, an absorbing liveliness which are compounded not only by paralinguistic features (stress, changes of pitch and tempo), but also by various negotiating features: her drawing in of her guest (*vous savez* [7], *vous l'savez bien* [22], her shifts from the first person singular to the other-inclusive third singular and second plural (*on, vous*), and her switches from an omnitemporal present to a punctual present (cf. . . . *la fatigue/qui fait que* [8] vs. . . . *on dit/zut/mais qu'est-ce qu'i vient d' dire . . . j'ai pas écouté . . . vous_êtes complètement gâteuse* [13–14]). In the end, her pauses and filled pauses, false starts, changes of mind, time-gaining gimmicks, slips in construction, in a word all the hesitation phenomena that are also present in her speech, pass largely unnoticed, as does her blunder in . . . *on dit/zut/mais qu'est-ce qu'i vient d' dire/c'est_épouvantable/j'ai pas écouté/et avoir à rebondir derrière c'est quelquefois prendre le risque de dire écoutez j'vous en prie madame/je j'viens d'vous l'dire* [13–16] (vs. *prendre le risque de s'entendre dire*): I only picked it out when I transcribed the piece after I had listened to it several times (here again a token of the subjectivity of the listening process, and a token too, of the subjectivity of fluency judgements).

There is little factual padding in the teenager's turns in Extract 3. The volume/main content discrepancy is small, and largely a function of message construction (cf. drawls, filled pauses, repetitions, false starts (e.g. in *c'était un/un truc[e] pour euh/pour euh/soi-disant qu'on . . voulait . . .* [3–4]), grappling with lexis and syntax (e.g. . . . *soi-disant qu'on . . voulait se rendre intéressant/quoi euh/qu'on_apporte une . remarque sur nous/dans les journaux* [3–5]). His message features reformulations (cf. previous example; also *de la nettoyer quoi/de la sauver quoi* [6]), but they are bound to the illustrative: unlike (B) in 4, he does not display the mental confidence, linguistic agility or public ease to capitalise on the shift between general and specific for padding — to go from statement to explanation to example, for instance. All the same, the message he puts across, in what must be an intimidating situation (interview for the public with an adult he does not know) is quite involved. He has the advantage over the children in Extract 1 of being familiar with what he is talking about, of being able to make sense of it in relation to the world at large, and of greater linguistic means. But what also marks him out is precisely those strategies he makes available to himself for coping when the resources he needs are not forthcoming:

- those that give him time, and give his messages continuity — filled pauses, repetitions, drawls, platforms (cf. for instance *soi-disant qu'on . . voulait se rendre intéressant* [3–4], *mais c'est pas du tout ça* [5], which, unlike contiguous utterances, are uttered in one breath, as a packaged whole, without support of filled pauses, drawls or *passe-partout* words (e.g. *truc* [3]); *quoi* [4, 6] perhaps deserves special notice: in giving statements a self-evident finality (particularly after a repetition, e.g. . . . *de la nettoyer/nous/et de la nettoyer quoi/* [5–6], it hands over responsibility for clarifying their implications to the interlocutor and has thus, in addition to being a filler, a dual function — avoidance tactic and interactive device;

- his language tactics — reliance on formulae (see previous example), and circumlocution, even if clumsy (*qu'on apporte une . remarque sur nous/dans les journaux* [4–5]).

His turns in the second half of the exchange are interesting for the way they deal with a tricky problem: getting round saying something that he does not want to say directly, because it is offensive (i.e. that no, he and the fellow members of his group do not get much support from people), and then tempering its impact when called upon to be more explicit. *ben oui/un p'tit peu* in [10] has the feel of an effort-avoiding, wishy-washy answer, yet its minimalism and hesitancy turn out to be a token of discretion. It is not an outright *oui*: the apparent hesitation on *ben* in fact introduces a note of mild denial, which endows *un p'tit peu* with negative undertones (compare with '*oui/un p'tit peu*' and '*oui*' on its own); it is a '*oui*' that wants to be a '*non*'. (B)'s temporising only really becomes clear in his response to (A)'s prompting (*un p'tit peu/c't'-à-dire/* [11]), where his feelings are spelled out: . . . */du moment qu'i qu'i sont pas contraints/et ben/i s'en foutent* [13–14]. The forcefulness of *i s'en foutent* is, however, toned down by the positive statement that precedes (. . . *les gens euh/quand ils voyent* [sic] *ça/ça leur fait quelque chose/* [12–13]), by the pragmatic impact of repetitions/hesitations — which help soften the blow, and also by the choice of a semantically negative, yet formally positive, lexical item ('*s'en foutre*'). (A), the host, could not have meant to embarrass (B) with his prompting, but his expectations betrayed him, and led him to mistake discretion for lack of cooperation.

But what *are* (A)'s expectations? His second question [7–9] provides some clues. There is a contrast between the question as it is first uttered, in one extended, continuous and lexically concise spurt (*est-ce que vous sentez une certaine solidarité autour de vous quand vous prenez une telle initiative/*), and its reformulation in chunks which spell out in simple everyday language the meaning of '*solidarité*' (*est-ce que vous vous r'trouvez avec plein d'gens/qui sont du même avis/et qui ont envie d'vous aider/*). Why should a fairly straightforward question need to be paraphrased in this way to elicit an answer? And if it is the reformulation that is counted on to elicit an answer, why bother with the initial question? (A), as this two-fold request could have told us, is addressing different parties: the TV audience, whom he expects to take in the meaning of '*solidarité*' and '*initiative*', and (B), the teenager, for whom he thinks it needs to be made clear. His assumption may be based on the age of his guest, and his supposed linguistic maturity, or on evidence from earlier on in the exchange; and it may or may not be justified. But the example confirms what was also manifest in Extract 1, namely that speakers adapt to the perceived capacities of their interlocutors, and simplify their messages accordingly. This is reassuring for students. What (B)'s response also points to, however, is something that was discussed in Chapter 2, namely that interlocutors may need to be encouraged to adjust their sights.

Additional features from the wider context of the extracts

The wider context of the extracts helps to confirm initial hypotheses if need be — contextual details in particular (see Extract 3 for instance). But it also provides further insights, or helps to nuance earlier observations (cf. Extract 1 in particular). The examples below, which will be discussed more briefly, pick out a few other points relevant to students' practical concerns. Overall implications will be reviewed in the next section.

Relativity

Individual variations in fluency:

(*a*) In Extract 4 see variations in the TV personality's degree of fluency in her second answer [cf. B: 33–49], where her speech is characterised:

- overall, by a more conspicuous planning effort; hesitations present in her previous turn (filled pauses, repetitions) are here compounded by the frequency of false starts (e.g. /*c'est que j'pense que/c'était* [33–34], drawls, time-gaining platforms (e.g. *j'pense que* [33, 35, 37]; tonal groups are shorter; there is a concomitant lack of focus in form and content, making the message more demanding to reconstruct (cf. for example *euh y a euh/moi je n'ai/je je pense que y a une sorte de euh euh/comment dire/là un réflexe* . . . [37–38]);
- in places, however, by greater fluidity, less conspicuous planning, evidenced in longer tonal groups, more spaced out hesitation phenomena, increased cohesion, denser content, (also faster tempo); cf. for example:

     . . . /*surtout Saddam Hussein qui utilisait si complaisamment euh les média/euh et les réseaux de télévision euh étrangère/il n'y a pas for-forcément . 'lieu de 'mettre au service de ben d'une puissance . totalitaire /euh* [↑] *les moyens d'information dont on dispose/tout simplement pour faire des taux d'audience et des taux d'écoute [-]/* . . . [39–43].

(B) seems here to experience greater task stress, at least initially: (A)'s question exposes a flaw in her previous answer (cf. *et pourtant* [27]) and confronts her with a sensitive issue (to do with her refusal to interview Saddam Hussein [27–32]); she is caught off guard, in unfamiliar territory, and cannot here so readily draw on personal anecdotal material for padding; instead, she falls back on familiar, well-rehearsed arguments, lexis and formulations, which give her a platform for the elaboration of the more demanding part of her answer.

(B) is in fact Anne Sinclair, an experienced public speaker, and it is reassuring to note that someone as practiced as she is can, too, be at a loss for words. She does, however, have strategies for coping: use of time-gaining devices, and a reliance on the language and arguments of her trade which echoes (A)'s shift, for different reasons, to the professional register in Extract 2. As she herself insists in another part of the interview, there is no substitute for knowing what you are talking about if you want to remain in control.

(*b*) In Extract 3 see variations in the teenager's fluency, whose turn in ll. 16–19 displays a more confined, yet comparable, increase in ease of expression when he is able to draw on a rehearsed lexical and factual stock (even though he has difficulties retrieving '*aménager*', or adapting it from '*aménagement*' in his interviewer's question); cf:

> . . . /*on avait parlé avec le maire de Roquevert/pour euh/'emmenager [sic] cette rivière/mettre des bancs/des poubelles/des sentiers de promenade/* [16–17];
> (note also his use of more specialised vocabulary with *faune* [19]).

Negotiation

Build-up and use of shared reference within exchanges:
(*a*) In Extract 1 see the function of shared reference in the build-up of speech and exchange which takes place after the introduction of *roulotte en glace/galerie des glaces* [10, 11], and later *voitures tamponneuses* [20].

The shift from the generic (*fête, manèges*) to the specific (*roulotte en glace/galerie des glaces, voitures tamponneuses*) gives the children a shared focus for their experience and creates an interactive impetus which marks a new phase in the exchange: the simple dissociated statements of the beginning give way to more elaborate turns (both in form and content, despite slips), which now begin to build on from one another in a way they did not at the outset, e.g.:

> *quand/quand j'étais euh/au manège/ben j'étais allée . dans/dans la maison de de glaces/et pis j'a-j'arrive là/j'avais même pas vu qu'y avait une glace/j'me cogne d'un coup/* [14–16]
> *c'est normal/faut faut mettre les mains pour que/pour que ???//* [18].

Verbal resources, in other words, are not necessarily all invested at once from the very beginning of exchanges or phases in exchanges. Involvement is often progressive, gathers momentum with the gradual build-up of shared points of reference (e.g. lexical, factual, argumentative, syntactic even), which act as a catalyst in unleashing the verbal energy and confidence of protagonists.

(*b*) In Extract 3 see the function of the 'job' leitmotiv as a group-generated platform for argument, evidenced here in ll. 41–48:

écoutez c'est 'mon métier//
oui mais c'est aussi mon 'travail de l'savoir/hein//
écou// non mais si vous voulez mon métier c'est d'vendre des cigarettes tous
les jours/mon métier c'est d'connaître les ci-les les . consommateurs/
votre métier c'est la santé/je le respecte/respectez mon métier si vous voulez/ . . . .

This 'job' leitmotiv is jointly established early on in the discussion as a shared middle ground to recast argument: allusions to one's job and to what it entails are reinvested time and again in the debate to assert one's motives and credentials and question others'. It works as an anchorage point, on which participants can, and do, rely to vindicate themselves, and gives them readily available lexical and factual platforms for negotiation — for taking, holding and interrupting turns, contradicting others or siding with them — more or less disingenuously. For all the friction it generates, it is nonetheless a point of convergence for the guests, enables them to negotiate arguments on their *own* terms — rather than those laid down by the host in his management of topic and sub-topics, and thus to create their own space within it.

Like the example from Extract 1, this example is a reminder that exchanges are a joint undertaking, generate argumentative and linguistic islands of viability which everyone can use to suit their needs or intentions: to get a footing in the exchange, to secure a retreat when threatened or at a loss for words or ideas, or to launch a charge.

Strategies for responding to competing sources of input:
(*a*) In Extract 1 see the teacher's selective response to the children's input in ll. lines 24–8, when, confronted with input from several children, she acknowledges / . . . *j'suis restée deux minutes coincée là-bas/* [25] yet disregards it, to go on attending instead to the exchange about bumping cars already under way (*mais pourquoi on peut pas les grandes/* [28]).

When the exchange gets more animated, it becomes difficult for the teacher to give equal attention to all incoming messages, let alone keep track of them (as also applies to transcribing them). Her strategy, to avoid losing control, is to make choices, and to concentrate on some at the expense of others. Her predicament is not unusual: anyone involved in a multi-participant exchange is likely to experience the same kind of problem to a greater or lesser extent, depending on a range of factors (size of the group, context of exchange, patterns of involvement, etc.). In large groups where everyone speaks at once, it is almost physically impossible to attend globally to what is going on: unless the exchange is approached selectively, it is just perceived as noise. It takes experience to cope. But it can only help to know that foreign speakers are not alone in being confronted with this kind of problem, and that there are ways to get round it — such as listening selectively and breaking into the exchange by latching on to one individual or a small sub-group in the first instance.

Help adjustments in exchanges involving speakers of assorted maturity:
    (*a*) In Extract 1 see expanding/clarifying reiterations, e.g:

    [child] *c'est normal/faut faut mettre les mains pour que/pour que ???//*
    [teacher] *faut mettre les mains devant/pour pas s'cogner/.. ah ouais/* [18–19].

    (*b*) In Extract 1 see probings seeking clarification* or encouraging further involvement**, e.g:

    *[teacher] *oh là/toute seule/des p'tites . /ou des grandes/* [21]
    **[teacher] *mais pourquoi on peut pas les grandes/* [28].

    (*c*) In Extract 3 see reformulations supporting comprehension*, or prompting clarification**, e.g:

    * [adult] . . . *j'voudrais savoir si . . . il y a euh une limite d'âge/est-ce que ça va de sept à soixante-dix-sept ans ou ou n'y a-t-i/ou n'y a-t-il pas d'frontière/* [25–28]
    [boy] *ben y a les gens de euh/les jeunes/les le les tout p'tits jeunes/h//*
    ** [adult] *ça commence à quel âge/ . . . /les tout p'tits jeunes* [30 and 31].

    (*d*) In Extract 3 see acknowledgements/reiterations of support, e.g:

    [adult] . . . *il y a beaucoup d'gens qui sont 'de ton avis/qui sont sensibilisés à ça d'façon à c'que cette bataille/comme tu l'dis si bien/ne s'arrête pas/* [23–24]
    [adult] . . . *cet âge/comme tu l'disais euh/un p'tit peu jeune . . .* [35–36].

    (*e*) In Extracts 1 and 3 see syntheses/clarifying paraphrases, e.g:

    [teacher] *c'est-à-dire qu'y a des enfants qui montent dans les grandes avec leurs parents/ .. c'est ça/* [31–32] (Extract 1), which brings together the children's indirect comments about access to bumping cars
    [boy] . . . *parc' que les les personnes âgées elles peuvent pas/descendre les pentes/tout ça//*
    [adult] *elles peuvent vous soutenir/mais elles sont moins actives/disons/* (presumably also taken up for the benefit of the audience) [32–34] (Extract 3).

Involvement in verbal exchanges can be trying for anyone: it may be intimidating, tentative, take time to gather pace, call on unfamiliar language resources. Yet, by and large, speakers are seldom left alone to battle it out. Exchanges *are* cooperative ventures, and support, whether moral, linguistic or interactional, is at hand when experience is unequal. What matters is to take a step, and to respond to openings to keep channels of communication open and build on them: to take heed of repairs (e.g. *galerie des glaces*) and alternative formulations, pay attention to tips (e.g. *aménagement*), yet take care that help does not become invasive and take away initiative.

Implications of the Analyses for Learners

The significance for fluency in general of the kind of observations prompted by the study of these extracts was explored in earlier chapters. But what do they mean for students in practice, and how do they translate into exercises which provide first-hand experience of what the analyses have drawn attention to? The synthesis of their implications is in the end quite plain:

Fluency is relative; people are not, in particular, consistently fluent in all situations, or consistently fluent in each; but there are a number of things that help:

- being familiar with the topic (facts/arguments) — if known, i.e. knowing what one is talking about (see Exercise 4 in the next section);
- being familiar with relevant vocabulary (see Exercise 4);
- having ready-made formulae at one's fingertips (see Exercise 4);
- having strategies for coping when resources are not appropriate (see Exercise 1);
- drawing on everyday experience for examples and padding (see Exercise 5);
- using linguistic padding (reformulations, shifts from the general to the specific, form 3rd person to 1st person, repetitions, filled pauses etc.) (see Exercise 5);
- drawing on the lexical and other points of reference built up within the exchange (see Exercise 1);
- ensuring interlocutors are involved in one's message (phatic strategies) (see Exercise 6).

Verbal involvement and fluency are not one-sided ventures; interlocutors help by:

- prompting;
- supplying lexical items;
- putting speakers' intentions into words;
- reformulating;
- synthesising; (see Exercise 2).

Coping with multi-participant exchanges is difficult, not least when they are loud and aggressive; what can help?

- getting a hold on the exchange through selective listening (see Exercise 3);
- breaking into the exchange, latching on to one individual, or a subgroup (see Exercise 3);
- trusting one's ability to make a contribution, drawing on others protagonists' strategies for claiming turns, and holding one's ground (see Exercise 7).

This leaves out temporising to avoid being offensive (cf. example of the young boy in Extract 3), which does not fit neatly under any of these headings, but is socioculturally just as relevant as other points.

Some of these suggestions are not particularly new: they are part of the stock of advice many teachers tirelessly give to their students (e.g. 'know what you are talking about and how to talk about it', for instance). But there is a world of difference between being told something and finding it out for oneself, before trying it out on the strength of one's own conclusions. The analyses of native speaker extracts provide both teacher and students with a rationale for exercises, now not only justified by observation, but also clearly defined in their objectives. Work then can shift from the macro to the micro level, and suggestions be turned into exercises with a clear point of application, and complementary intentions:

- give students first-hand experience of general phenomena observed in the analyses (e.g. aspects of negotiation) — by way of further sensitisation;
- give them the opportunity to test what they have observed in the way of strategies (e.g. strategies for filling time with talk, for interrupting, repetitions and reformulations, etc.), for selective pratice.

A subset will be given and discussed in full below to illustrate the approach, others sketched out as ideas which can be taken up and developed along similar lines.

Practical Applications: Examples, Rationale and Further Suggestions

Examples of exercises and discussion

Exercise 1: Lego game (adapted from a standard type of communicative activity): Hands-on sensitisation to aspects of negotiation (see description in Table 12).

A and B's models seldom match exactly at the end of Stage 1. But the task becomes easier and more successful with each subsequent stage, for reasons which the set-up of the exercise helps to magnify. The task, at Stage 1 is constrained by two sets of factors:

- the stock of shared linguistic points of reference is limited: Lego pieces, apart from basic bricks, have no name; describing them, let alone explaining how they should be positioned in relation to one another is quite tricky, even for native speakers. Doing so does not necessarily involve drawing on sophisticated linguistic means, but

Table 12 Lego game

LEGO GAME
INSTRUCTING HOW TO DUPLICATE A MODEL, WITHOUT AND WITH NEGOTIATION

Time	Approximately 30 mn.
Aim	Sensitise students to aspects of negotiation: • building up of shared references • negotiation of the communication gap • complementarity of resources — verbal, non-verbal (also use of communication strategies).
Method	Variation on the same basic exercise with control of exchange parameters.
Material	Two identical sets of 5 or 6 Lego pieces (use quite different shapes — i.e. not just bricks).
Procedure	Divide the class into groups of three students: A, B, C: A to build a model with the Lego pieces and give B instructions to duplicate the model; C to act as observer and record how things proceed at each stage of the exercise [optional[1]] (roles can be exchanged in the course of the exercise to diversify experience); impose a time-limit for completing the exercise.
Stage 1	A and B work back to back, B is a silent partner, i.e. A cannot see what B is doing; B cannot ask clarification questions from A, nor get any form of feedback.
Stage 2	A and B still work back to back, but B can now ask questions from A if problems occur.
Stage 3	A and B work face to face, i.e. A can now see how B is proceeding with the task, adapt instructions accordingly and pre-empt B's questions.
	=> report, group discussion and generalisation to other contexts.
1 Having an observer is not absolutely necessary, but is useful both to oversee the exercise and to keep students alert to its meta-cognitive function

rather making effective use of available resources and communication strategies. What it also requires is verbal empathy: outlandish instructions are unlikely to strike home; they need to be adapted to the partner's perceived ability to respond;

- the exchange set-up is unlike most naturally occurring types: it cannot be negotiated, either verbally (as it can in telephone conversations), or by using visual feedback. The closest equivalent is perhaps leaving a message on an answerphone, and the task here is every bit as unsettling, for the same reasons. Both partners are left literally in the dark about their respective enterprise: A cannot see how B is proceeding and cannot adapt instructions to fit B's progress, or even provide support in the form of facial acknowledgements; conversely B cannot get any clues about his/her progress, either verbal or visual.

The time-limit gives urgency to the task (and makes the task pyschologically less damaging when it is not successful), though it is in the end completely ignored in most cases: completing the exercise soon becomes a challenging incentive in its own right, further fired by the anticipation of getting instant feedback on the outcome of the game.

By the end of Stage 1, the task has become familiar and easier to handle. But what really makes the difference thereafter, as the students do not fail to recognise, is that it can be managed more cooperatively:

- students by then have built up common references for naming Lego pieces and giving instructions, and can pool resources to share the exchange on a more even footing;
- as verbal and non-verbal negotiating possibilities are gradually restored, the outcome of the exchange can be checked at every move (e.g. using verbal confirmation checks at Stage 2, and both confirmation checks and visual feedback at Stage 3).

The step-by-step experience of the impact of different negotiating features brings home just how instrumental they are in interpersonal communication; communicating is not just about 'speaking', but also about finding common grounds for doing so and drawing on the resources made available in exchanges to sustain their viability and their efficiency.

Exercise 2: Silent partner: Hands-on sensitisation to the interlocutors' role in sustaining interpersonal communication (see description in Table 13).

B partners can seldom, in the end, resist the urge to speak. Speaking a foreign language may be intimidating, and difficult, but nowhere near as difficult as not speaking when you can, at least on a one-to-one basis, even if it only means 'making noises' to convey or support otherwise unvocalised

Table 13 Silent partner

SILENT PARTNER
DRAWING ON INTERLOCUTORS' SUPPORT TO CONVEY INFORMATION

Time	Approximately 15 mn.
Aim	Remind students that (more proficient) interlocutors are predisposed to be supportive; sensitise them to the kind of help exchange partners make available.
Method	Limiting speakers' ability to get verbally involved in a dyadic exchange (also use of non-verbal means to convey information).
Material	[Optional] pictures, e.g. newspaper photographs illustrating controversial issues.
Procedure	Divide the class into groups of three students — A, B, C: A to elicit information from B on a set topic; B is a silent partner whose only means of expression are gestures and facial mimicks; C acts as observer [optional] (rotate roles to diversify experience); the choice of topic, from simple (e.g. finding out about family background, plans for the future) to more complex (e.g. eliciting opinions on a controversial issue, with/without support of a picture), sets the level of difficulty of the exercise. => report, group discussion and generalisation to other contexts.

intentions. All the same, they usually manage to do so long enough for the exercise to fufil its primary function, i.e. put A partners under pressure to assist their interlocutor, which, as in the extracts, they can be observed to do within groups in several complementary ways:

- by asking closed questions;
- by providing both questions and answers, or a choice of possible; answers;
- by reformulating when questions or answers draw a blank;
- by putting B's mimicks into words;
- by prompting B to give more clues;
- by synthesising the information elicited to confirm that clues are interpreted as they were intended.

Exchanges tend to be slow to begin with, and a little clumsy, but draw momentum from the gradual convergence of means and reciprocal tuning of responses: A partners become more skilful at combining techniques to elicit more intricate information, and at adapting them to fit in with B's anticipated response; B partners for their part become more adept at taking leads and at adjusting their response signals to their partner's eliciting style. The main point, however, is simply to encourage students to observe what happens when partners in an exchange do not have matching expressive means, and to take stock of it for future reference. Prompting someone else to speak using techniques observed in NS data, and, more importantly, responding to help (including for instance using interlocutors' utterances as a platform to launch one's own) can be practised in separate exercises to systematise insights.

Exercise 3: Intruder: Practice in breaking into an exchange latching onto one individual, or a subgroup (see description in Table 14).

Classroom discussions amongst non-native speakers of French hardly ever match NS exchanges on polemical or indeed any other matters: they rarely get as intense, aggressive, or even loud, though in this instance the purpose of the exercise works as an incentive. All the same, this kind of practice can only give a muted taste of what it is like to find ways of getting involved against the odds. On the other hand, nothing is at stake in the classroom, other than practice, and learning, and the exercise at least creates opportunities to build up confidence and know-how at reduced psychological risk. It also invites discussion, and comparison with real-life

Table 14 Intruder

INTRUDER
JOINING AN ONGOING DISCUSSION

Time	30–40 minutes or longer as required.
Aim	Listen selectively; practice getting involved in multi-participant exchanges; assess the nature of difficulties.
	(also dispel fears about the imperviousness of groups)
Method	Launch parallel discussions and bring in late-comers.
Materials	[Optional] role cards to support involvement; use roles representing conflicting points of view to create plenty of room for argument.
Procedure	Divide the class into groups large enough to induce discussion (e.g. of 5 or 6), with a debate leader to initiate proceedings in each; select a contentious topic, i.e. likely to produce a suitably heated debate and kindle students' unprompted response after an initial warm-up period (discussion topics can be the same in all groups to make things easier, or different to make them more difficult); once discussions are under way, withdraw one student from each group, and give them directions to (a) join another group, (b) focus their attention on just one of its member's input, and (c) use it as a platform to join in the debate; repeat the procedure at 5 minutes' interval until all students have had a chance to get involved with another group.
	=> report, group discussion and generalisation to other contexts

examples (video or radio-recordings, students' own experience): if this is unlike the real thing, how is it different? To what extent is it a question of proficiency, to what extent a question of socio-cultural experience, or again motivation? What does it take for reserved foreign speakers to compete verbally with French people? Practice helps, but so too does mental and pyschological preparation.

Rationale for devising applications

As regards the aspects of communication and fluency covered in this chapter, exercises can, in most cases, be adapted from the substantial range covered in language teaching manuals devoted to communicative practice. The Lego game in example 1, for instance, is based on an archetypal communication game. What makes it different is that it goes beyond practice to promote a more critical outlook: its main feature is that by modulating the conditions of exchange, it creates opportunities for taking the measure of relevant parameters and assessing their impact meta-cognitively. In other words, it places students in the position not just of communicators, but of *observers*.

Practice, thus, is not an end in itself but also a means to the end of fostering meta-cognitive activity, and of giving students direction for subsequent work, both an essential proviso for continuous and independent learning. What matters is to keep the critical momentum going, to develop student's control over language through practice, but also to develop their control over learning by encouraging them to handle practice as inquisitively as the study of data. There are different ways of promoting a discriminating outlook, e.g:

- directly, i.e. within tasks — by controlling exchange variables (e.g. Lego game), by magnifying specific features of verbal behaviour (cf. Silent partner, Intruder), or again by handling the same task from different angles to make room for comparison (see examples below);
- indirectly, at the end of exercises, by giving students the opportunity to verbalise findings and rationalise experience for now and later.

But it can also be fostered by involving them in the problem-solving process of devising adapted activities in the first place: identifying what aspects of verbal interaction deserve attention, specifying objectives, and finding ways of fulfilling them, are all part of developing control over one's learning and taking responsibility for it.

Once objectives are justified inductively by reference to actual data, jointly devising applications is relatively straightforward: motivation is already taken care of, and the authenticity of needs legitimises exercises, however contrived or plain they may be in other respects. Once it becomes clear, for example, that Anne Sinclair's fluency in Extract 4 goes hand in hand with her filling time with talk, and once the strategies she uses to this end have been identified, what to do next can be, in the first instance, a simple question of trying some out (e.g. use of personal or other anecdotes to pad a pre-set assertion, use of examples to illustrate or introduce general statements; see Exercise 5 below), testing them in different contexts, and comparing their effectiveness. But it also sets the stage for further work: further data enquiries (what other forms of factual and linguistic padding can people be observed to use in different exchange set-ups?), integrated language study (e.g. is the shift from general to specific only a matter of content? what are its form/language correlates?), and related exercises (practice shifting from first to third person and vice-versa, reformulating, shifting from verb to nominalisation and vice-versa, using fillers for linguistic padding, switching registers).

Outline of further possibilities

These principles and procedures can be applied to any other observation elicited from the study of data, in exercises which, because they are already contextualised and validated, need not be particularly sophisticated to motivate participation. Here are just a few additional basic suggestions to set the ball rolling:

Exercise 4: Assessing the merits of being familiar with tasks, topics, and relevant vocabulary/ready-made formulae:

- get students to make a short (2/3 mn) improvised presentation to several different partners in succession (e.g. summary of a text just read, report on a favourite film/book, news report); compare and discuss resulting differences, taking in both speakers and listeners' points of view (does the exercise become easier? why? implications?);
- organise micro discussions (a) on topics factually and lexically very familiar to students and (b) on topics far removed from anything they know (also a good exercise to practice communication strategies); compare, and discuss the impact of the difference on performance and confidence;
- set up exercises to be carried out first without, then with, factual and/or lexical priming; compare the outcome of the tasks and students' assessment of their performance in each.

These exercises are quite standard, but can expand in other directions, e.g. be used to alert students to priorities for individual study (what kind of people are they likely to come into contact with when abroad? what are these people likely to talk about in their day-to-day conversations? what kind of resources are available locally to build up a factual/linguistic repertoire to cope with it? how can these resources be used?).

Exercise 5: Filling time with talk/padding

Give students a set of general statements and factual/linguistic padding instructions, e.g:

> *Les étudiants travaillent trop*
> (pad with personal examples, first in the 3rd person then in the 1st)
> *Le stress qui en résulte nuit à leurs études*
> (same thing)
> *Il nuit aussi à leur équilibre affectif*
> (same thing);

and the other way round to drive strategies home:

> *Les étudiants ne travaillent pas assez*
> *Ils accordent trop d'importance à leur vie sociale*
> *Leurs résultats ne sont pas à la mesure de leur potentiel.*

Exercise 6: Using phatic strategies to involve interlocutors

- refer to data to identify sets of options (e.g. *si vous voulez, vous l'savez comme moi, écoutez, vous croyez pas que . . .* in Extract 2);
- practice in pairs, then in larger groups, discuss and use as a platform to build up a more diversified repertoire through observation and practice.

Exercise 7: Building up strategies for keeping or claiming turns

- again refer to data to identify a limited number of possible strategies and highlight their supporting features (e.g. in Extract 2: use of basic adversatives (*non, ah non, mais, oui mais, non mais si, c'est faux*) in conjunction with voice and/or body projection, repetition/ reformulation of the interrupted speaker's assertion, repetition of one's assertion to hold the ground);
- set up micro-discussions involving conflicting partners, whose brief is to outwit (the) other/s using turn taking/keeping devices as their main strategy (the gist of the arguments to be used as a basic framework can be agreed upon beforehand to make it easier for

students to concentrate on interrupting and holding the floor); discuss, taking in other options students may have used spontaneously, and use as a platform for building a working repertoire through observation and practice.

Pedagogical Considerations

There is nothing particularly uncommon about this set of practical applications, and little in them that does not fit in with normal classroom routine. The study of data to set them within a working context, on the other hand, is perhaps more contentious.

One possible objection, as was mentioned before, is that analyses are too difficult. Like any other demanding task, however, they can be graded, and like them they require a guiding framework. In this case, contextualising extracts (see under 'Investigating Data', p. 66–73) is a stepping stone; it could be skipped over, but is useful in focusing students' attention on data, giving them confidence to handle them and setting the scene for contrasting extracts: it is relatively familiar territory (who is speaking, about what, in what sequence, where? are speakers old, young, what do they do in life, what is their status in the exchange? how is it possible to tell?), and the detective work involved hangs in the first instance on fairly simple clues (e.g. topical lexical items, gender, forms of address). Work at the next stage, i.e. tracing aspects of relativity and negotiation in the extracts (see pp. 73–86), is arguably more intimidating, because qualitative. Making it manageable is a question of setting realistic targets to support incremental comparison:

- giving focus to the search for clues, e.g. by limiting the number of observations to make (look for two or three differences between the children and the adults', in extracts y and z) or their scope (how do speakers begin their turns? do they wait to be given a turn to speak? if they don't, what do they do?);
- rooting qualitative remarks in quantitative evidence (length/syntactic characteristics of utterances, nature of content, relationship volume/content), e.g. providing paradigms of options to look into (are the children's utterances easier/more difficult to understand than the adults', and why? are they long/short, simple/complex? what kind of information do they convey — facts, personal responses, general opinions? how does that affect the form of utterances? how much do they actually say, in how many words?);
- working on minimal contrasting pairs (general/specific, first person/third person, professional/everyday);

- exercising selectivity (see Chapter 3 — use shorter/simpler samples, deal only with the subset of features most relevant to students' current experience), and sharing tasks out amongst students.

Approaching data selectively, and capitalising on group work to pool resources, is the answer to another possible objection, namely that analyses are time-consuming. Then again, so is any other kind of work once it is handled in any depth: why devote time to the study of written texts, and confine the spoken word to practice, when both the written and the oral medium are at least equally relevant to students' concerns, yet exhibit significant differences above and beyond their similarities?

Besides, analysing verbal interactions, though in this instance harnessed primarily to fluency concerns, involves much language work with implications for other activities: dealing with questions of pragmatics, register, lexis and syntax makes for a better *overall* understanding of language; drawing on strategies such as inferencing contributes to language learning. Perhaps more importantly, it gives direction to oral work, and combines with exercises to provide incentives and anchorage points for subsequent study and practice, as must already be clear from some of the applications. The interruption strategies used by the various speakers in the debate on anti-smoking campaigns, or by students in related exercises, for example, may lack variety; all the more reason to look out for alternatives in other data.

Notes
1. Extract from a private recording made in a French *école maternelle* (1996).
2. *Ciel mon mardi — Le Tabac* (presented by Christophe Dechavannes. Recorded from TV5 Europe, 1990).
3. *C'est pas juste — Rivière sans retour* (presented by Vincent Perrot. Recorded from TV5 Europe, 1990).
4. *Scully rencontre — Anne Sinclair* (Recorded from TV5 Europe, 1993).

Chapter 5

Discourse/Form Features of Verbal Fluency: Spontaneous Speech

This chapter and the next work as a pair. They both look at discourse/form features, the first in spontaneous speech, the second in planned speech, with the function of assessing the relationship between form and fluency in different contexts. They also share a common set of preliminary activities which can be handled separately, but fulfil their contrastive and grading functions better when introduced together.

Form, as a rule, is not something with which students feel very comfortable, particularly in the spoken language: more often than not, their oral/aural procedural grip on speech, acquired through practice, is only patchily matched by a conscious grasp of how it works. Nor is it something that they are particularly willing to look into, or perceive as particularly relevant, beyond certain traditional limits (e.g. phonology, or register). Developing critical processes to convince them that it *is* relevant, for both aural and oral functions, is what these two chapters are about.

As in the previous chapter, comparison is the main analytical device in handling the data. Its purpose in this case is to draw attention to discourse parameters of oral and aural fluency, in two distinct samples: one of ad-lib speech set against written transpositions in this chapter, the other of planned speech, set against written text in Chapter 6.

The call for a graded approach, however, is more compelling. With relativity and negotiation, work options are quite open: start with sensitisation activities to bring on analyses of data, or go straight into analysis before moving on to hands-on sensitisation and practice. With form and related discourse features, there is a strong case for pre-analysis groundwork: the scope of the question, and students' possible misgivings or inexperience, militate against tackling it head on.

This first chapter in the pair will thus open, as a preamble, with the description of an example of introductory exercises to bring on the kind of comparative investigation illustrated in the set. They are designed to form an integral part of the overall enquiry, but can just as well be treated as

stand-alone activities with more self-contained objectives. This also applies
to components of the analyses and to other exercises covered in these two
chapters, which will otherwise proceed as the previous one, starting with
the investigation of the sets of samples, moving on to a summary of
implications for learners, before turning to applications.

Preliminary Groundwork: Functions and Outcome

In the examples used here (see worksheet in Table 15), preparation hangs
on transcription, handled not as a dictation exercise, with emphasis on
precision and accuracy, but as a means of bringing out differences in form
between pieces and of motivating further study. Apart from two transcriptions (Exercises 1 and 2d), and a comparison of the transcription work
involved in each case (Exercise 3), it includes tasks with greater emphasis
on textual characteristics, also intended to prepare the ground for the
second (more difficult) transcription.

Exercise 2a involves combining simple topically-linked sentences into
complex clusters, using appropriate coordinating, subordinating or other
syntactic devices to bring out the logical relationship between them and
allow for subordination and embedding (see examples of written transpositions in Table 17 p. 103).

It is, in other words, a conventional exercise in syntactic transformation,
which focuses attention on syntactic options available in written discourse.
It also produces, after feedback, a sample of connected written texts.

Exercise 2b takes up related concerns, but with a preliminary shift to the
oral medium: students are asked to read aloud text-only transcriptions of
passages from the same radio programme as the extract they have to
transcribe later (in 2d), and to recover their segmentation, using the first
line of the first passage as a guide (see passages 1 and 2 in Table 15).

Making sense of the passages requires prosodic projection, a necessary
condition to recover their coherence/cohesion and proceed with 2c, i.e.
produce written reformulations/summaries of the pieces; this, too, entails
turning utterances into connected sentences, using the same kinds of
principles as in Exercise 2a, while simultaneously exposing other significant features (e.g. ellipsis), e.g. for passage 2:

> *La technique pour éviter de se faire voler son scooter, comme le savent
> tous ceux qui, comme moi, en ont un, est de se mettre dans un endroit
> éclairé, car les voleurs ne vont pas prendre le risque de se faire voir à
> l'oeuvre, et à côté d'un scooter plus neuf ou dont l'antivol est plus vieux,
> ce qui est facile puisqu'on peut se déplacer pour en trouver un qui
> remplisse ces conditions.*

Table 15 Discourse/form features of verbal fluency: preparation worksheet

---

PREPARATION A LA COMPARAISON ECRIT/ORAL

1   *Transcrivez l'introduction du cours magistral de P-L Blanc,* Bilan des années de Gaulle *('bon/ avant de vous parler . . . c'est la diplomatie') (en tout ou en partie)*

2.a   *Transformez les phrases simples qui suivent en phrases complexes/composées de façon à produire un passage écrit continu*
     Le journal Soixante millions de consommateurs *du numéro de février a testé tous les antivols pour les motos, les scooters, les vélos.*
     Le numéro de février vient de sortir.
     Il n'y a pas un antivol qui résiste.
     Il y en a trois marques.
     Je ne vais pas vous les citer.
     Ce sont les fameux U.
     Ce sont les meilleurs, les plus résistants.
     Avec un (certain) moyen, il faut seulement une minute et huit secondes pour ouvrir n'importe quel antivol.
     Soixante millions de consommateurs *ne veut pas dévoiler ce moyen.*

  b   *Essayez de recréer les passages transcrits ci-dessous tels qu'ils seraient produits oralement (extraits de l'émission* Les déjeuners de Laurent Ruquier, *France Inter, février 96): lisez-les à voix haute, retrouvez-en le découpage en groupes de mots de façon à en faire émerger la structure orale et à en retrouver le sens (cf. 1ère ligne du passage 1 pour exemple)*
     Passage 1: mais c'est parc'que/c'est c'est/Einstein l'a dit/tout est relatif/ l'antivol/moi j'vais l'donner puisque j'connais la combine/c'est exactement comme la serrure fichée dans les immeubles tout l'monde enfin tous les cambrioleurs savent l'ouvrir simplement si y a deux serrures celle-ci est plus dure que l'autre i suffit d'se mettre à côté d'un scooter plus facile à voler que l'sien
     Passage 2: mais mais voilà c'est ça la technique i faut toujours se mettre euh tous les gens qu'ont des scooters moi j'en ai un il faut toujours s'mettre devant une vitrine qu'est éclairée parc'que le type va pas prendre le risque de s'faire voir si y a d'la lumière en train d'essayer d'le voler ou alors à côté d'un d'un truc qu'a l'air un p'tit peu plus vieux ou alors plus neuf. . . pacque i faut toujours mettre plus beau [mais si l'autre scooter connaît aussi l'coup] pardon [si l'autre scooter connaît aussi la combine] oui mais l'avantage en scooter c'est qu'on est mobile [oui] donc on va dix mètres plus loin jusqu'à ce qu'on en trouve un [ah d'accord] mieux avec un antivol plus vieux [ouais]

  c   *Reformulez/résumez ces passages sous forme écrite, en en rétablissant la cohérence*
  d   *Transcrivez le début de l'extrait dont ces passages sont tirés ('euh/vous roulez en moto . . . n'importe quel antivol)*

3   *Comparez le processus de transcription pour les deux extraits (i.e. cours magistral/extrait France Inter)*

Producing appropriately cohesive and coherent stretches of written text in Exercise 2 is not so simple, for reasons which become apparent later. It is particularly tricky in 2b, where it can hardly be achieved fully without some major transformations or padding in (see example on p. 98), and no doubt teacher support at the end of the exercise. But the actual outcome of the students' work on their own matters less than what it is intended to induce, i.e. a mental toggle between the written and the oral mode, both applied to the same topic, with the following purposes:

- setting comparison in motion by drawing attention to differences in form between written and oral text;
- anticipating Exercise 2d, i.e. the transcription of the beginning of the extract from which the passages in 2b are taken; the piece, a sample of radio talk, is difficult, and the task is intimidating; but students by then are at least familiar with topic and lexis, and familiar, too, with the propositional content of what they have to transcribe: it turns out to correspond with the sentences given in 2a; they also have an idea of what to expect aurally, and of what the transcription might look like (from 2b).

The same applies to comparing the experience of transcribing the two set pieces (Exercise 3): the end result of the process matters less than its alerting students, if only impressionistically, to the general characteristics, underscored by the demands of transcription, of what are two contrasting pieces:

- the introduction to an academic lecture given to university students[1] (see transcription in Chapter 6, Table 21), i.e. a planned, monologic piece delivered by someone with experience of public speaking, and something of a half-way house, with a grading function: it exhibits features typical of verbal delivery, yet, as we shall see, has similarities with the written medium students are used to handling; it is by and large straightforward to transcribe: its register, form and lexis should, in type at least, be familiar to them, even if its topic is not;
- the extract from the radio talk programme[2], i.e. a piece exhibiting typical characteristics of ad-lib speech, and accordingly difficult to grasp and put down on paper (see transcription in Table 16).

The sample of radio talk is clearly far more demanding to transcribe than the introduction to the lecture. As ever, speed of delivery is usually mentioned as the main obstacle to comprehension, and, *a fortiori*, to transcription. But hesitation phenomena and brokenness of utterance do not lag very far behind. They are magnified by transcription, make its process strenuous, and its product untidy: what it looks like on paper is a far cry from the written transposition produced from the propositional content given at the beginning of the worksheet; yet it is transactionally equivalent, and is recognised to convey, on-line for a native audience, a similar message. The lecture extract is credited with converse qualities: its

Table 16 Transcription of the bike-lock exchange (ad-lib speech) (the passages in bold are the passages dealt with in the worksheet)

> *Extrait de l'émission* **Les déjeuners de Laurent Ruquier** — *France Inter 9/2/96*
> 1 *euh/vous roulez en moto vous aussi/*
> 2 *en scooter/*
> 3 *en scooter/*
> 4 *vous_avez un antivol/j'imagine/*
> 5 *oui/*
> 7 **bon alors y a une/euh/le journal Soixan-Soixante millions de consommateurs du**
> 8 **numéro/le numéro d'février qui vient de sortir/et qui a testé 'tous les_antivols . /pour**
> 9 **les motos les scooters les vélos/euh ben y en_a pas un . qui résiste hein heu en**
> 10 **fait/alors y en_a trois marques hein/j'vais pas vous les citer/qui sont euh les fameux**
> 11 **U/hein euh/(oui)/euh qui sont euh les meilleurs (en)fin les les les plus résistants**
> 12 *(l'histoire de ???) mais en tout cas a-avec euh . un moyen euh que ne veut 'pas*
> 13 *dévoiler euh Soixante millions de consommateurs/il faut seulement 'une minute et*
> 14 *'huit secondes pour ouvrir 'n'importe quel euh . antivol/*
> 15 *oui sur ce point d'vue si j'peux m'permettre/j'ai connu/et ça n'est pas d'la blague/j'ai connu un*
> 16 *collectionneur d'antivols/c'est-à-dire un voleur d'antivols/il ne volait que d'ça/*
> 17 *(il laissait les/*
> 18 *(c'était vous/* [laughs]
> 19 *oui oui absolument/il il mettait un point d'honneur à ne voler que l'antivol/il laissait l'vélo et il*
> 20 *avait une 'très jolie collection/une bonne centaine/*
> 21 *il est dans votr'livre/il est dans l'livre des Biz(arres/*
> 22 *(non c'était_après euh c'était_après la publication*
> 23 *de la dernière euh édition du livre des Bizarres/*
> 24 *mais dans les_années 68 euh/justement (y avait eu un scan-/un un scandale avec les sa//*
> 25 *(ouais mais c'est_assez joli (hein/*
> 26 *(oui c'est joli/*
> 27 *les sa-les fameux sabots d'Denver/Jean Yanne avait réussi à euh ouvrir un un sabot*
> 28 *d'Denver/à défaire un sabot d'Denver/avec une épingle à ch'veux d'une dame qu'avait*
> 29 *traîné dans sa voiture/*
> 30 *c'était vous/*
> 31 *non/et pis quoi encore/et tant d'autres/* [laughs]
> 32 **bon/euh alors le le là l'antivol/j'trouve que/une minute huit secondes pour ouvrir/alors Libé/**
> 33 **pisque c'est dans Libé qu'je lis euh cet_article/dit/une seule solution transformer la moto**
> 34 **en_arbre de Noël 'orné d'antivols histoire de prolonger l'plaisir euh des voleurs/c'est**
> 35 **vrai qu'quinze antivols/ça fait quand même quinze fois quinze minutes et quinze fois huit**
> 36 *(secondes quoi/*
> 37 *(mais non/[comment]/c'est pas comme ça du tout qu'ça*
> 38 *marche/*
> 39 *alors qu'est-ce qu'i faut faire/*
> 40 *mais c'est pa(r)c'que/c'est c'est/Einstein l'a dit/tout_est relatif/l'antivol/moi j'vais*
> 41 *l'donner puisque j'connais la combine/c'est exactement comme la serrure fichée dans*
> 42 *les_immeubles/. tout l'monde/enfin tous les cambrioleurs savent l'ouvrir/simplement*
> 43 *si y a deux fi-deux serrures/celle-ci est plus dure que l'autre/i suffit d's'mettre à côté*
> 44 *d'un scooter plus facile à voler que l'sien/*
> 45 *ah oui/*

46 *mais mais voilà c'est ça la technique/i faut toujours se mettre euh tous les gens*
47 *qu'ont des scooters/moi j'en_ai un/il faut toujours s'mettre devant une vitrine qu'est*
48 *éclairée/pa(r)c'que le type va pas prendre le risque de s'faire voir si y a d'la*
49 *lumière/en train d'essayer d'le voler/ou alors à côté d'un d'un truc qu'a l'air un p'tit*
50 *peu plus vieux/ou alors plus neuf . . . /parcque i faut toujours mettre plus beau {mais*
51 *si l'autre scooter connaît aussi l'coup} pardon/{si l'autre scooter connaît aussi la*
52 *combine} oui mais l'avantage en scooter c'est qu'on_est mobile {oui} donc on va dix*
53 *mètres plus loin jusqu'à c'qu'on_en trouve un {ah d'accord} mieux avec un antivol*
54 *plus vieux {ouais}/*
55 *c'est un malin Vandel hein/*
56 *oui oui oui/ (.)*

more manageable pace is, in particular, unanimously described by students as the single most facilitating feature; other help features mentioned include greater continuity, use of pausing and stress, and a degree of predictivity which facilitates anticipation.

At this point, then, the outcome of the work is this:

- on-paper data illustrating different forms of discourse — planned speech and spontaneous speech in transcription, written transpositions and written renderings of spontaneous speech (in cleaned-up versions agreed upon when work with the worksheet is complete), to which can be added a sample of written text for comparison (see Chapter 6);
- a set of more or less impressionistic observations about features of the data, which need to be rationalised, but have, all the same, produced some awareness of their particularities, and provided a platform for clarification and expansion.

There is enough material for rounding off the work at this stage with a broad discussion of students' response, and so treat it as a self-contained activity leading straight into implications and follow-up work (see end of this chapter and the next). Alternatively, it can justify branching out into more involved investigations of form in the modes of expression illustrated by the data — the next stage here (for ad-lib speech) and in the corresponding section of the next chapter (planned speech).

Investigating Ad-lib Speech Data: Comparison of Radio Talk Samples (Transcriptions vs. Written Transpositions)

The written transpositions of the radio talk extract in Table 17 do not, strictly speaking, qualify as genuine samples of written French: keeping to the propositional content of the oral version (see Transposition 1 in particular) cuts out options otherwise available in writing (by, for instance, restricting lexical freedom). But because they share with the oral version this basic propositional content, they make it easier, in the first instance, to assess features of the two mediums.

Eliciting observations about form

One way of bringing out contrasts is simply to separate out what the various versions have in common from what makes them different (see Table 17). This drives home what the line count also makes clear: the oral version is longer, albeit only slightly. It also helps, as a crude first step, to map out and label roughly what each version features above and beyond shared matter (see Table 18).

Table 17 Oral version and written transpositions of the passage studied, with shared matter in a lighter font.

Oral version

1. *bon alors y a une/euh/le journal* **Soixan**-Soixante millions de consommateurs *du numéro/le*
2. *numéro d'février qui vient de sortir/et qui a testé 'tous les antivols. /pour les motos les*
3. *scooters les vélos/euh ben y en a pas 'un . qui résiste hein heu en fait/alors y en a trois*
4. *marques hein/j'vais pas vous les citer/qui sont euh les fameux U/hein euh/ (oui)/euh qui sont*
5. *euh les meilleurs (en)fin les les les plus résistants (l'histoire de ?) mais en tout cas a-*
6. *avec euh . un 'moyen euh que ne veut 'pas dévoiler euh Soixante millions de consommateurs/il*
7. *faut seulement 'une minute et 'huit secondes pour ouvrir 'n'importe quel euh . antivol/*

Written transposition 1 (close to the oral version's propositional content)

1. *Le journal* Soixante millions de consommateurs *du numéro de février, qui vient de sortir, a*
2. *testé tous les antivols, pour les motos, les scooters, les vélos.* **Parmi ceux des** *trois*
3. *marques* **considérées, que je ne vais pas vous citer, mais qui sont** *celles des fameux U, les*
4. *meilleurs, les plus résistants, pas un ne résiste. Avec un moyen que ne veut pas dévoiler*
5. Soixante millions de consommateurs, *il faut seulement une minute et huit secondes pour ouvrir*
6. *n'importe quel antivol.*

Written transposition 2 (NS produced, without reference to the oral version)

1. *Selon le numéro de février de* Soixante millions de consommateurs, *qui vient de sortir, sur*
2. *tous les antivols pour motos, scooters, vélos de trois marques, que je ne vais pas vous*
3. *citer,* **aucun ne résiste, puisqu'il** *faut seulement une minute et huit secondes pour ouvrir*
4. *n'importe* **lequel des** *fameux U — les meilleurs, les plus résistants — avec un moyen que le*
5. *journal ne veut pas dévoiler.*

Making sense of observations

According to the information in Table 18, fillers and repetitions in the oral version are the most conspicuous attributes accounting for the difference in length. Like the omission of the negative particle *ne* and other

Table 18 Features differentiating the various versions of the radio talk basic text

	Oral version	Transposition 1	Transposition 2
Fillers/ adverbial fillers	*bon* *alors* [× 2] *euh* [× 11] *ben* *hein* [× 3] *en fait* *enfin* *en tout cas*		
Repetitions	*Soixan-Soixante* *(du) numéro/(le) numéro* *les/les/les* *a-avec*		
VPs	*y a une/* *y en a (pas un qui . . .)* *y en a (trois marques)* *(qui) sont (les meilleurs)* *a testé***		
Grammatical connectors	*et qui (a testé . . .)* *qui (résiste)* **qui (sont les fameux U)**** *qui (sont les meilleurs)* *mais [en tout cas]*	*que (je ne vais pas)* *mais (qui sont celles)*	*que (je ne vais pas)* *puisqu'(il faut . . .)*
Pronouns	*(y) en (a pas un qui . . .)* *(vous) les (citer)*		*aucun (ne résiste)*
Determinants	**les (motos, etc) [×3]**** *les (fameux U)*	*ceux des (3 marques)* *celles des (fameux U)*	
Prepositional phrases		*parmi (ceux des . . .)*	*Selon (le journal)* *sur (tous les antivols)*
Adjectival elements	*(n'importe) quel***	*(marques) considérées*	*(n'importe) lequel des*
Negative particle		*ne (vais pas vous citer)* *ne (résiste)*	*ne (vais pas vous citer)* *ne (résiste)*

** compared with transposition 2 only

forms of elision (*y a* vs. *il y a*) (whose impact on length is negligible), their occurrence as features of spontaneous spoken French is hardly an eye-opener: their presence is merely heightened in the transcription of the extract, where it adds to the sense of fragmentation. Nor is their most obvious function much of a revelation: students know well enough from their own experience what happens when there is little time to think of what to say, though they may not be fully, or consciously, aware of just how much native speakers, too, rely on time-gaining gambits in spontaneous speech, or of the other functions they fulfil in it. But why should their perception be so restricted?

The table gives no direct answer to this question. But it raises others, and is an invitation to look at the way utterances and sentences are put together:

- why, for instance, are there extra VPs in the oral version?
- is the number and nature of grammatical connectors significant?
- what justifies the occurrence of prepositional phrases in the written transpositions?

Form of utterances

The first additional VP in the oral version (*y a une* [1] in Table 17) is a false start, and evidence of how else time pressure affects the production of oral messages: with no time to think ahead, utterance planning can be hit-or-miss, and changes of mind or backtracking difficult to avoid, here as at other points, e.g:

- this *y a une* is a handy ready-made platform, which may have been meant to turn into '*y a une enquête*'; but perhaps because of the perceived need to introduce the name of the magazine first, or the sense that the utterance would become too complex to handle, it is rejected as an opening gambit and gives way to a different construction with *le journal Soixan-Soixante millions de consommateurs* [1];
- [*le journal*] . . . *du numéro* [1] is abandoned, under pressure of introducing additional information, in favour of *le numéro d'février qui vient de sortir* [1–2], which, too, may have given cause to anticipate subsequent planning difficulties; the repetition of *numéro* is thus a function of message construction rather than a straight hesitation.

Lateral information is at times sufficiently prepackaged to be inserted parenthetically within the ongoing message without much disruption (e.g. *y en_a trois marques hein/j'vais pas vous les citer/qui sont* [4]). This is not always so. Feeding in *pour les motos, les scooters, les vélos* [2–3], for instance, or *qui sont <u>euh</u> les meilleurs (en)fin les les plus résistants* [4–5] does not help: it takes attention away from the main thrust of the utterance, diverts it from its original track, and again prompts shifts in construction:

> /alors y en_a trois marques hein/j'vais pas vous les citer/qui sont euh les fameux U/hein euh/euh **qui sont <u>euh</u> les meilleurs (en)fin les les les plus résistants<u>/</u> <u>mais en tout cas a-avec euh . un 'moyen</u>** ... [4–5] (see also [2–3]).

It also accounts for the occurrence of other additional VPs:

- the first *y (en) a*, in /*<u>euh</u> ben y en_a pas 'un . qui résiste <u>hein</u> <u>euh</u> en fait*/ [3], as indeed the second in /*alors y en_a trois marques hein*/ [3–4], herald new starts at points where utterance is in danger of stopping in its tracks: like *y a une*, both are used as a launching pad (supported by *alors* for the second) after tell-tale hesitations (see *<u>euh</u> ben*, and *<u>hein</u> <u>euh</u> en fait* — also a closing sequence; see later); this time they are allowed to develop into a foreseeable *'qui'* relative construction, with *qui résiste* [3] and the referentially inappropriate *qui sont euh les fameux U* [4]: U is not a brand but a type of lock. This lapse in cohesion, hardly noticeable when the text is heard live, is not tolerated in the first written transposition, which deals with it by means of syntactic padding with a demonstrative (cf. *celles des (fameux U)* [WT 1: 3]; it is avoided in the second, where the syntax is completely different;
- *sont* is part and parcel of *qui sont* in /*euh **qui sont <u>euh</u> les meilleurs** ...* / [4–5], and a straight echo of the same in the immediately preceding clause (***qui sont** euh les fameux U*) (same line). This second *qui sont* turns out to be redundant (compare with *'qui sont les fameux U/les meilleurs/ les plus résistants'*); but it is a convenient backtracking stopgap at an uneasy juncture point where (a) it occurs to the speaker that it may be necessary to justify *'fameux'*, and (b) control in any case appears to be slipping away (cf. hesitation fillers *hein heu/euh*). Like the other additional VPs at other planning points, then, it works as a readily retrievable platform, a springboard which lunges utterance forward.

The written transpositions dispense with such padding, and with concomitant redundancies: the *'qui'* brought on by *'y en a pas un'* in *y en_a pas 'un qui . résiste* [3], for instance (compare with *pas un ne résiste* or *aucun ne résiste*); cf. also *qui sont* in *qui sont <u>euh</u> les meilleurs* above). No task stress means no playing for time, and fewer clauses: 7 and 5 respectively as against 11 in the oral version overall. But the table calls for modulations and complementary explanations: content *is* the same, but it is introduced differently:

- there are additional, or different, grammatical linking devices, manifest in the use of subordination to:
  - flag the status of *j'vais pas vous les citer* [4] as embedded matter: cf. *que je ne vais pas vous citer* in both WT1 and 2 (where the object relative pronoun *'que'* cancels the need for the object personal pronoun *'les'* as cohesion marker); there is a knock-on effect in WT1, where *'mais'* is introduced to signal the restrictive function of the now also embedded *[mais] qui sont celles des fameux U . . .* [WT1: 3];
  - spell out the causal relationship between statement (*aucun ne résiste*) and explanation (*il faut seulement . . .*) with *'puisque'* in *aucun ne résiste puisqu'il faut seulement . . .* [WT2: 3];

- prepositional phrases are used as economical substitutes for some clauses, and syntactically bring out the semantic relationship between pieces of information, cf:
  - *parmi ceux des trois marques considérées* [WT1: 2] (vs. *y en_a trois marques . . . qui* [3] in the oral version]);
  - *selon le numéro de février de . . .* [WT2: 1] (which gets round *le journal . . . a testé* [1–2], the propositional backbone in the oral version and a main clause in WT1) and *sur tous les antivols . . .* [WT2: 1–2].

The result in the written transpositions is neat. It is simpler to decode on paper, not least because logical connections emerge more forcefully, yet it appears syntactically more complex. The second transposition, in particular, reorganises information around a single main clause (*aucun ne résiste*) in what is a highly structured network of subordination and embeddings. Transposition 1 is little more than a cleaned up version of the oral piece, but involves conspicuous syntactic tightening up, either to do away with superfluous features (e.g. planning platforms), create syntactic continuity (cf. the first sentence for instance) or restore coherence and cohesion (e.g. *Parmi ceux des trois marques considérées* [2–3], *qui sont celles des fameux U* [3]). Time for planning makes all the difference. So, too, does retrospective thinking and editing: content and language to express it can be retrieved, sorted and arranged at leisure, with economy, precision, coherence and cohesion.

The oral version, in contrast, reflects the temporal constraints under which it was produced on-line, with limited scope for forward projection and backward referencing. Instead of a synoptic whole, it presents itself as a sequence of accruing components, strung into the message more or less as thoughts are gathered, by whatever means task stress seems to make expedient: juxtaposition, coordination, prepackaged, recycled or quite basic subordination, interspersed with time-gaining devices. Recovering their composite meaning from the transcription takes quite some effort. Yet it is aurally just as effective in conveying the message's overall propositional content, the relative status of its constituent parts and the relationship between them, as the written transpositions on paper. One has only to refer back to the initial groundwork, and to listen again to the recording, to pinpoint the key to the difference: prosodic and related temporal/sequential features, including fillers and other so-called hesitation features. Now that attention is drawn to them from a different angle, it becomes easier to pinpoint their less conspicuous functions.

Prosodic and temporal/sequential features

The contrast between main building-blocks themselves, and between them and secondary matter, is thus achieved by a variety of combined means, including the following.

Shifts in speech rate and loudness. There is a noticeable quickening of pace and lowering of pitch on strings appended as asides, or subscript, to the main fabric of the utterance, e.g.

> */le numéro d'février qui vient de sortir/* [2]
> */pour les motos les scooters les vélos/* [2–3]
> */j'vais pas vous les citer/* [4]
> */ . . . (en)fin les les les plus résistants/* [5].

Conversely, pace slows down and pitch rises when it comes to those core chunks of information, which, for the most part, correspond to main clauses in the more literal first written transposition:

> */le journal . . . numéro/* [1], */et qui a testé 'tous les_antivols . /* [2]
> */euh ben y en_a pas 'un . qui résiste hein euh en fait/* [3]
> */mais en tout cas a-avec euh . un 'moyen euh . . . /* [5–6]
> */il faut seulement 'une minute . . . /* [6–7]

Stress and silent pausing. Both feature almost exclusively in core strings (see above) where they play a role in slowing down the pace and thus in superscripting content; but they also have a framing effect which aurally lifts out items from their context and creates an additional layer in the hierarchical structure of the message: the groups prefaced by stressed items in:

> */[et qui a testé] 'tous les_antivols ./* [2]
> */pas 'un . [qui résiste]/* [3]
> */[il faut seulement] 'une minute et 'huit secondes pour ouvrir 'n'importe quel euh . antivol/* [6–7],

where accentuation is compounded by pausing, are almost sufficient to reconstruct the gist of the overall message, by virtue, also, of the semantic contrasts they generate (*'tous'/pas 'un/n'importe quel'*); the most significant piece of information further required to complete this general picture — *'qui résiste'*— itself acquires salience from the proactive impact of the preceding pause, from the downwards pitch change it generates, and the closing of the frame with fillers (see below);

Framing with fillers and drawls. There are hesitation markers within tonal groups (e.g. */euh qui sont euh les meilleurs (en)fin les les les plus résistants/* [filled pauses (cum drawl), repetition]); most filled pauses (e.g. *euh, ben, hein*), however, occur at major planning points, where task stress is greatest, and where their presence coincides with syntactic and topic shifts; in this sense, they act as formal signals between main clusters of information, where their function is boosted not only by accumulation and drawls, but also by their use in combination with platforms (see above) and adverbial fillers or coordinating conjunctions (e.g. *en fait, alors, mais, en tout cas*), thus:

> **bon alors ... euh [... journal ... a testé ... antivols] euh ben [y en_a pas un qui résiste] hein heu en fait/alors [y en_a trois marques]/hein heu/euh [...]/mais en tous cas [... il faut seulement ... pour ouvrir].**

Filled pauses and adverbial fillers no doubt provide thinking-space to proceed with constructing the message, but by the same token underscore its segmentation. They are also expressive in their own right, and fulfil significant strategic and interactional functions:

- *bon alors*, at the beginning of the turn, introduces a shift to a different mode: *bon* has a summing up value which brings the preceding prefatory question/answer exchange to a close; *alors* takes hold of the floor and settles attention in anticipation of what is to follow; (*bon alors* is a standard transitional gambit, and is typically used by teachers as a phatic attention-switching device);
- *ben* and *hein*, in **euh ben** [y en_a pas un qui résiste] **hein euh** en fait/alors [3], reinforce the framing and slowing down function of the two *euhs*; *ben*, however, also gives clues about what is to follow by suggesting that some predictable conclusion is to be drawn from the preceding build-up of information, and involves interlocutors in the process by giving them space to reach their own; *hein* is likewise interactive: it invites interlocutors to recognise with the speaker that there was indeed nothing unexpected in *'y en_a pas un qui résiste'*, and gives them credit for anticipating the same conclusion; like *bon alors* at the beginning of the turn, *en fait/alors* then work as a hinge, with *en fait*

simultaneously reinforcing *hein's* functions and closing the frame, and *alors* shifting attention to the next. Etc.

The transcription of the passage makes fillers, filled pauses and silent pauses graphically conspicuous. Because it does not record prosodic phenomena, nor the interplay between the various features involved in verbalising its propositional content, its record on paper projects them all too exclusively as hesitation markers. It thus fails to do justice to the diversity of the roles they play in the production of the message, and in its aural reconstruction. They may well provide evidence of task stress. Yet, together with accentual stress, changes of rhythm, of pitch and loudness, they are instrumental in giving listeners clues they need in order to grasp the value of the message's ingredients and the connection between them.

What scrutiny of a short piece like this one makes clear to students then, is that if these features pass largely unnoticed — as hesitations — during actual interaction or decoding, it is precisely because they are as crucial for interlocutors or listeners as they are for speakers. They are part and parcel of the fabric of the message, break it down into manageable units, guide its reconstruction, foster continuity and fluidity. But they also make room for decoding, anticipating and absorbing its content: the respite speakers get from filled/unfilled pauses, continuity fillers, or again repetitions and platforms, is time, too, for interlocutors to process messages and respond to interactive signals — as demanding a task as producing them in the first place. They are, in short, a key ingredient sustaining the viability of exchange, and as important to decode as words themselves, usually the main focus of students' effort.

Additional observations

Passages 1 and 2 of the worksheet would, by and large, produce similar observations, give or take individual variations: speakers draw on the same stock of strategies to construct utterance, and use them to comparable ends, but there is room for flexiblility in their application. Both, however, contain tell-tale examples of other reasons why interlocutors need all the help they can get, and give themselves, including drawing on their own knowledge of the world, e.g:

- to juggle with information when changes of mind or the flow of utterance put pressure on cohesion and coherence, as in, for instance:
  — *l'antivol/moi j'vais l'donner puisque j'connais la combine/c'est exacte-ment comme la serrure fichée* . . . (passage 1, [40–1] in the Table 16 transcription, pp. 101–2)

where '*l*'' non-sensically appears to refer to '*antivol*', but in fact does not: *moi j'vais l'donner* turns out to be parenthetical matter, presumably to be interpreted as something like '*je vais donner/dire ce qu'il faut faire puisque je connais la combine*', with '*le*' projecting forward to the end of the turn (*i suffit d'se mettre à côté d'un scooter plus facile à voler que l'sien* [43–4]

— [*il faut toujours se mettre*] . . . *à côté d'un truc qu'a l'air un p'tit peu plus vieux/ou alors plus neuf . . . /parc'que i faut toujours mettre plus beau/* (passage 2, [49–50] in Table 16)

which leaves it to interlocutors to unpackage two utterances compressed into one: as it transpires later (cf. . . . *jusqu'à c'qu'on en trouve un mieux avec un antivol plus vieux/* [53–4], '*vieux*' refers to locks, '*neuf*' to scooters and the passe-partout referent '*truc*' to both interchangeably; typically, the speaker who steps in at this point, with *mais si l'autre scooter connaît aussi l'coup* [50–1], has already correctly interpreted the string, using his own resources, and clearly does not need this post-hoc clarification;

• to fill in the gaps of ellipses, e.g:
/*simplement si y a deux fi-deux serrures/celle-ci est plus dure que l'autre/i suffit d'se mettre à côté d'un scooter plus facile à voler que l'sien/* (passage 1, [42–4] in Table 16) which jumps straight from door locks to scooters without spelling out the connection.

There is little to be gained from making claims about the relative syntactic complexity of these samples of unplanned speech and written transpositions, except to concur with Halliday: both are more complex in their own way. But they do make different demands. Significantly, oral turns are driven on by a forward dynamic which has a critical impact on the way utterance shapes up, unfolds, and is received. They may score low on synthesis, but make up for it by capitalising on the distinctive resources of their medium, to, at one and the same time, circumvent task stress, hand out syntactic clues and bond participants in their build up. For, crucially, they involve interlocutors as much as speakers, make them partners in the shared undertaking of message construction — and fluency: thus, transactional efficiency is achieved by pooling resources, with all parties contributing pieces to a jigsaw whose whole is greater than the sum of its parts on paper, as the transcription makes clear.

This is something students often find difficult to recognise when dealing with a foreign language: they do not always realise that if they are missing something, it is not necessarily because they have not understood, but because it may not be there and is left to them to contribute top-down, i.e.

using their own knowledge of the world. On the other hand, and as teachers know only too well, they are often over-anxious to catch every single word, at the expense of other signals, and at the expense, too, of contextual clues which provide opportunities to recover meaning, again top-down, when words or parts of messages are not clear or properly understood (e.g. the word *'antivol'* here, which some students found they did not know, and looked up, only to realise later that they could just as easily have inferred its meaning from what followed had they given themselves a chance to do so).

In any case, it is not as if the exchange is particularly compact. Because the pieces compared are based on the same propositional content, little can be said about transactional density (which tends to be low in this kind of interaction), or indeed word choices (see next chapter on these points). All the same, it seems plain, even without points of comparison, that the amount of raw information the full passage conveys is quite small in relation to the amount of speech it generates. What it boils down to is that cycle locks, even of the best kind, take little time to force open, for those who know how. The anecdotes which otherwise make it up give it texture, but their function is as social as it is transactional. They are a useful gambit for getting involved in conversation, sustaining participation, maintaining viability (see Chapter 4). Yet what is important for learners to bear in mind is (a) that missing out on details does not necessarily prevent them from getting the overall gist of exchanges of this kind, nor from keeping involved as listeners or interlocutors, so long as they are prepared to take it in their stride and, in particular, do not stop in their tracks when there are attention or comprehension gaps; and (b) that, in this kind of exchange, keeping pace with social and interactional moves, attending to viability, is as important as attending to the minutiae of transactional content.

The scope of this kind of work is necessarily limited: the sample is very small, idiosyncratic, a source of insights rather than generalisations. But it has made at least one thing clear, or confirmed it: learners are not alone in experiencing task stress in spontaneous interactions. Native speakers have greater linguistic means at their disposal, and can encode messages very fast, but, like them, they are susceptible to time pressure: words elude them, they hesitate, change their minds, they string messages as they come, produce discontinuous utterances, rely on their interlocutors to make sense of elliptic messages and to make up for lapses in coherence — even when, as those involved in the radio talk, they can be assumed to be rather more proficient than average. It is all part of coping. It is, too, what gives speech its distinctive shape, yet makes it viable, orally, and, significantly, aurally and interactionally: what makes speaking easier can also make listening and responding easier. On the other hand, if the form of messages is modulated by the strategies used for coping with production and interaction, then responding to their impact, and in particular to the range of signals used to sustain the viability of exchange and put information across, is, also, an integral part of comprehension, and an integral part of aural and interactive fluency for FL learners. How to handle these tactics from the complementary point of view of speaking and oral fluency is a more sensitive matter, which immediately reopens perennial issues.

Implications for Learners

Production and oral fluency

The radio talk extract gives examples of strategies native speakers have to cope with the demands of on-line communication, proceed with planning, negotiate the transfer of meaning and the balance between viability and efficiency:

- they rely on filled and unfilled pauses, some with little actual sense (e.g. *euh*), others with greater semantic value (e.g. *bon, alors*) to create space at pressure points, maintain continuity, keep hold of utterance, involve interlocutors;
- they use platforms and prepackaged formulae, to launch utterances or sustain their flow e.g. *'il y a'*, *'qui sont'* (see other examples elsewhere in the transcription, e.g., *'ça n'est pas d'la blague'* (15), *'et pis quoi encore'* [31], etc.);
- they adapt their syntax to the fast flowing forward dynamic of utterance — rely on juxtaposition, coordination (c.f. *'et . . . '*, *'mais . . . '*), routine or readily implemented subordination (i.e. not involving distant backward or forward projection), use shifts in speech rate and loudness, combined with performative features, as a substitute for grammatical devices to hierarchise information and bring out syntactic relationships;
- they tend to unpackage information, e.g. into simple verb clauses rather than, for instance, synthetic prepositional phrases;
- they make new starts when they experience planning difficulties;
- they associate interlocutors in the construction of message, covertly or overtly invite them to cooperate in it.

But learners, too, rely on these kinds of strategies. The first question that arises, then, is how to treat the overlap between what native speakers and FL learners do to cope, and the impact it has on the shape of the speech they each produce. The second takes us back to pending questions raised in Chapter 2: to what extent should learners actually be encouraged to emulate native speakers' tactics — where does viability end and inefficiency begin, when do such features become counterproductive conversational irritants?

What became apparent from the work on the radio talk, however, and corroborates earlier hypotheses, was (a) that these features were used in combination, and (b) that where hesitation features, as other task stress features, passed undetected on-line, it was because they fulfilled instrumental functions for interlocutors. The point, then, is not that learners should assimilate such features into their speech at all costs, and indiscriminately, on the assumption that it will give it a native speaker-like ring: where they cease to serve the interests of interlocutors, and of interaction, they are likely to stand out as a weakness and to impinge not only on viability, but also on efficiency; all things being equal, coherent speech makes the transmission of meaning more effective, and puts less strain on interaction (Kerbrat-Orecchioni, 1990: 44–5). What is important, however, is that they should be alerted to what they are, to the range native speakers use and where, and to the way they work in different kinds of exchange, including their own, so as to be in a position to assess overlaps and differences between their and native speaker practice, and integrate them more discriminatingly into their own. This means a range of possible activities:

- further observation, to:
  - test findings in other contexts and expand on them (see Exercises 9 and 10 in the next section; also next chapter);
  - assess individual speakers' style (see Exercise 11);
  - build up a repertoire of options within and across types of features (e.g. filled pauses, prosodic devices, interactive and phatic devices, time-gaining platforms) (see next section generally);
- selective practice, to:
  - test the functions of the features identified and rationalise their use by applying it to specific ends, e.g. introducing lateral information, contrasting information, involving interlocutors, unpackaging information, giving oneself thinking space (see Exercises 1, 2, 3, 4);
  - develop or review individual paradigms, i.e. assess personal preferences, develop a feel for those strategies that are most comfortable and effective in sustaining viability while freeing attention to concentrate on efficiency (see Exercises 3 and 4);
- diagnosis and self-monitoring, i.e.
  - use the framework generated by observation to assess individual strengths and weaknesses in the use of viability features and their

relationship with efficiency (see exercises' post-mortems, or use videotaped interactions of students oral activities).

Comprehension and aural fluency

What can be done to make the task of coping with NS spontaneous speech more manageable and give direction to listening activities is easier to circumscribe. The work so far has thus shown that:

- this kind of speech draws on a range of resources to construct utterance; hence the need to get used to responding to different kinds of signals, including filled and unfilled pauses, drawls, repetitions, stress, changes in pace and loudness and, in particular, to the way they help:
  — break down utterances into manageable chunks;
  — signal changes of mind;
  — recreate temporarily severed semantic or syntactic connections;
  — bring out syntactic relationships;
  — contrast information with different functions;
  — hierarchise information, e.g. by highlighting the most relevant words or strings (See Exercise 5.)
- what is uttered may have different functions — convey information, yet also sustain the flow of utterance and maintain contact with interlocutors; hence the need to sort what is to do with viability from what is transfer of information proper to modulate processing, and in particular to be able to:
  — detect platforms, redundancies, repetitions, i.e. features which make the task of speakers easier, help them pace delivery, and similarly help regulate listening and processing efforts (see Exercise 5);
  — take clues from performative features (see above).
- not every word needs to be understood, or processed, for messages to be recovered; there is, in any case, no time for it on-line, and it is likely to obscure other signals or other processes instrumental in keeping up with overall comprehension; hence the need to be able to:
  — put up with attention or comprehension gaps and attend to whole messages rather than individual bits (see Exercise 6);
  — anticipate how messages are likely to unfold (see Exercise 7);
  — listen for gist (see Exercise 6);
  — draw on context and one's own knowledge of the world to recover meaning (see Exercise 8);

- comprehension is not a passive activity, i.e. putting messages together, negotiating meaning involves interlocutors as much as speakers, is an interactive venture which calls on:
    — use of one's own world knowledge not only to anticipate messages but also to fill in gaps left by speakers, make up for vagueness, incoherences and inconsistencies, for instance;
    — response to interactive clues. (See Exercise 8).

Practical Applications

Once the implications of the work with actual samples have been mapped out, there are, here again, plenty of options for follow-up work (see rationale at the end of Chapter 4), either practical applications taking up specific points (practice or further sensitisation) or supplementary activities. What follows are just a few possibilities, briefly outlined.

Examples of exercises

Production

Exercise 1: Hands-on sensitisation to form/discourse features of ad-lib speech.
Get students to extract the propositional content of ad-lib messages or short interactions (e.g. recorded from the radio; two different sets to share out equally amongst the class), and to present it as a set of simple sentences in writing, as in the radio-talk example given at the beginning of this chapter (use already transcribed pieces, or get students to do the transcription themselves as a warm up for focusing on form). Once this is done, groups exchange scripts and, in pairs, use them for producing the text orally as connected discourse, with listening partners taking special notice of the form/discourse features of the messages uttered by the other in the pair. Discuss the work and observations collectively, focusing on (a) linguistic differences between the acted-out version of the pieces and their original, and (b) the performative features used in verbal projection. Repeat the exercise to give students the opportunity to built on their work.

Exercise 2: Unpackaging written language in oral delivery.
Give students in pairs short written texts (a different one for each member of a pair), e.g. short anecdotes, jokes, pieces of news in brief; ask them to read their text carefully to assimilate its content and prepare to produce it orally, taking down essential details if necessary, and bearing in mind differences between written and spoken language, i.e. noting, in the written text, what syntactic features and lexical items will need to be adapted when shifting to the oral medium (an intermediary note-comparing step

can be introduced at this point). Students then recount their piece orally to their partner, focusing on unpackaging the information as observed in NS data, with listening partners making a mental or written note of relevant aspects of the speaker's oral account (including comprehension problems). Round off the exercise with a post-mortem dicussion (of strategies/devices used, difficulties experienced in production and reception, alternatives/diversification, etc.), and repeat it to give students the opportunity to build on their work (change texts round).

Variation: Introduce contextual constraints: e.g. produce the piece as if speaking in front of a camera/for an audience, as if speaking to a friend, etc.

Exercise 3: Using platforms, phatic devices, fillers and other hesitation phenomena to create thinking space and support the construction of utterance.

Give students in pairs a one line prompt (e.g. for an anecdote: *'Madame Dupont aimait beaucoup les nains de jardins'*, a piece of news: *'le Front de libération des nains de jardins a encore frappé'*, for expressing an opinion: *'le vol des nains de jardin est inadmissible'*, etc.); each student in the pair then composes the piece orally, without preparation: the object of the exercise is to concentrate on using time-gaining, planning and phatic devices observed in NS data to create space for thinking of what to say and how to say it, and keep utterance going without undue breaks/silences or the listener losing track (again with the listening partner keeping track of relevant aspects of the speaker's performance: amount and nature of information added, devices used, effectiveness, lapses). Round off the exercise with a post-mortem discussion (of strategies/devices used, difficulties experienced, alternatives, etc.), and repeat it to give students the opportunity to build on their work (change prompts round).

Variations: Same exercise but with speakers focusing on involving interlocutors (without, however, letting them break the story line), and with interlocutors, for their part, focusing on trying to take the narrative over.

'Parler pour ne rien dire' — same exercise but adding as little transactional information as possible, or even none at all, and sustaining utterance as long as possible, convincingly, with strings drawing on viability/performative/prosodic features mostly, or only, i.e. projecting something like the string below orally:

> *bon alors là hein euh effectivement les nains de jardin hein euh enfin euh y a pas on peut pas enfin j'veux dire là quand même j'vois pas mais si enfin euh toi je sais pas mais* (see also example in Anne Sinclair's second answer, Table 11, [37–38]).

This is a very contrived exercise, and a real test for students, but it can
be turned into a game to ease the pressure off: who can hold the floor longest
without adding anything to the transactional content of the prompt? It can
also be done in English first, as a warm up, to help students assess the nature
of the demands it makes.

Exercise 4:   Introducing lateral information/hierarchising information.

Give students in pairs a message in note form (a different one for each
member of the pair), with the main message interspersed with addenda in
brackets, or gaps indicating that additional information will need to be
inserted at these points, e.g:

> **Le football** *[passion personnelle pour le football => intérêt]* **fait toujours
> beaucoup de bruit dans les média** *[pas seulement dans les médias;
> également dans la vie quotidienne => exemples]* **mais on peut se demander**
> *[vrai aussi pour d'autres types de sports => exemples]* **si la place qu'on lui
> fait** *[. . .]* **peut se justifier** *[. . .]*, etc.

Allow students a few minutes to absorb the message, prepare to fill in
the gaps and/or think of ways to insert the additional information into the
main message (bearing in mind observations about NS data), before
reconstructing it orally in turn. Round off as in previous exercises.

Note: The effectiveness of these exercises is enhanced by recording or
filming students, and using samples of their oral work in the post-mortems
to verify on-line observations and boost discussion (of positive aspects,
difficulties, alternatives, possibilities for further work); the back-up recorded samples provide is not, however, a substitute for on-line monitoring: getting students used to responding critically to discourse features of
verbal messages during actual exchanges is a key aspect of the exercises, a
means to the end of fostering more active and discriminating listening.

Reception

*Exercise 5:   Variations on the use of transcription to focus attention on
performative/prosodic features and on their functions in spontaneous
speech.*

- give students word-only transcriptions of short ad-lib messages or
  exchanges (or get them to do the transcription themselves) with the
  brief to supplement them with performative and prosodic features,
  either all at once, or step-by-step to grade the exercise (e.g. concentrating first on filled and unfilled pauses, moving on to stress and drawls,
  then to shifts in speech rate and loudness, etc.); compare, verify and

discuss work at each stage, then globally to review the functions of the features identified, with reference to earlier analyses where applicable (the exercise can also be used for pre-analysis sensitisation to performative/prosodic features and elicitation of data for subsequent study);

- selective transcription: focus transcription on particular features or message components, e.g. main transactional building-blocks, strings introducing lateral information, platforms and time-gaining devices, stressed items only; pool, verify and discuss work, reviewing the contributions of the features/components transcribed to the overall message (content, production, decoding) in the light of earlier analyses (e.g. value of stressed items in assisting message reconstruction).

Exercise 6: Listening for gist vs. intensive listening; transactional vs. interactional content.

Select an ad-lib passage or short exchange likely to challenge students' comprehension (e.g. on an unfamiliar topic) and get them to:

- listen to the recording (once or twice only, without stopping the tape) to extract the main thrust of its transactional meaning, compare their work in small groups or pairs, listen again to verify or come to an agreement if necessary; check/discuss in whole group;
- listen to the passage again, without stopping the tape, this time to retrieve all information necessary to provide a more comprehensive account of its content, pool work in small groups (going back to the recording to resolve disagreements and fill gaps if, and where, necessary), and report to the whole group for corroboration.

Discuss the exercise in the group at large both to compare strategies used/involved in (a) listening for gist and (b) intensive listening, and to assess the nature and value of the information retrieved in each case (e.g. transactional information vs. information with padding or social value).

Variation: Similar exercise, but with focus on contextual inferencing: select an ad-lib passage or exchange containing lexical items/idioms students are unlikely to know but which will not jeopardise overall comprehension; ask students to pinpoint comprehension blackspots under (a), and to concentrate on narrowing down meaning options for what they did not grasp under (b); use the group discussion to catalogue the clues used in the process and assess their value.

Exercise 7: Using world knowledge to anticipate messages.

Recount an anecdote, joke, short piece of news, stopping at intervals to allow students to anticipate what is to follow and make a brief note of it (or use a pre-recorded message and stop the tape at appropriate intervals); students should tick correctly anticipated matter in their notes when the narrative is taken up (or the tape started again); discuss predictions and the degree of convergence with the actual message at the end of the exercise, focusing on what prompted predictions (appropriate or not).

Exercise 8: Using world knowledge to make sense of messages.

Give students a recording of a short elliptical passage or exchange, and ask them first to take notes on its content, then to assess what additional information is required to recover meaning. Compare work at the end of the exercise (first in pairs then in whole group) to identify the nature of the additional information required and discuss implications for comprehension.

Variation: Same exercise but with focus (a) on presuppositions and references shared by speakers in interactions, or (b) the value of interactive clues.

Examples of supplementary activities

Exercise 9: Using available dictionary entries as a platform for investigating the functions, and building up a repertoire, of viability features (fillers, platforms, etc.).

Words like *'alors', 'bien'/'ben', 'bon', 'enfin', 'euh'* have dictionary entries which cover their occurrence as performative features, or, rather, as what is described, in most cases, as 'interjections' — the closest they are to being acknowledged as fillers (see examples from *Le Nouveau Petit Robert* in Table 19a). The reason for using such entries to prompt work on viability features is clear from their content: they hardly do justice to the expressive range or functional diversity of the items they describe, and they say nothing of their interdependence with other features of speech in fulfilling their role/s in oral discourse (the reference to Colette in the *Robert* entry for *euh* suggests that examples are, in any case, taken from written texts, at least in this instance).

In the short example given in Table 19b[3], for instance, *alors* and *bon* have none of the 'meanings' described in the *Robert* entries, but are expressive on other counts, not least for their strategic functions. Both are time-gaining devices, planning platforms, yet also double up as syntactic markers signalling the introduction, in the message, of information with a different status: *alors* introduces a qualification; *bon* introduces a series of examples, a 'taking-of-stock' as it were, and marks a shift from general to specific

Table 19 Performative inserts (a) as described in dictionary entries, and (b) in a speech sample

---

ALORS [I.2.] (Introd. une conséquence) Dans ce cas, dans ces conditions. *Alors, n'en parlons plus.* — En conséquence. *Il n'y a pas de train aujourd'hui, alors je suis venu en voiture.* = > **aussi.** ♦ (Pour demander une suite, une précision) *"Ils rentrent de voyage. — Et alors, ça leur a plu?"* (Pour réfuter une objection) *Et alors? Qu'est-ce que ça change?* (cf. Et puis*). [I.3.] permet de renforcer l'expression, d'insister. — (Pour amorcer la conversation). *Alors, ça va?* — (Pour marquer l'impatience). *Alors, ça vient?* — (L'étonnement, la surprise). *Ça alors!* — (L'indignation). *Non, mais alors!*

BON [1.I.9.] — Interj. *Bon!* marque la satisfaction, notamment après une affaire faite, terminée. = > 1. **Bien.** *Bon on y va!* — Marque la surprise. Ah, bon? — IRON. Marque le mécontentement. *Allons bon! voilà que ça recommence! Bon, bon, nous verrons qui a raison.* ♦ *C'est bon! cela suffit.*

EUH interj. — XVIIe; onomat. ♦ Marque le doute, l'hésitation, l'embarras, la recherche d'un mot. "un taxi s'arrêta. "Au restaurant . . . euh . . . au restaurant du <u>Dragon Bleu</u>" (Colette).

a. **Entries for '*alors*', '*bon*', '*euh*', *Le Nouveau Petit Robert* (1993 edn)**

---

et vous avez aussi cette formule qui est jolie/c'est ./vous dites c'est/vous êtes une a-n-anar'chiviste . alors de sa de sa mémoire/et ./moi j'ajouterais/vous n'employez pas l'mot/mais j'dirais même de son 'savoir-faire . euh/parc'que . /c'est vrai c'que vous dites/elle/bon elle gardait tout/la peau du <u>lait</u>/l'pain rassis pour faire des gâteaux/la cendre de bois pour la lessive/y a toute une énumération/et c'est vrai qu'c'était tout un savoir faire/ . <u>qui</u> <u>qui</u> di-va disparaître avec vous/

b. **'*alors*', '*bon*', '*euh*' in a sample of speech (B. Pivot, *Apostrophes*)[3]**

---

which is then reversed when the parenthesis is closed, i.e. with *y a toute une une énumération*. But their impact depends on their use in combination with other features to which dictionary entries make no reference at all (slowing down on *de sa mémoire* — heralded by the pause which precedes *alors*, speeding up and lowering of pitch after *bon*). Similar remarks extend to *euh*: while it does have the hesitational value described in the *Robert* entry, it, too, has a framing function, and in fact combines with *bon* to punctuate the interplay between main message and inserts, between general and specific, here again with support of other features: it is drawled, and together with the preceding silent pause, compounds the stress on '*savoir-faire*, in a string which contrasts in its slower speech rate with subsequent strings with a different status (addenda to the main thrust of the message).

These kinds of points have already been made on several occasions in the context of earlier analyses (see discussion of '*ben*', '*hien*', '*euh*' in this chapter; also *'ben'*, *'quoi'* in Chapter 4). Supplementing dictionaries entries by observing what value and functions these performative features take in samples of speech, and how they combine with other features to achieve this, is a way of giving direction to enquiries from a different angle; it is initially more focused, yet soon builds into a network of observations which highlight not only the instrumentality of these items in speech, but also the discourse specificities of the spoken medium.

Exercise 10: Using film dialogues and their version in a written narrative (where available) as counterpoints for spontaneous speech.

(See example of matching dialogue extracts from Djian's 1985 novel *37°2 le matin* (pp. 30–1) (Table 20a) and its film version (Beineix, 1986)[4] (Table 20b), to which brief references will be made below by way of illustration; see ad-lib radio-talk used at the beginning of this chapter for a counterpoint.

There are as many different kinds of film dialogue as there are film genres or varieties of language, hence their versatility as a resource for language teaching/learning (see other possible uses in Chapter 7). But they have one thing in common: they are idealised, and even at their least constrained, contrast with real-life examples in a way which peculiarly highlights both the demands exchanges produced in real time make on those involved, and the impact of these demands on the make-up of speech.

It is this common characteristic that this exercice draws on, in a film (and book) whose language students experience as very natural — close to what they expect native speakers to produce live, and close to what they expect to produce themselves. But how close is it? The work is a variation on what was illustrated in the first part of this chapter, and has the same overall objectives: to draw students' attention to the impact of different conditions of production on the shape of discourse and to the specificities of ad-lib speech produced in real time, now in contrast to fictional scripts. But it prompts additional remarks and reinforces others, in particular about the effect of different kinds of pressure on the relationship between viability and efficiency.

The discussion of the radio-talk sample made no reference to the role of body behaviour and interaction with physical context in verbal communication: there was no evidence of it in the transcription, and the audio recording precluded observation. Their function is conspicuous in film dialogues, even, in this case, in the transcription alone (see reference to coffee making in Table 20b [8–9, 22]; see also Table 20a [1–3] vs. Table 20b [1–3]). It is not the purpose of this particular exercise to assess the part they play in speech; this will be dealt with in Chapter 7. But the way film dialogues rely on their expressive value is significant on other grounds. It is all part of achieving peak effectiveness in the face of constraints otherwise

Table 20 Matching dialogue extracts from _37°2 le matin_ (novel and film soundtrack)

1A	_Dites-moi, il a fait, est-ce que c'est à cause de cette_	1A	_dites euh/c'est_à cause de cette_
2	_jeune femme qu'on vous trouve encore au lit à dix_	2	_. euh/jeune femme . /qu'on_
3	_heures du matin . . . ?_	3	_vous trouve encore emmêlé à_
4	_J'ai enfoncé mes mains dans mes poches en regardant_	4	_dix heures/_
5	_par terre, ça me donnait l'air du type ennuyé et ça_	5B	_oh il est déjà dix heures/_
6	_m'évitait de voir sa gueule._	6A	_ah vous_êtes formidable/il est_
7B	_Non, non, j'ai fait. Elle y est pour rien._	7	_onze heures/ 'toujours_
8A	_Il ne faudrait pas, voyez-vous, il ne faudrait surtout pas_	8	_'humecter la_
9	_qu'elle vous fasse oublier pourquoi vous êtes ici,_	9	_mouture/toujours/vous savez/i_
10	_pourquoi je vous loge et vous paye, comprenez-vous . . . ?_	10	_suffirait que j'passe une petite_
11B	_Oui, bien sûr, mais . . ._	11	_annonce . / demain matin_
12A	_Vous savez, il m'a coupé, il suffirait que je passe une_	12	_j'aurais une foule en émeute_
13	_petite annonce et demain matin j'aurai une centaine de_	13	_pour vot'place . /j'n'veux pas_
14	_types qui se bousculeront devant l'entrée en priant_	14	_vous prendre en_
15	_pour avoir votre place. Je ne veux pas vous prendre en_	15	_traître/vous_êtes ici d'puis_
16	_traître parce que vous êtes ici depuis longtemps et je_	16	_longtemps/j'ai jamais eu à_
17	_n'ai jamais eu à me plaindre vraiment de vous, mais ça_	17	_m'plaindre de vous . /mais je_
18	_ne me plaît pas. Je ne pense pas que vous puissiez loger_	18	_n'pense 'pas que vous puissiez_
19	_ce genre de filles et faire votre travail convenablement,_	19	_. garder cette fille ici/ . et faire_
20	_vous voyez ce que je veux dire . . . ?_	20	_convenablement votre boulot/_
21B	_Vous avez discuté avec Georges? j'ai demandé._	21	_voyez c'que j'veux dire ._
22	_Il a hoché la tête. Ce type était repoussant et il_	22	_/regardez comme ça gonfle/_
23	_le savait. Il s'en servait comme d'une arme._	23B	_c'est vieux George qui vous_a_
24B	_Bon, j'ai enchaîné, alors il a dû vous dire aussi qu'elle_	24	_dit pour elle/_
25	_nous avait bien aidés. Je vous jure qu'on n'en serait pas_	25A	_eh / vous vous_affichez non/_
26	_là sans elle. Si vous aviez vu les dégâts après ce foutu_	26B	_d'accord/d'accord/mais il_
27	_cyclone, il y avait plus grand-chose qui tenait debout et_	27	_aurait 'aussi dû vous dire_
28	_elle s'est occupée des courses pendant que Georges et_	28	_qu'elle s'occupe de tout ici/elle_
29	_moi on essayait de réparer tout ça en vitesse. Elle a posé_	29	_tient la baraque elle fait les_
30	_le mastic aux fenêtres, elle a ramassé les branches_	30	_courses/elle vérifie un peu tout_
31	_mortes, elle courait dans tous les coins, elle . . . elle_	31	_quoi/hé hé hé ça compte dans_
32	_restait pas une seconde à rien faire, elle . . ._	32	_une journée ça/[(A) ouais j'dis_
33A	_Je ne dis pas . . ._	33	_pas j'dis pas]/ouais ouais mais_
34B	_Et j'ajouterai une chose, monsieur, elle a jamais_	34	_elle me fait gagner un max de_
35	_demandé à être payée pour ça. Georges peut vous dire_	35	_temps à moi/pis en plus_
36	_qu'elle nous a fait gagner un temps fou . . ._	36	_euh/elle a jamais d'mandé à_
37A	_En somme, vous voudriez que je ferme_	37	_êt(r)e payée/_
38	_les yeux là dessus, c'est bien ça . . . ?_	38A	_en somme vous voudriez que ._
39B	_Ecoutez . . . je me suis peut-être levé un peu tard, ce_	39	_j'ferme les yeux/c'est ça hein/_
40	_matin, mais en ce moment je fais mes dix-douze heures_	40B	_bon c'matin j'ai eu une panne_
41	_par jour. On a eu un boulot épouvantable, vous avez_	41	_d'oreiller/ hein/mais_
42	_qu'à jeter un coup d'oeil. Normalement, je suis debout_	42	_aujourd'hui on va bosser ça va_
43	_avec le jour, je sais pas ce qui est arrivé. Ça_	43	_usiner/et surtout après un bon_
44	_m'étonnerait que ça se reproduise._	44	_café/j'vous sers/ . . ._
20a: book version of the extract (pp. 30–1)		**20b: dialogue extract in the film**	

exposed, in the example, by the adaptations the script undergoes in the shift from novel to film version (omissions, e.g. Table 20a [8–11, 17]; abridgements, e.g. Table 20b [11–13] vs. Table 20a [13–15]; substitutions, e.g. Table 20b [18–19] vs. Table 20a [18–19], where the details conveyed in the book are made redundant by the visual support in the film): the need to convey a maximum of information in a limited time, and the need to sustain the attention of an audience who is not actively engaged in the negotiation and construction of exchange. Whatever concessions film dialogues make to convey the feel of the spoken medium, over and above those the book dialogues make too (cf. elisions, oral form of questions, phatic interpellations, presence of *some* fillers, colloquial nature or vagueness of some lexical items/phrases; see Table 20), their priority is efficiency.

This is manifest, in the example, in the form and density of content of the screen script, which contrast noticeably in both respects with the text of the radio-talk (greater cohesion and coherence, reduced syntactic fragmentation, lexical, syntactic and transactional density, intelligibility on paper), and in the almost total absence of viability features, including task stress features (e.g. changes of mind, planning platforms, hesitations). There is no real call for them in films: dialogues are rehearsed, acted out from a written script, and make no planning demands; and they could only distract audiences who do not need them anyway, because they are only engaged receptively, and because the coherence and cohesion of planned messages minimise processing efforts (see also Chapter 6 on this point): this greater coherence/cohesion, together with visual clues, offsets the demands created by the efficiency of film dialogues enough to make the performative features observed in the radio-talk surplus to requirements, both as syntactic markers and as decoding breathing spaces. The same applies to book dialogues, for comparable reasons, but with the difference that the absence of visual and sound support means an even greater reliance on text and narrative devices to give readers clues for the interpretation of the materials (e.g. register shifts: cf. for example the interplay between oral and written forms in (A)'s questions, used to convey his cynicism and unpleasantness [e.g. Table 20a [1, 10] vs. the use, to the same end, of matter-of-fact asides in a message whose ominous tones are reinforced by quite deliberate unfilled pauses in Table 20b [6–22]). In a piece like the ad-lib radio talk, on the other hand, performative and prosodic features are all the more instrumental that (a) audiences are deprived of any other signals to assist them in decoding speech, and (b) as speech is not planned, it makes greater processing demands: even though listeners are, as with film dialogues, only engaged receptively, and even though the transactional content of the radio-talk is spaced out, and in this sense less taxing, the impact of task stress on the form of messages means that the audience needs almost as much help to reconstruct messages as the interlocutors directly involved in the exchange; so that task stress features, far from being a distraction, are a crucial asset.

The contrast, while illustrating the impact of different modes of production/reception on the form of messages, is thus a reminder of just how much ad-lib speech is given over to constructing and sustaining viability. By the same token, it drives home the extent to which efficiency itself is modulated by the conditions under which speech is produced, as the next chapter, with its focus on planned speech, will also make clear.

Exercise 11: Identifying and trying styles of fluency.

The question of style has already come up, if indirectly, in Chapter 4, with references to Anne Sinclair's partiality to anecdotal padding, and to the recurrent use of register shifts in the debate on tobacco advertising (see interplay between vernacular and professional). These practices were then discussed as strategies for sustaining utterance, and are by no means unusual or idiosyncratic. Nor are they the only strategies that can be observed. The example below illustrates other options:

> *écoutez/vous croyez qu'c'est une vie vous monsieur Pivot/de réussir . dans son entreprise/de réussir son couple/de réussir ses_enfants/d'être une super-maman euh formidable/qui écoute les psydiatres [sic] Dolto Braselton etc./qui fait tout bien comme tout l'monde/d'être une femme séduisante intelligente euh cultivée drôle/parc'qu'i faut êt'drôle effectivement/i faut avoir beaucoup d'humour/ça c'est très important/d'ailleurs j'ai essayé de le faire passer dans l'livre/et puis de faire tout ça à la fois et/vous croyez qu'c'est facile/est-ce qu'on d'mande tout ça à un homme/* (M. Fitoussi, *Apostrophes*[5])

The speaker in this case draws energy from an enumerative style which hinges on the reiteration of syntactic platforms, used in two ways: to encode lexical information, and to generate new platforms which are then reinvested in a similar fashion, in a cumulative, snowball-like process from which she derives her verbal stamina, thus:

vous croyez qu'c'est une vie
de réussir — dans son entreprise
>>> *— son couple*
>>> *— ses enfants*
d'être — une supermaman euh formidable — qui écoute les psychiatres
>>>>>> *— qui fait tout bien*
>>> *— une femme séduisante intelligente euh cultivée drôle*
de faire tout ça à la fois
vous croyez qu'c'est facile.

[Note the rounding up of the turn with a come-back to the plaftform which launched it in the first place, see *vous croyez que*].

Styles are not easy to emulate. But they can be identified, rationalised and practised, as a way both of getting a sense of one's own style and preferences, and of widening one's options — by, for instance, applying observed patterns to other contexts or topics (student life, life of the unemployed, etc.) on the basis of a basic frame, e.g:

> *vous croyez que c'est une vie d'être étudiant, d'apprendre à . . . , d'être . . . qui . . . qui . . . , de se retrouver . . . etc;*

> *vous croyez que c'est facile d'être au chômage . . . , de ne pas savoir . . . , d'être obligé de . . . etc.*

Notes

1. *Bilan des années De Gaulle 1958–69* (Pierre-Louis Blanc. Lecture given at the University of East Anglia, 1974).
2. *Les déjeuners de Laurent Ruquier* (presented by Laurent Ruquier. France Inter, 1996).
3. *Apostrophes* (presented by Bernard Pivot, 1988. Recorded from TV5 Europe).
4. *37°2 le matin* (Jean-Jacques Beineix, 1986. Paris: Gaumont).
5. *Apostrophes* (presented by Bernard Pivot, 1987. Recorded from TV5 Europe).

Chapter 6

Discourse/Form Features of Verbal Fluency: Planned Speech

This second chapter about discourse features of speech and their relationship with oral and aural fluency focuses on planned speech, and by way of example, on the lecture extract designed to serve as a counterpoint to the radio-talk sample in the set of preparatory exercises described at the beginning of Chapter 5.

This lecture piece contrasts with the ad-lib interactive radio-talk analysed in the previous chapter in at least three respects: it is prepared, its main function is to impart information, and, crucially, it addresses an audience of listeners rather than interlocutors. Because it is projected verbally, it is bound, on the other hand, to exhibit features which set it apart from comparable written texts, whatever characteristics it may otherwise share with them by virtue of being planned. What effects does all this have on its form? And how does it bear on students' handling of types of text which, whether in the shape of lectures or other kinds of monologic presentations — those to which they are likely to be exposed (e.g. TV and radio broadcasts) or called upon to produce (e.g. exposés, verbal reports) — are aurally and orally as relevant to their concerns as spontaneous speech, not least for the opportunities they create to concentrate on efficiency?

Investigating Planned Speech Data: Academic Lecture vs. Written Text and Ad-Lib Radio Talk

Eliciting observations about form

Here again, the students' response to the transcription exercises set in the worksheet (see beginning of Chapter 5) are a natural starting point. Just why should they find it comparatively easy to cope with the introduction to the academic lecture (see transcription in Table 21)? Its pace is admittedly manageable, some mention the use of pausing and stress, some the relative 'continuity' of the text — but what do they mean? In any case, it is quite demanding in other respects: it conveys a good deal of information, about

Table 21 Sample of planned speech: introduction to an academic lecture

---

Pierre-Louis Blanc — *Bilan des années de Gaulle 1958–69* — **Introduction**

1   *bon/avant de/avant de vous .'parler . sur le sujet de ma . de ma p'tite_ . 'causerie ou*
2   *conférence/je voudrais/au préalable/vous dire un certain nombre de 'choses/la première/c'est*
3   *que je ne suis pas un universitaire/je ne suis pas un 'savant/et . j'ai été . . . /comment*
4   *dirais-je/j'ai été amené à faire ce que vous_a dit . le . Professeur 'Masson/c'est-à-dire les*
5   *euh/j'ai 'conscience . que les réflexions que je vous 'ferai/sont_empreintes d'une certaine .*
6   *'subjectivité/cela dit/il y a un_historien qui a dit/être objectif . en_histoire/c'est_avoir*
7   *conscience . de sa 'sub'jectivité/donc de ce point de vue là/si vous voulez/j'ai le 'sentiment*
8   *d'une certaine façon d'être objectif/la . 'deuxième chose que je voudrais vous dire/c'est que .*
9   *le . 'personnage du général de Gaulle/est_un personnage . 'compliqué/et/c'est_un*
10 *personnage qui est compliqué parce qu'il était . 'psychologiquement . 'compliqué/c'est_un*
11 *personnage_'compliqué aussi/parce qu'il est_intervenu . 'plusieurs fois . dans . 'l'histoire .*
12 *de . mon 'pays/alors je suis un peu . 'désolé de/m'adressant à un public où je vois qu'il y a .*
13 *des gens de ma . 'génération/et des gens d'une génération plus 'récente/il faut que vous*
14 *sachiez . qu'il y a . 'trois 'notions qui sont_assez . 'différentes/il y a la notion . de . 'de*
15 *Gaulle . en tant que . 'personnage . historique/c'est_un homme qui comme vous le savez a*
16 *été pendant deux fois . responsable des 'destinées de son pays/de 1944 à 1946/et de 1958 à*
17 *19'69/il y a ensuite . un mot qui ressemble et qui s'appelle le . 'gaullisme/alors le gaullisme*
18 *c'est déjà une notion plus . . plus 'floue . /parce qu'au fond . c'est_un ensemble de 'principes/*
19 *assez généraux d'ailleurs/qui ont . 'marqué/l'action du général de Gaulle/et qui . euh ont*
20 *'marqué aussi/un certain nombre de gens/qui ont travaillé . avec lui/ à . 'différentes_*
21 *époques/il faut d'ailleurs que vous sachiez/que . le général de Gaulle a jusqu'ici/dans*
22 *l'histoire de France le seul/dans l'histoire de la 'République française/le seul privilège*
23 *d'avoir eu . comme . 'ministres/ les . représentants de la 'totalité . des . 'tendances de la vie*
24 *politique française/puisqu'il a eu à la fois/à différentes_époques/des ministres .*
25 *'communistes/des ministres_'socialistes/des ministres_'radicaux/des ministres_de droite/à*
26 *'l'exception . des ministres d'extrême-droite/parce que . il y a toujours eu/entre 'de Gaulle et*
27 *. la droite qui avait collaboré avec l'Allemagne en 1940 et 1944/une opposition .*
28 *'fondamentale et . 'irréductible/donc si vous voulez/l'idée de gaullisme est est_une idée/qui*
29 *est . 'différente/déjà de celle . du personnage qui l'a créée/la troisième idée qui est*
30 *différente/c'est celle de . 'gaulliste et de . 'parti gaulliste/le 'parti gaulliste/c'est_un 'parti/qui*
31 *avait été créé/par le général/pour 'l'aider à remplir sa mission/et qui après/à la disparition*
32 *du général/a . essayé d'avoir l'existence_qu'il 'pouvait/mais . ce parti/le général de Gaulle*
33 *d'ailleurs a été très clair là-dessus/n'engage . en rien . la responsabilité de son_'auteur/cela*
34 *dit/si . euh on_essaie de voir/maintenant/la 'période qui va de 1958 à 19'69'/c'est-à -dire la*
35 *période/qui s'ouvre . sur __euh_ 'l'arrivée du général de Gaulle aux_affaires/'et . __sur__ . __le__ .*
36 *'départ du général de Gaulle au mois d'avril 1969/c'est_une période intéressante . pour*
37 *'deux 'raisons/d'abord parce que c'est_une période qui est 'finie/et euh au point de vue*
38 *historique/il est toujours facile/d'étudier une_période qui se . 'termine/c'est_aussi une*
39 *période qui est_intéressante/parce que/à 'beaucoup 'd'égards/elle apparaîtra/je crois/comme*
40 *une période . 'importante . de . 'transition/dans . la vie . française/et . c'est . 'sur ce point .*
41 *que . je . voudrais . essayer . de . vous donner .. un . certain nombre .*
42 *'d'indications/pourquoi . euh cette période est_intéressante/parce que/dans . 'trois*
43 *domaines/on voit/ .. lorsque le général quitte les_affaires/en 1969/il laisse un pays . 'très*
44 *'différent . de celui . qu'il a pris . /quand il est_arrivé au pouvoir/onze 'ans plus tôt/ces trois*
45 *domaines/ce sont . 'les_institutions/c'est . 'l'économie/et c'est . la ' diplomatie./*
46 *pour les_institutions/quelle est la situation (.)*

a topic which is probably not very familiar to them and, unlike the subject of cycle locks, bears little relation to their everyday experience; and it features a number of conceptual terms or notions, which, even if they are, at times, quite close to English equivalents, students often find cumulatively intimidating (e.g. *réflexions . . . empreintes d'une certaine subjectivité* [5–6], *ensemble de principes . . . qui ont marqué l'action du général* [18–19]), not least when they are part of alien-sounding strings of genitive constructions (e.g. *les représentants de la totalité des tendances de la vie politique française* [23–24]). On the other hand, it formally bends to its audience in a number of ways which can be readily pinpointed by mapping out, in note form, the function of the passage's various transactional parts (i.e. leaving aside for the moment anything phatic), the textual transitions between them, and their content, as shown in Table 22.

Making sense of observations

Structural characteristics of the lecture extract

With this outline, features which help project the piece verbally and make it easier to cope with aurally become conspicuous.

The overall structure of the passage is very clear: It is a model textbook introduction (which warrants looking at the whole rather than a shorter sample). Each section, delineated by discourse markers (see next paragraph), typifies a standard function: establishing contact (see preliminary remarks in Table 22), contextualising the topic (see background remarks + focus on topic), introducing the topic (see topic of lecture proper), introducing the framework of the lecture (see framework of the lecture). Any listener familiar with this archetypal pattern, this orderly narrowing of focus — so common in French —, can use it to anticipate, and check, the sequence of verbal events, just as the speaker himself can use it to pace delivery. Recognising the structural make-up of planned pieces, and harnessing it to their own ends, is something pupils learn to do early on in French schools; it is equally relevant to the needs of students of French, for comprehension, for production, yet also to blend in with a French way of thinking.

The way it unfolds is very clear: For every new piece of topic-related information (see right-hand column of the outline), there is a discourse marker signalling its impending disclosure and its status in relation to preceding details (see left-hand column of the outline); the same holds true for every new section. What, for the speaker, are platforms for the rhetorical organisation of the presentation, islands of reliability enabling him to keep

Table 22 Outline of the lecture extract

Preliminary Remarks

au préalable . . . vous dire un
certain nombre de choses
        la première   • *pas un universitaire*
                          — *réflexions empreintes de subjectivité, mais*
                          — *objectivité en histoire: conscience de sa subjectivité*
                          → *d'une certaine façon: objectif*
        la deuxième   • *de Gaulle personnage compliqué*
                          — *pyschologiquement compliqué*
                          — *est intervenu plusieurs fois dans histoire du pays*

Background Remarks

il faut que vous sachiez qu'il
y a 3 notions . . . différentes
      il y a la notion de   • *de Gaulle personnage historique*
                          — *2 fois responsable destinées pays (1944–46, 1958–69)*
        il y a ensuite . . . • *le gaullisme (notion plus floue)*
                          — *principes qui ont marqué action de Gaulle/gens qui ont*
                            travaillé avec lui
[+ **additional remark:** *il faut* *[ministres toutes tendances politiques — communistes,*
d'ailleurs que vous sachiez . . .] *etc. sauf extrême-droite (collaboration Allemagne = >*
                         opposition fondamentable et irréductible)]
       la troisième idée . . . • *gaulliste/parti gaulliste*
                          — *créé par le général → l'aider à remplir sa mission*
                          — *lui a survécu mais n'engage en rien sa responsabilité*

Focus on Topic

     cela dit si on essaie de voir • *période 1958–69: arrivée de Gaulle aux affaires/départ*
                         → *période intéressante*
2 raisons . . . d'abord parce que • *période finie → plus facile à étudier*
          aussi . . . parce que • *période importante de transition dans la vie française*

Topic of Lecture Proper

         c'est sur ce point *[i.e. période importante de transition (see above)]*
     → *donner . . . indications*

Introduction Framework Lecture

               pourquoi *période intéressante*
parce que dans trois domaines → *pays très différent de celui de 11 ans plus tôt*
   ces trois domaines ce sont • *les institutions*
                    c'est • *l'économie*
               et c'est • *la diplomatie*

control over its course, and 'breathing' spaces, too, have comparable help functions for listeners: the meta-statements which punctuate the text and flag its structure, also allow them to digest what they have just heard, and to prepare for what is to come next, with the support of earlier structure-tagging prompts (e.g. *il y a trois notions . . . différentes, il y a la notion de . . . , il y a ensuite . . . , la troisième idée*), where coherence is created, here as elsewhere, by progressive reiteration of motifs: *[trois]* **notions/[il y a]** *la notion de, il y a [la notion de]/il y a [ensuite]*, **trois** *[notions]/la* **troisième** *[idée]*.

The way it unfolds is modulated by fluctuations in register: The difference in function between structural markers and lecture text is underscored by language shifts which further help to pace processing, and delivery: the contrast between the standard vernacular used to convey meta-statements (left-hand column of the outline) and the more subject-specific language and lexical items used to convey topic-related information (right-hand column of the outline) creates opportunities for grading efforts.

Its progression is unimpeded by backtracking, its content sufficient unto itself: The outline scrupulously keeps to the sequence of presentation of its content, and adds nothing to it. Yet there is enough material in it to reconstruct the overall gist of the piece without any to-ing and fro-ing between pieces of information, nor any padding with materials other than those explanations or illustrations which are given in the full text: there are no backtrackings or ellipses, no demands made on the audience to juggle with information to recover meaning, or to step in to fill gaps with their own world knowledge. Information is prepackaged in a way which eases the burden of receptive processing: listeners are involved in responding to incoming messages, but not, as they are with the radio-talk extracts, in constructing them jointly with the speaker.

Form

Reasons why students should experience the passage as less demanding, and also more 'continuous', are already building up. The way information is labelled, paced and spelled out makes it easier to follow and process: it assists reception, guides comprehension, and makes for smoother listening and perception of listening. And it has knock-on effects, which a brief look at a likewise clearly structured and articulated piece, but meant for reading (see *Francoscopie* text in Table 23), helps to bring into sharper focus.

The content of the lecture is not particularly dense: Where the lecture passage swarms with strings bringing on transactional content (see above)/introducing topic-related information and/or creating or main-

Table 23 Sample of written text: Introduction to *Francoscopie* (Mermet, 1996: 8; reproduced with kind permission of Larousse-Bordas)

METHODOLOGIE *La veille sociologique*

1 *La raison d'être de Francoscopie est*
2 *d'aider ses lecteurs à connaître et à*
3 *comprendre l'état de la France et des*
4 *Français, à mesurer son évolution au*
5 *fil du temps et à établir des compa-*
6 *raisons avec d'autres pays développés.*
7 *On peut qualifier la* **démarche utilisée**
8 de **veille sociologique.**
9   **Cette démarche repose sur deux idées-**
10 **forces. La première est que** *le fonc-*
11 *tionnement de la société est en*
12 *permanence le résultat des attitudes et*
13 *des comportements des individus qui la*
14 *composent, tels des atomes qui font*
15 *partie de molécules (les foyers et les*
16 *familles) et constituent ensemble la*
17 *matière sociale. S'il n'existe pas à*
18 *proprement parler de volonté ou*
19 *d'inconscient collectif, la société se*
20 *présente à tout moment comme l'agrégat*
21 *algébrique de forces qui s'additionnent*
22 *ou se soustraient (selon qu'elles vont*
23 *dans la même direction ou s'opposent),*
24 *se multiplient ou se divisent lorsque*
25 *naissent de véritables mouvements*
26 *sociaux. La seconde idée-force est que,*
27 *dans une société de type libéral et*
28 *démocratique, les actes, les décisions*
29 *et les choix des individus-citoyens-*
30 *consommateurs (c'est-à-dire en fait*
31 *leurs modes de vie) ne sont jamais dus*
32 *au hasard. Ils sont dictés par leurs*
33 *attitudes, leurs opinions, et leurs*
34 *valeurs. Celles-ci sont à leur tour*
35 *largement conditionnées par les*
36 *facteurs d'environnement comme le*
37 *climat social, le contenu et la*
38 *tonalité des médias, l'action des*
39 *institutions et des grands acteurs de*
40 *la vie politique, administrative,*
41 *économique, syndicale, scientifique,*
42 *culturelle, etc.*
43   *L'observation et la compréhension de*
44 *cette alchimie complexe est l'objet de*
45 *la veille sociologique. Elle permet de*
46 *mesurer de façon continue le changement*

47 social, d'identifier les tendances
48 lourdes et les "signaux" de faible
49 amplitude qui apparaissent dans la
50 société, d'évaluer leurs conséquences
51 présentes ou futures pour les organi-
52 sations dans leurs domaines d'activité.
53   *Cette approche permet aussi de*
54 *vérifier que le sociologique se situe*
55 *généralement en amont du politique et*
56 *de l'économique et qu'il aide donc à*
57 *l'expliquer, parfois à le prévoir. Bien*
58 *sûr, le contexte économique (national*
59 *et international) et les décisions*
60 *politiques ont une influence sur la vie*
61 *sociale, à l'intérieur d'un système*
62 *cybernétique qui fonctionne en boucle.*
63 *Mais il est illusoire de penser qu'ils*
64 *déterminent l'état de la société. Car*
65 *l'offre ne crée jamais vraiment la*
66 *demande; elle ne réussit que si elle la*
67 *rencontre, c'est-à-dire si elle est en*
68 *phase avec les grandes tendances qui*
69 *sont à l'oeuvre dans la société. C'est*
70 *ainsi que les comportements de consom-*
71 *mation ou d'épargne ne peuvent être*
72 *induits par les exhortations des hommes*
73 *politiques, des institutions ou des*
74 *entreprises.*
75   *Les informations mentionnées sont les*
76 *plus récentes disponibles au moment de*
77 *la rédaction (terminée en août 1996).*
78 *Elles émanent d'un grand nombre de*
79 *sources, publiques ou privées, dont les*
80 *plus importantes sont indiquées en*
81 *annexe (Remerciements). De nombreux*
82 *chiffres proviennent d'enquêtes et de*
83 *sondages d'opinions, sélectionnés parmi*
84 *ceux qui présentent les meilleures*
85 *garanties de représentativité et de*
86 *fiabilité (méthodologie, échantillon,*
87 *libellé des questions . . .). Sauf indi-*
88 *cation contraire, les enquêtes portent*
89 *sur des échantillons représentatifs de*
90 *la population âgée de 18 ans et plus.*

(emphasis in bold added)

taining contact with listeners (compare for instance *il faut d'ailleurs que vous sachiez/que . le général de Gaulle a jusqu'ici* [21] with *'le général de Gaulle a d'ailleurs jusqu'ici'*; cf. also the significant number of verb phrases prompted by first-person involvement, particularly at the beginning, and sequences including *'vous'*), there are only three fully explicit discourse markers in the *Francoscopie* text, i.e:

> *cette démarche repose sur deux idées-forces* [9–10]
> *la première est que . . .* [10]
> *la seconde idée-force est que . . .* [26]

The rest just blend in with the text, using lexical repetition as a bond (e.g: *on peut qualifier la démarche utilisée . . .* [7]/*cette démarche repose . . .* [9]; *Elle permet de mesurer . . .* [45–6]/*Cette approche permet aussi de vérifier . . .* [53–4], etc.). This integrated use of textual hinges brings home just how much of the lecture passage is, in contrast, given over to spelled-out meta-statements and affiliated matter, including phatic strings, which tend to thin down its subject-specific content, and make it easier to digest, not least because they also make the passage lexically and syntaxically less compact.

It is lexically spaced out and heterogeneous in its register: Phatic   strings and explicit discourse markers, as the text of the lecture passage generally, feature a high proportion of non-content items to total discourse, and/or semantically undemanding passe-partout words (e.g. *'être'*, *'avoir'*, *'choses'*, *'dire'*, *'faire'*, *'gens'*, *'aller'*, *'voir'*, etc.) which add little to the topical substance of the piece but mesh it together and spread out the processing effort, particularly at the beginning: there is a gradual easing into greater lexical density and precision with the shift from general to specific, from opening remarks to direct treatment of the topic, and with the concomitant phasing out of first-person involvement. Yet even at its densest (see [21–28] for example), it is nowhere near as lexically charged as the *Francoscopie* text. Content words tend to be more abstract and have greater definition in the *Francoscopie* piece (see for example *'l'agrégat algébrique'* [20–1] vs. a lexical alternative like *'la somme'*, against *'période finie'* [37] vs. *'révolue'* in the lecture passage). But, as is becoming clear, it owes just as much, if not more, to the form of utterances, and to the relationship between form and delivery medium.

It is syntactically drawn out: Like the radio-talk samples, it features matter which would be surplus to syntactic requirements in a written transposition, and are sidestepped in the *Francoscopie* text:

- deictic redundancies, e.g:

  /*la première [chose]/c'est que . . .* / [3] [and other similar examples]
  vs. *la première est que* [10] in the written text), or again
  /*alors le gaullisme c'est déjà une notion plus . . plus 'floue .* / [17–18],
  where the occurence of *'c'est'* causes *'le gaullisme'* to stand alone at
  the beginning at the utterance and to be singled out for attention
  (compare with *'le gaullisme est déjà une notion plus floue'* or *'la notion
  de gaullisme est plus floue'*);

- VP platforms which launch or re-launch utterances, sustain their flow,
  or unpackage syntactic or lexical information (i.e. encode in several
  clauses what could be compressed into one using embedding in
  prepositional/ adverbial/adjectival clauses or nominalisations) e.g:

  /*c'est-à-dire les euh/j'ai 'conscience . que les réflexions que je vous
  'ferai/sont_empreintes . . .* / [4–5]
  (compare with *'c'est-à-dire que les réflexions que je vous ferai'*, or again
  'mes réflexions seront donc empreintes')

  /*il y a un historien qui a dit/être objectif . en histoire/c'est_avoir conscience
  de sa 'sub'jectivité/* [6–7]
  (vs. *'un historien a dit/selon un historien, l'objectivité en histoire est
  fonction de/va de pair avec la conscience de sa subjectivité'*)

  /*c'est_une période intéressante . pour deux 'raisons/d'abord parce que
  c'est_une période qui est 'finie/* [36–37]
  (vs. *'cette période est intéressante pour deux raisons; elle est d'une part
  finie . . . '*)

  / *. . . le . 'personnage du général de Gaulle/est_un personnage .
  'compliqué/et/ c'est_un personnage qui est compliqué parce qu'il était .
  'psychologiquement . 'compliqué/c'est_un personnage compliqué aussi/
  parce qu'il est_intervenu . 'plusieurs fois . dans . l'histoire . de . mon 'pays/*
  [9–12]
  (vs. *'le général de Gaulle est un personnage compliqué, psychologiquement, et du fait de ses interventions répétées* (see comments on
  repetition below);

- repetitions, or, rather, incremental reiterations — highly conspicuous
  both on paper and aurally, and the main lexical and syntactic padding
  ingredient; some repetitions result from hesitations (e.g. *avant de/avant
  de vous . 'parler* [1], *. . . j'ai été . . . /comment dirais-je/j'ai été amené à* [3–4]),
  but very few; the majority work as overlapping motifs gradually
  blending new lexical items, new syntactic patterns and new ideas with

some introduced before, like progressive variations on themes. They are of course rhetorical devices, and combine with stress and pausing to steer listeners' attention and keep it on track (see under 'Prosodic and Performative Features, pp. 136–138) to follow); in so doing, they take up matter which could be omitted, or otherwise integrated (e.g. using pronominal reference, embeddings), yet buoy up delivery and decoding (see last example above in particular; also / . . . *c'est_un ensemble de principes . . . qui ont . 'marqué l'action du général de Gaulle/et qui . euh ont 'marqué aussi/un certain nombre de gens/qui ont travaillé . avec lui* [18–20] vs. *'qui ont marqué l'action du général de Gaulle et celle, aussi, d'un certain nombre de gens qui ont travaillé avec lui* [or *'de ses collaborateurs'* — see comments on lexis above] etc.).

All in all, the lecture passage relies to a great extent on subordination, associated, in earlier comments about written transpositions in Chapter 5, with the spelling out and tightening up, within sentences, of logical relations either loosely expressed in corresponding utterances, or underscored paralinguistically. Some subordinate clauses in the lecture passage are similarly expressive (*puisqu'il a eu à la fois/à différentes_époques, des ministres* . . . [24–25] for instance). But the great majority are just a by-product of padding with those ready-made platforms, phatic formulae, and repetitions, a vehicle for unpackaging information and spreading its load hypotactically, rather than a means of generating the kind of complex interdependency relations evidenced in the second written transposition (see WT2 in Chapter 6, p. 103), and also illustrated at their peak, in the *Francoscopie* text, by the longest sentence in it (cf. *S'il n'existe pas à proprement parler de volonté* . . . [17–26]).

The overall effects of planning *on the text* of the lecture passage are now plain to see: its thorough structure, its controlled progression, mostly unimpeded by backtracking and ellipses, affiliate it to a similarly planned written piece, and make it aurally more manageable than ad-lib speech. So, too, are the overall effects of its delivery medium, and the way they set it apart from the text of the written piece: the way it conveys information is less compact all round — in content, lexis and syntax, and is bound to make it aurally less demanding than a written text read aloud. This is food for thought for students who, in oral exposés, prefer the security of a fully scripted text to speaking from notes. They know some of the risks: lack of control over reading and voice projection, loss of contact with their audience. They are not always aware that it can also mean putting too much across in too little time. Evidence that written discourse is, in this sense, ill-adapted to oral presentations may persuade them to think again: using a spelled-out script, where it fails to make allowances for the efforts involved in listening, is as likely to jeopardise the viability and transactional efficiency of their oral work as poor verbal projection. But verbal projection *is* a relevant feature. How does it work in the lecture passage, how does it compare with projection in the ad-lib radio talk samples, and how does it relate to planning?

Prosodic and performative features

Silent pausing and stress, in this case consciously experienced as help features by students, would be natural candidates for eliciting initial comments. But there is perhaps something else to look into first, for the central questions it raises. The lecture passage is noticeably easier to piece together from the transcription than the radio-talk samples, that is to say even without the benefit of prosodic and performative features which, in the radio pieces, proved critical for recovering the coherence and cohesion of messages. Why? And what, then, *is* the function of such features in the lecture passage? Why indeed should some, unregistered in the radio piece, so conspicuously attract students' notice in the lecture?

There are clues in the script itself. Just as it contains few topic shifts (see Table 22 and under 'Structural Characteristics of the Lecture Extract', pp. 129–135), the lecture passage, unlike the radio-talk extracts, contains few shifts in construction (three in all) or message abandonments (just one). When these do occur, it is, significantly, mostly in phatic strings, that is to say in utterances inserted on the spur of the moment, without prior planning, e.g:

[phatic strings] *et . j'ai été . . . /comment dirais-je/j'ai été amené à faire ce que vous_a dit . le . Professeur 'Masson/c'est-à-dire les* <u>euh</u>/j'ai 'conscience que . . . [3–5]; alors je suis un peu . 'désolé de/m'adressant à un public où je vois .. génération plus 'récente/il faut que vous sachiez . . . [12–14]*

[[other] *. . . parce que/dans . 'trois domaines/on voit/.. lorsque le général quitte les_affaires/en 1969/ il laisse un pays . . . [42–43]*

And unlike the radio-talk extracts, it contains very few filled pauses of hesitation (six *'euh's*), as indeed few other kinds of filled pauses (a settling-in *'bon'* at the very beginning, a couple of *'alors'* — the first [12] flagging a topic shift, the second [17] an explanation).

Bearing in mind what these pieces are, and with work on the ad-lib radio-talk not so far from mind, it does not take long to get to the bottom of these differences. They must be something to do with the degree of control which planning gives the speaker, evidenced, within the passage itself, in the contrast between phatic strings and transactional utterances: knowing what is going to be said, in what sequence, and having the requisite language to put it into words means less task stress, fewer encoding hiatuses and fewer tell-tale time-gaining hesitations. It also means that the audience gets less help with syntactic segmentation, at least in the form of filled pauses; but it is not as if they need it: the text does not just give the *impression* of being more continuous aurally, it *is* by and large more continuous, and, in particular, syntactically more cohesive than the radio-talk sample, thus easier to grasp in this respect. Nor do they need the respite provided by filled pauses, for the same reasons, and because, as listeners rather than interlocutors, they are not called upon to engage interactively, or jointly to construct messages with a locutor: the speaker, as was noted earlier, does much of the work for them.

This leaves stress and silent pauses to account for, as well as other features or factors also manifest in the radio talk (e.g. shifts in speech rate and loudness). If there is no pressing call for the function they fulfilled in ad-lib speech, namely backing up filled pauses in the business of syntactic segmentation, what role do they play?

Stress and silent pausing work in ways which students are quick to recognise: their first-hand taste of the way both types of feature drew their attention to parts of utterances, and what they know about their rhetorical effect, is a trigger for detecting, or confirming, how this is achieved, and how it helps. With stress — reinforced in many cases by a preceding silent pause (.'xxx) —, words are lifted out of utterance and given a prominence which singles them out for attention: essential ingredients — discourse markers and key lexical items — thus stand out as a super-scripted layer of information underpinning the structural and transactional fabric of the passage:

> /la . *'deuxième chose* que je voudrais vous dire/c'est que . le . *'personnage*/du général de Gaulle/est un personnage . *'compliqué*/et/c'est un personnage qui est compliqué parce qu'il était . *'psychologiquement* . *'compliqué*/c'est un personnage *'compliqué aussi*/parce qu'il est *'intervenu* . *'plusieurs fois* . dans . *'l'histoire* . de . mon *'pays*/ [8–12].

Silent pauses, when, as is mostly the case, they do not result from hesitation, are part of the same underscoring process. Apart from slowing down the pace of the strings in which they occur, they break tonal groups into aurally conspicuous stand-alone units, and are, on their own or combined with stress, equally effective in flagging crucial information and focalising attention, as they do so flagrantly when the topic of the lecture is introduced towards the end of the passage:

> /c'est aussi une période qui est intéressante/parce que/à *'beaucoup* *'d'égards*/elle apparaîtra/je crois/comme une période . *'importante* . de . *'transition*/dans . la vie . française/et . c'est . *'sur ce point* . que . je

*voudrais . essayer . de . vous donner . . un . certain nombre .
'd'indications/* [38–42]

What stress and silent pauses do, in other words, is create hierarchised
layers of information, thereby enabling the audience to assess the relative
status of information, both within utterance and within the passage at large,
and thereby, too, giving direction to decoding priorities: what is emphasised is what the speaker thinks important; it is also what is necessary and
sufficient to get the gist of what he says. This is a function they had in the
ad-lib talk, but it was not the only one. Because they are, in this case, freed
from doing anything other than create emphases, they take on far greater
rhetorical force, and stand out aurally in a way which students did not fail
to register and capitalise on for help.

Conversely, what is not emphasised by stress and silent pausing recedes
into the background of utterance, simply by contrast with slowed-down
strings, or because, as in the radio-talk, it is further marked out as secondary
information or asides by shifts in speech rate and loudness (speeding up
and lowering of pitch); this applies for instance to:

- phatic inserts, e.g. */c'est un homme qui ↓ comme vous le savez ↑ a été
  pendant deux fois . responsable . . . /* [15–16];
- qualifying asides, e.g. */c'est un ensemble de 'principes/↓ assez généraux
  d'ailleurs/↑ qui ont . 'marqué . . .* [18–19];
- illustrations/explanations, e.g. *. . . deux fois . responsable des 'destinées
  de son pays/↓ de 1944 à 1946/et de 1958 à 19'69/↑ il y a ensuite . . .* [16–17];
  /et qui après/↓ à la disparition du général/↑ a . essayé d'avoir . . . [31–32];
- nuancing reiterations, e.g. *. . . le général de Gaulle a jusqu'ici/dans
  l'histoire de France le seul/↓ dans l'histoire de la 'République française/↑
  le seul privilège . . .* [21–22].

What is ultimately most striking about all these features, is how much
more confined they are in their function than in the radio talk — when, that
is, unlike filled pauses, their function is a legitimate one. Planning and
monologic delivery make some of these functions simply redundant. By the
same token, they enable the speaker to capitalise on what performative
features, i.e. those, like most of his silent pauses, that do not result from
hesitation/task stress, can do as rhetorical devices: what help he gives the
audience with structural markers, changes of register, lexical and syntactic
spacing out, reiterations, is compounded by the contrasts and emphases
with which he performatively underscores the status of transactional
information, thereby also keeping himself on track and increasing his
control over his material. But what does all this mean for students' own
practice?

Implications for Learners

Let us, here again, begin with a table, this time reviewing not the framework and transactional content of the lecture piece, but the main features observed in it and their overall functions for speaker and listeners (see Table 24).

The 'whys' of this table are perhaps already clear. First of all, it is a recapitulative summary, which brings into sharper focus the main points elicited in the analysis. But what it peculiarly highlights, is, on the one hand,

Table 24 Features observed in the lecture passage and their function

FEATURES RELIED ON	FUNCTIONS FOR	
	SPEAKER	LISTENERS
Structure/Organisational Features		

Clear structure/progression
=> archetypal structural patterns
  eg introduction (context/topic/framework)
=> markers of discourse organisation
  (metastatements)
=> shifts in register
  (vernacular vs. subject specific)
	Plotting/Pacing of Delivery	Plotting/Pacing of Listening (anticipation/check on sequence of verbal events)

Content		
Prepackaging of information => spelling out of information no ellipsis/backtracking		
Transactional spacing out => with metastatements, phatic strings vs. topic specific content		
Language	Spacing out of Delivery Effort	Spacing out of Listening Effort
Lexical spacing out => heterogeneity: vernacular vs. topic specific vague vs. precise		
Syntactic drawing out => padding with platforms, redundancies, repetitions		
Rhetorical reiterations => repetition of lexis, syntactic patterns		
Performative Features	Encoding Support (monitoring of pace)	Decoding Support (assessment of value of info.)
Rhetorical hierarchisation of information => stress, silent pausing, shifts in speech rate/loudness		

the convergence and overlap in functions of the various structural, linguistic and performative features observed, and, on the other, the direct correspondence there is in the way they serve the interests of speaker and of listeners. The common denominator of what are, in the end, three main mutually supporting functions (plotting/pacing of information, spacing out of effort, and support), all playing a complementary role in delivery and listening/comprehension, is *control*:

- the control the speaker gives himself in the delivery of his material, and the control he gives his listeners in the apprehension and comprehension of this material;
- the control he secures from being prepared, and which is, on-line, safeguarded from the unpredictabilities of spontaneous interaction by the monologic nature of his performance.

That control is the essence of planned speech, and is what most strikingly sets it apart from spontaneous speech, is probably nothing new for students. But that does not necessarily tell them very much about how it is achieved, or how to achieve it. That is where the table can further come into its own. Approached from the end they know — control — (see Table 25), it can begin to fulfil other functions. Turned round this way, it becomes a record of implications, yet also a checklist, and a guide:

- for preparation:
  - for using archetypal patterns to give an exposé a recognisable structure and for organising arguments logically (see Exercises 3 and 8 in the next section);

Table 25 Checklist for the preparation, evaluation and practice of planned speech

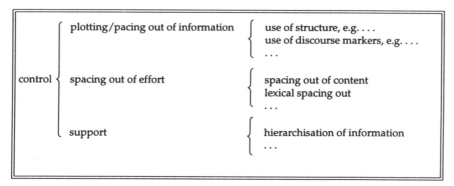

— for discriminating between main ideas, explanations and examples, and making use of shifts in register accordingly — which entails having relevant subject-specific vocabulary at hand (see Exercise 8);

— for making sure that listeners are given all the guidance they need to process, and appreciate, what the speaker means to convey (e.g. with organisational markers, linking devices, rhetorical markers), all the information they need to attend to messages without undue effort (e.g. without having to cope with unyielding ellipsis, backtracking, equivocations, or lexical and syntactic density) (see Exercises 2 and 3);

— for making sure, too, that the materials, the notes to be used for actual delivery give the speaker all that he needs to produce the exposé, keep control over its course, yet also to pace it for the audience, bearing in mind what risks there are in relying on fully written scripts: loss of one's bearings in it, yet also loss of contact with the audience, taxing speed of delivery, undue transactional, lexical and syntactic density (see Exercise 1);

• for evaluation (individual review, group review and/or teacher's review) — along similar lines (see other option in Exercise 7);

• for the corroborative study of other pieces (see Exercise 8);

• for focused oral and aural practice — concentrating on particular features one by one, or in subsets, to further assess their impact and experience it hands-on: those shown in Table 24 (see Exercises 1, 2, 3, 4, 5, 6), and those, instrumental too — supporting gestures and other paralinguisitic features — which dealing with an audio-recording has not yet made possible to observe (see next chapter on this question.

There is of course some overlap between what implications were drawn from the work with ad-lib speech in the previous chapter and those that emerge here from the work with a sample of planned speech. Performative and prosodic features, in particular, can be seen to play comparable functions, here magnified by rhetorical force and greater singleness of purpose: what they do to pace the flow of utterance, flag the relative value and syntactic status of information, is highlighted in a way which confirms their relevance to speech production and reception, and further justifies placing them high on the teaching/learning agenda: far from being the icing on the cake, the final touch to add on when everything else has been attended to, they are integral to the very texture of speech.

Practical Applications

Examples of exercises

Production

Exercise 1: Verbal projection: Control of delivery and pace through (a) reading out loud and (b) reconstructing a text orally from notes.

This exercise uses the kind of material produced by the work illustrated in this chapter, i.e. transcription of a sample of planned speech (including prosodic markers) and outline in note form (see Tables 21 and 22), to spark off practice on verbal projection and intonation. Once students are familiar with the transactional content of the sample, as they should be after they have studied it, their attention can be focused on making use of temporal, prosodic and discourse markers to achieve greater control over its oral delivery, in two complementary activities:

- reading the transcription out loud, with each student taking a few lines in turn, paying particular attention to silent pauses, stressed items, shifts in pitch and speech rate to pace delivery and hierarchise information for the benefit of the audience;
- reconstructing the piece orally from the outline, again with each student taking a short section, this time harnessing the use of prosodic features and discourse markers (see left-hand side of the outline) to piece the notes together and make *their* task easier as speakers.

Compare the outcome of the work for the two parts of the exercise, highlighting in particular the way speaking from notes, more daunting though it is, regulates delivery and keeps the pace manageable for the audience: what tends to happen during the first part of the exercise (reading out loud) is that students gradually speed up delivery to the point where the audience can no longer cope, i.e. where the effort of keeping up with the pace set by the speaker takes over from attending to transactional content.

Suggestion: Project texts up from a transparency, both to keep the group engaged with the performance of individual speakers and to compel speakers to look up and project their voice more forcefully than they would if they were working head down from their own script.

Expansions: Same exercise, this time with a sample of planned speech that has not yet been studied (e.g. cf. *Le Monde* on CD-ROM under '*Intégral*' for printed samples of speeches): use a transcription *without* prosodic/performative markers for the first part of the exercise (reading out loud), and a pre-drafted outline for the second (speaking from notes); the work, apart from giving further practice, serves to confirm, albeit the hard way, the functions, and importance, of prosodic/performative features in oral delivery and, by default, the virtues of being familiar with one's material/notes. (Alternatively, students can, for the second part, be asked to produce outlines themselves, provided they do so in two groups, i.e. with each preparing notes for the other for a different section of text, to ensure that the outlines used to reconstruct the text orally are not familiar).

Individual practice: Once students are sensitised to features of verbal projection by dint of analysis and guided practice, they can be prompted to practice reading out loud in self-directed mode, with the help of a tape recorder (i.e. repetition/recording of verbal strings from a taped sample and listening for comparison, with the objective of reproducing the pronunciation and intonation patterns of the source speaker).

Exercise 2: Preparing material for oral presentation:

Give students a piece of *written* text of fairly high transactional, lexical and syntactic density (e.g. *Le Monde* article of manageable length), first to read out loud, in full or in parts, to draw their attention to features likely to impede aural response (in particular those connected with transactional, lexical and syntactic density), then, in small groups, to adapt/prepare for oral presentation along the lines outlined in Tables 24 and 25).

Compare the outcome of the work of the different groups after oral presentation of the various pieces (strategies used, alternatives), single out for each a limited number of options for improvement, and reassess after revisions.

Exercise 3: Micro-practice with pre-specified focus:

Get students to prepare and make two-minute presentations with a specific objective, i.e. practice one of the aspects outlined in Table 24 (the topic and transactional content of the presentations can be agreed beforehand to make greater room for comparison); follow individual presentations with self- and group-diagnosis of strengths and weaknesses (e.g. with each student contributing two comments, one positive, the other a suggestion for improvement); follow up with repeat presentations integrating the comments made in the first part of the exercise and round off with a post-mortem evaluation.

Note: The activity is less intimidating and quicker-paced when carried out in small sub-groups (with whole group post-mortem to round it off at the end); video-recording (some of the) presentations provides tangible back-up for both critical discussion and evaluation of progress.

Reception

The exercises below, like Exercise 5 in Chapter 5, are based on the same, very basic, principle: they are simply a matter of using selective note-taking or transcription to focus attention on the facilitating function of particular features of speech in the comprehension of planned pieces (e.g. lecture, speech, news or documentary broadcast), and, by the same token, to promote a more discriminating approach to listening. They are complementary and can serve either:

- to assess the relative value of those different features in one particular sample of planned speech (e.g. lecture *or* speech *or* news or documentary broadcast), or
- to compare the relative value of these features across different samples (e.g. use of discourse markers in lectures as opposed to news broadcasts, stress patterns in the same).

The notes which follow are general guidelines, i.e. apply to any piece without reference to specificities or contrastive features, and only detail basic steps; the choice of sample(s) to use and the minutiae of the procedure to adopt depend on the objective assigned to the exercise(s), and need to be selected/adapted accordingly (e.g. by including comparative stages where appropriate).

Exercise 4: Focus on discourse markers as a guide for listening:

- get students to transcribe discourse markers only for the set piece(s);
- check the work collectively and use the framework to anticipate the status of the transactional information included in the piece(s);
- get students to fill in the framework, i.e. to take notes on the information flagged by the discourse markers identified (this can be done in several stages, e.g. with focus on main ideas only in the first instance [often introduced immediately after their flagging, though not always], then on secondary or illustrative matter); check collectively;
- get students to take notes on remaining matter (e.g. phatic matter), if any;
- discuss the work collectively along the lines defined by the objectives of the exercise and summarise conclusions; apply to another piece in extensive listening mode to test applicability on-line.

Note: The exercise can be extended to include a study of the linguistic correlates of the different types of information transcribed.

Exercise 5: Focus on prosodic markers as a guide for listening (e.g. stressed words/strings, as in the example below; also shifts in speech rate/loudness [see analysis in the early part of this chapter for reference]):

- get students to transcribe stressed words/strings in the set piece(s) (using stress itself for identification, but other marks also where present [e.g. silent pauses]);
- compare the outcome of the work collectively and assess the extent to which transcribed matter makes it possible to reconstruct whole messages;
- get students to take notes on unstressed material;
- compare the outcome of the work collectively and review the status/ function of stressed and unstressed items, with particular reference to patterns of hierarchisation; apply the work to another piece to test/nuance observations.

Note: As in the previous exercise, work can be extended to studying the linguistic correlates of the different types of information transcribed. News broadcasts, where silent pausing before words and stress on their first syllable has become a standard means of lifting them out of the fabric of utterance to sustain listeners attention (see Callamand, 1987), produce interesting patterns in this respect.

Exercise 6: Focus on particular class words as a guide for listening:

- get students to transcribe some classes of words or types of items only (e.g. abstract nouns, verbs, words accompanied with figures);
- check the work collectively and study (a) the value of the different types of words or items for predicting the status of the information conveyed (e.g. abstract/concrete, main/secondary) and (b) the extent to which they make it possible to reconstruct messages/get the gist of the passage (nominalisations and abstract nouns usually point to main ideas, figures/dates to examples or reformulations at a less abstract level; verbs tend to have greater weight at more concrete levels of expression, but unlike abstract nouns, are, for obvious reasons, not usually sufficient on their own to reconstruct messages);
- check the distribution of these various types of words or items in the text, and assess implications for listening with reference to [linguistically achieved] patterns of hierachisation and anticipation strategies.

Note: It is not always easy for students to identify relevant items for transcription: in some cases (e.g. word classes), it presupposes some knowledge of the distinctions the exercise is intended to highlight; pooling the resources of the group, however, usually makes it possible to elicit sufficient, and sufficiently relevant, data.

Examples of supplementary activities

Exercise 7:   Development of a general framework for preparation/evaluation using students' own productions:

The frameworks for preparation/group evaluation in Tables 24 and 25 grew out of the study of a sample of native speaker speech. Students' own oral productions can be used to the same end, as part of diagnostic activities later to set against, and supplement work, with native speaker material:

- get students to make short (two/three minutes) formal presentations on a topic of their choice (e.g. expository accounts, response to a contentious issue);
- during the presentations, get each student in the audience to make a note of strengths and weaknesses (e.g. two of each for each presentation);
- when all students have had their turn, write comments on the board and sort them by type: even in a small group, the range is usually wide enough to bring out main prospective goals; the verbal and non-verbal resources necessary to achieve these goals in practice can then be investigated step-by-step using NS samples.

Exercise 8: Study of additional material for corroboration and expansion:

The characteristics of the lecture extract studied in this chapter confines the range of observations: keeping to the introduction is a restrictive factor, in terms of both structure and content; so, too, is the register of the text in relation to the target audience. But the kind of framework produced is a working basis to explore other texts, and observe further how features of planned speech regulate production and comprehension, for instance by:

- extending comments about structure to sections other than introductions, and studying what patterns obtain in the development of argument (including bridging passages; cf. also use of introduction/ development/conclusion pattern within main sub-sections in long pieces);
- studying the relationship between the function of information used to convey particular points and patterns of hierarchisation (e.g. general statement —> explanation (cause, consequence), or reformulation at a less abstract level —> illustration (with concrete facts, figures), and taking stock of the linguistic and prosodic correlates of these patterns (see Exercise 6);
- confirming, and nuancing, observations about discourse markers (which are often far more implicit than in the lecture passage; cf. examples in the *Francoscopie* text, also found in oral pieces);

- studying the interplay between form, function and projection in different kinds of samples of planned speech, depending on their nature (e.g. speeches or lectures vs. news broadcasts), the audience for whom they are intended, or the conditions under which they are produced, with particular reference to the impact of such factors on the balance between viability and efficiency (how do politicians, for instance, when they want to make an impact on people from all walks of life and socio-cultural backgrounds, make their speeches manageable and fittingly authoritative without being patronisingly simple?).

There is perhaps no need to dwell on these possibilities, which correspond to quite conventional lines of textual study, not least because of the degree of overlap there is, in more formal registers, between planned speech and the kinds of written texts traditionally used in teaching. As in earlier instances, what matters is to give analyses a point of application: to underscore the relationship between fluency and control, and to equip students to capitalise on those features of planned speech which can promote the development of their fluency through control.

Chapter 7

Paralinguistic Features and Fluency

Paralinguistic features are generally understood to cover 'non-vocal phe-nomena such as facial expressions, head or eye movements, and gestures, which may add support, emphasis or particular shades of meaning to what people are saying', as well, for some linguists, as 'those vocal charac-teristics such as tone of voice which may express the speaker's attitude to what he or she is saying' (Richards *et al.*, 1985: 206). There are more technical definitions, but this is how the term will be used here, i.e. to refer to non-verbal, or kinesic, behaviour, and to features of voice and prosody in functions so far mostly left aside (expression of attitude, emotions, etc.).

There is, by and large, no getting round paralinguistic behaviour: no matter what we do or do not do with our bodies when we speak or do not speak, or with our voices when we do, it is irrepressibly integrated into, and modulates, speech and exchange (see exercises in Chapter 4). Paralin-guistic features, as is generally acknowledged, are part and parcel of communication, and warrant being treated as such in FL teaching, i.e. as 'essential' rather than merely 'incidental' to the communication process (Kellerman, 1992: 239). The issue for this chapter is also to assess how they fit in with fluency.

The film extract used in the first part to highlight issues and illustrate how paralinguistic features attune to verbal expression, interaction and compre-hension will, as in previous examples, be handled inductively and from the same teacher/students point of view. Accounting for these features involves long descriptions on paper (the alternative preferred, for the sake of clarity, to complex and problematic codified transcription), and the guided discovery approach established in previous chapters will gradually give way to a more direct treatment of the material, implications and applications.

Investigating Data: Film Extract

Vincent, François, Paul . . . et les autres (Sautet, 1974)[1], the film from which the extract used here is taken, is a fairly light-hearted sociocultural and psychological study of a group of long-standing friends, and of how various events in their personal, social and professional lives shape the course of their existences and relationships. The sequence in question gathers them all for a Sunday lunch in the country residence of one of the main characters. The scene is genial, but turns sour, and is, in this respect, quite typical of meal scenes in French films, which, with their language and behaviour shifts, are well suited for the kind of work to be illustrated here. That, and the diversity of features at play, is the reason for preferring a multi-participant film extract to more manageable or perhaps more standard alternatives (e.g. TV expository material) as a starting point here: it gives greater scope for discussion, and for exposing perhaps less obvious ins-and-outs of paralinguistic features with which students need to be able to cope, in films (or other types of samples) and, though perhaps less dramatically, in face-to-face interaction.

Eliciting observations about the relationship between linguistic messages and paralinguistic clues

The intricate network of signals involved in exchanges, which, as in the sample used here (see transcription in Table 26), gather together several participants and build on references unfamiliar to students, makes them difficult to grasp fully first time round. The urge to fill in comprehension gaps and to settle differences of interpretation is an incentive to search for further clues to solve the puzzle, but also to disentangle them from their different sources: visual track, transcript and soundtrack.

In this example, the actual outcome of the sequence, which culminates in one of the main characters (François) abruptly losing his temper, is itself quite plain from the start, both aurally and visually, as is, broadly speaking, the reason why he does:

- François' unmistakable verbal coarseness and expostulations at the end of the scene set the tone unequivocally and leave no doubt about his anger (see [48–52] and [54–55] in Table 26); his tone of voice — loud, inflamed — matches both his words and his behaviour (see below);
- the visual track is equally eloquent: François, who had so far been mostly absorbed in carving the Sunday joint, bone in one hand, knife in the other, briefly stops in his tracks, launches into what the expression on his face and the distortions of his mouth project as a bout of exasperated talk, waves knife and joint about, then furiously drops both on the plate in front of him; after a short pause, he resumes his angry shouting, all the while thrusting his arms/hands forward accusingly, before getting up from the table and storming off;

Table 26 Extract from *Vincent, François, Paul . . . et les autres* (Sautet, 1974)

1 Pierre	*Vincent/ . . . ton verre/*
2 Vincent	*oui/*
3 [?]	*tu finis pas ton saucisson /*
4 Vincent	*oui oui/*
5 [?]	*tiens/Pierre passe la bouteille s'il te plaît/*
6 [?]	*merci/*
7 François	*Julia/impeccable/ça c'est un gigot/*
8 Paul	*ben qu'est-ce tu crois/*
9 Jean	*alors/Jacques/tu disais la banlieue/*
10 Jacques	*je dis pas la banlieue/mais un peu plus loin/quand tu traverses/tu reconnais plus rien/*
11 Paul	*ben ni personne/*
12 [?]	*c'était pourtant bien ces p'tites maisons/on se croyait à la campagne/assez merci/*
13 Marie	*en tout cas/c'était moins laid qu'ces tours/*
14 François	*ça dépend lesquelles/*
15 Jacques	*ah hein c'est vrai/il y a des tours qui sont belles/*
16 Marie	*oui mais en général dans celles-là y a des bureaux/*
17 Pierre	*pis les autres t'as qu'à voir les prix/*
18 Paul	*eh Julia t'as pas un aut' couteau/*
19 François	*non non non non ça va ça//*
20 Julia	*euh oui y en a un sans manche là dedans/*
21 Paul	*sans manche ???/ [laughs]*
22 François	*ça va ça va ça va regarde/*
23 Pierre	*en tout cas les gens qu'habitaient là/i s'[sont] fait expulser eux . /sans_histoire/*
24 François	*on les r'loge/*
25 Pierre	*oui dans les HLM/avec des loyers qu'i peuvent pas payer/*
26 François	*z'ont qu'à s'installer plus loin/*
27 Vincent	*oui dans la Creuse/c'est pas mal y paraît/ . . . [laughs] /ou dans l'Ardèche/ [laughs]*
28 Pierre	*tu rigoles/mais les types qui sont déjà à soixante ou cent kilomètres de leur travail/c'est*
29	*pas une rigolade pour eux/ . . . en attendant qu'on qu'on les éjecte un peu plus loin/*
30 François	*c'est l'évolution urbaine/c't'inévitable/faut savoir s'adapter/*
31 Pierre	*s'adapter/t'es très marrant toi/faut avoir les moyens d's'adapter/*
32 Julia	*Pierre/*
33 Paul	*ben c'est François qu'a raison . . . / ceux qui n'ont pas d'argent i n'ont qu'à*
34	*s'arranger/ou pour en avoir/ou pour s'en passer/mais pas pour emmerder les_autres/*
35	*qu'est-ce que ça veut dire/ . . . /s'adapter ça signifie quoi/ça signifie . . . vivre avec*
36	*son temps/savoir bouger avec la société/comme François/. naturellement une seule*
37	*devise/pour changer d'vie/changez la vie/hein/ . . . /ah autrefois c'était autre chose/*
38	*fallait pas rire avec le progrès social sinon i s'fâchait/seulement c'était la grande*
39	*époque du dispensaire/créons et multiplions les dispensaires de banlieue/nous d'vons*
40	*soigner les pauvres gratuitement//*
41 Marie	*la science n'est pas à vendre/*
42 Paul	*nous sommes au service du monde etc. etc./voilà c'qu'on entendait à Maison Alfort .*
43	*dans les_années cinquante/pis alors/j'sais pas c'qui s'est passé là/pfft/tout d'un*
44	*coup coup de baguette/plus de dispensaire dis donc/ . . . et à la place une*
45	*clinique toute blanche à l'Etoile/nous sommes au service du monde mais . du beau*
46	*monde/c'est ça l'évolution urbaine mon p'tit garçon/les autres i n'ont qu'à*
47	*s'installer plus loin/c'est 'ça s'adapter/t'as compris/*

> 48 François *non mais j'vais pas entendre des conneries toute ma vie/recevoir des leçons imbéciles*
> 49 *jusqu'à la fin des temps/écoutez/un_écrivain qui n'écrit rien/un boxeur qui veut pas boxer/*
> 50 *des bonnes femmes qui couchent avec n'importe quoi/ merde/ . . . /et quand on s'ra*
> 51 *parti celui-là qui va rester avec sa danseuse . qu'a une jambe mécanique/qu'est-ce*
> 52 *que j'en_ai à foutre/*
> 53 Vincent *écoute François/arrê//*
> 54 François *ta gueule toi/tu m'emmerdes toi/j't'emmerde/ . . . j'vous_emmerde tous avec votre*
> 55 *dimanche et vot' gigot à la con/ merde/*

- there is no mistaking that François has been on the spot: his words in the lines that so dramatically close the scene suggest that he interprets whatever has been said before as a personal slight (cf. *j'vais pas . . . recevoir des leçons imbéciles jusqu'à la fin des temps/* [43–49]; see also [54]); but even if these words are not understood first time round, his outburst as observed on screen can leave no doubt that that is how he feels.

The degree of convergence between verbal and non-verbal behaviour, at this point in the sequence, can hardly be greater. The linguistic and visual evidence for François' presumed victimisation earlier on, however, is more elusive, more difficult to piece together, at least after just one viewing: students, even when they have perceived a growing sense of unease in the scene, find it testing to pinpoint what brings the bout of anger on, or fully to explain the reasons for it. Dealing with visual track and script separately, before bringing in the soundtrack, soon makes clear why.

Visual track
The sequence, viewed without sound, is a cameo example of the kind of conviviality often associated with French meals: food is dished out and passed round, drinks are poured, there is a bustle of ten people at once eating, drinking, talking, all in apparent cheerfulness and good humour — until the outburst. Watching the sequence again, without distraction from the soundtrack, confirms, however, that something is indeed amiss, from quite early on:

- it is now easier to register signs of embarrassment or irritation in some of those present (fixed stares, slightly averted gazes, pinched lips, raised eyebrows, stiffening postures, sighs), presumably triggered by something in the conversation: there is no evidence of anyone doing anything overtly offensive;
- the pace of activity also seems to slow down gradually and there are, here and there, uncomfortable-looking pauses.

But there are conflicting signs:

- others around the table are smiling and talking on, including the last person to take the floor before François' outburst — Paul, the host;
- Paul's manner, in this last turn before François' outburst, does not seem to tally at all with the violent response it sparks off in François; he seems quite amiable, and appears in fact to address the company at large rather than François specifically; his long turn is punctuated by various evenly paced activities, with no obvious trace of aggressivity: opening a bottle, pouring a drink, smoking — elbows on the table, hand accenting his speech — lifting arms and head in emphatic upward motion, stubbing out his cigarette, gazing about him; the camera at this point briefly cuts to one of the women (Marie, François' wife), who takes up Paul's emphatic upward hand/head motion in a short verbal contribution (41 in the script); but it soon returns to Paul, who resumes his talking, still stubbing out his cigarette, and is seen to make a few swift sideways cutting movements with his hand, before concluding, after a lateral sweeping arm gesture, with a nudging of the arm of the person on his immediate right (Pierre, the last speaker before Paul); Paul's gaze, except on a couple of occasions when it rests on François, circles round without resting on anyone in particular, save Pierre, at the end, and his demeamour throughout is affable: the sparkle in his eyes and benign smile when he takes up his turn hardly leave his face at all.

The contrast between Paul's congenial-looking performance and François' ensuing outburst is striking. Judging both by François' reaction (including a pause in his carving of the joint and intermittent looks of annoyance), and the signs of embarrassment in others (see above), what Paul says must somehow be offensive. But it is not projected as such: there must, accordingly, be some kind of mismatch between what he says and the way he says it.

Script (see Table 26)

From a purely lexical or even syntactic point of view, the sequence is not all that demanding, save for the mention of locations which may not ring a bell, because unfamiliar (*la Creuse* [27], *Maison Alfort* [42]), not sufficiently explicit (*l'Etoile* [45]), or potentially misleading because they have different connotations for French and English people (c.f. *l'Ardèche* [27] (ex-)back of beyond for the French vs. desirable holiday destination for the British). It is very allusive, however, and the illocutionary force of the turns is hardly transparent, at least without restrospective interpretation, and with the text as the only source of information: clearly, the text on its own simply does not give all the clues.

Apart from two episodes connected with meal activities ([1–8], [18–22]), the conversation revolves around changing aspects of housing and its damaging impact on the landscape [10–16], the cost of accommodation [17, 25] and the inconvenience of having to live further and further away from the work place [23–29]. The consequences of the changes are not unanimously or unconditionally deplored, but there is nothing blatantly acrimonious about the discussion on paper, or blatantly personal. There are only two personal rebukes, both uttered by the same character (Pierre), the first directed at someone other than François (Vincent), and the second at François himself:

- *tu rigoles/mais les types qui sont déjà à soixante ou cent kilomètres de leur travail/c'est pas une rigolade pour eux . . . /* [28–29], which sets Vincent straight after a statement marked out as ironical by references to undesirable geographical areas for relocation (*oui dans la Creuse/c'est pas mal y paraît/. . . ou dans l'Ardèche* [27]);
- *s'adapter/t'es très marrant toi/faut avoir les moyens d's'adapter* [31], which reproves François after a set of uncompromising sweeping statements (*c'est l'évolution urbaine/c't' inévitable/faut savoir s'adapter/* [30]).

This second rebuttal is the first and only fully overt sign in the text of François being put on the spot. It is strong enough (see reiterations of *s'adapter* — which takes up François' point — intensification and focalisation of the antagonistic *t'es marrant* with *très* and *toi*, implications of *faut avoir les moyens de s'adapter*), but not so strong that it justifies the magnitude of his exasperation at the end of the sequence.

This leaves the final turn before the outburst to account for (i.e. Paul's). It is not addressed to François directly, but refers to him and to his statement about the need to adapt, in what is ostensibly a vindication: see *ben c'est François qu'a raison . . . /* [33]. But the disingenuousness implicit in *ceux qui n'ont pas d'argent i n'ont qu'à s'arranger/ou pour en avoir/ou pour s'en passer/mais pas pour emmerder les_autres/qu'est-ce que ça veut dire/. . . /*[33–35]) sets the tone: the vindication is sarcastic, a devil's advocate tactic to expose François's bad faith (see *s'adapter . . . ça signifie . . . savoir bouger avec la société/comme François* [35–36]). Paul's subsequent denunciation of a change of attitude over the years, from social idealism and militancy to bourgeois opulence and complacency, proceeds in a similar vein, and is taunting on other counts:

- it is full of debasing clichés (*s'adapter . . . ça signifie . . . vivre avec son temps* [35–36]) and quixotic catch-phrases (*c'était la grande époque du*

>   *dispensaire* [38–39], *créons_et multiplions* <u>les</u> *dispensaires de banlieue* [39],
>   *nous d'vons soigner les pauvr<u>es</u> gratuitement* [39–40]);
> - it plays equivocal games with pronominal reference and the intended
>   application of its pronouncements: impersonal statements (e.g.
>   *s'adapter, ça signifie* [35], *pour changer de ne/ changez la vie* [37], *fallait
>   pas rire avec le progrès social* [38]) and all-inclusive plural imperatives
>   (*créons_et multiplions . . .* [39], *nous sommes_au service du monde* [45],
>   *voilà c'qu'on_entendait à Maison Alfort* [42]) ostensibly refer to no one in
>   particular; however, the *'il'* in [*fallait pas rire avec le progrès social*] *sinon
>   i s'fâchait* [38], i.e. in a phrase which is not impersonal and for which
>   the only possible referent is François (see *comme François* [36]), points
>   the finger at François specifically and restricts the application of what
>   is being said to him alone (or those he typifies);
> - as if referring to someone in his presence in the third person was not
>   enough, this *'il'* [François] of *'i s'fâchait'* adds insult to injury by giving
>   presumptuous overtones to the ensuing covert quoting of François
>   (see *créons_et multiplions . . . , nous d'vons soigner les pauvres . . . , nous
>   sommes_au service du monde* [39–40, 42]).

Together with references which, even if they are not familiar, can in
context be interpreted as giving the full measure of the turncoat change
(from *dispensaire de banlieue* to *clinique toute blanche à l'Etoile*) and a few other
touches (e.g. the allusion to magic to justify a baffling change in */pfft/tout
d'un coup coup de baguette/plus de dispensaire/dis donc/* [43–44], the qualification in *au service du monde* <u>mais</u> *. du beau monde* [45]), there are, in other
words, plenty of ingredients in what Paul says to work François up, and
account for his exasperation. There is also plenty in it to confirm that it *is*
offensive, even though it is not projected as such.

The contrast between Paul and François's behaviour on screen now
makes better sense. In both cases however, their manner is in fact in keeping
with their words, even, at least initially, where Paul is concerned: his overt
good humour matches his overt vindication of François at the beginning of
the turn. But as the attack gets more direct and closes in on François (see *i
s'fâchait*), Paul's affability is increasingly at odds with what his words
convey, and all the more infuriating as a result: the growing *décalage*, in
bringing the verbal sarcasm which permeates the turn out into the open,
gives the full measure of Paul's tactic, of his manipulative use of verbal and
non-verbal means of expression, and the full measure of his illocutionary
intentions.

What is still not entirely clear, however, is why there should have been
signs of unease amongst some of the guests *before* Paul set to expose
François. There are clues for this in the script: François' contributions to the

discussion up to the statement which triggers Paul's attack (cf. Paul's borrowings — *s'adapter* [35, 47], *l'évolution urbaine* [46] from François *c'est l'évolution urbaine/c't'inévitable/faut savoir s'adapter/* [30]) strike the only discordant note in an exchange otherwise characterised by social empathy and converging opinions. This, however, only becomes manifest *retrospectively*, i.e. when going back over the script and reinterpreting François' early assertions in the light of his increasingly callous later ones: on the basis of the script alone, *ça dépend lesquelles/* [14], in particular, can only really be perceived as a first taste of his contrary attitude when it is reassessed against his subsequent more openly contentious pronouncements, i.e. *on les r'loge/* [24], *z'ont qu'à s'installer plus loin/* [26] and *c'est l'évolution urbaine/c't'inévitable/faut savoir s'adapter/* [30]. In other words, his actual comments on their own are not enough to explain the build-up of tension observed visually, at least early on. Either, then, there is more to account for visually than has been done so far, or the explanation of the puzzle lies in the soundtrack, or both.

Soundtrack

The soundtrack, and what it reveals about the characters' vocal characteristics in the exchange, gives important clues, about François' attitude in the discussion about housing, but also about the role played, in the build-up of tension, by so far less conspicuous characters, not least Pierre:

- François' tone of voice is in keeping with the unsympathetic thrust of his utterances about housing: it gets more curt, more openly uncompromising with each; but it is already noticeably aloof from the start, at least when compared with the tone of other people in the exchange: thus, the way he utters *ça dépend lesquelles* [14], under his breath almost, and with a rising intonation, leaves no doubt that he *is* being contrary — even though the propositional content of the utterance is not, in itself, necessarily offensive;

- Pierre too, however, emerges as a key actor in the deterioration of the exchange: *his* contributions are uttered with an impassioned, obstinate earnestness which is at odds with the relative offhandedness of the other speakers, confirms François in his defiance, and sets them both on a collision course; despite attempts to defuse conflict, either through conciliation (cf. *ah hein c'est vrai/il y a des tours qui sont belles/* [15]), meal-related talk (*eh Julia t'as pas un aut' couteau/... ça va regarde/* [18–22]) or humourous irony (*oui dans la Creuse/c'est pas mal y paraît/.. . ou dans l'Ardèche/* [27]), he and François thus become engaged in a verbal feud, evidenced in the script in the pairing of their turns (23/24,

25/26, 30/31), which culminates in a direct appeal for moderation (cf. Julia's *Pierre* [32] whose pleading despondency is conveyed through falling intonation) before being appropriated by Paul.

The soundtrack also corroborates earlier points, about Paul, for instance, whose expression, in his attack on François, is as overtly affable as his manner, yet has overtones, in turn empathetic [33], emphatic [37–39, 45–46], incredulous [44], ironic [36, 46–47] (conveyed by variations in speed, pitch and loudness), which fully confirm his illocutionary intentions.

With the build up of clues, it becomes easier, too, when watching the sequence again, to take in other tell-tale details about the behaviour of the people involved in the discussion, e.g.

- about François, whose body language sets him apart from the group: unlike the others, whose looks and head movements by and large coincide with turn-taking patterns, he keeps his head obstinately down and avoids eye contact, both when he speaks and when he is spoken to; he has the excuse of being absorbed in carving the joint, but the deliberateness of his manner and his growing irritation are given away by shifts in the pace of his meat-carving in response to ongoing talk, short pauses with deep sighs, and some pinched-lipped, annoyed raising of the head/eyes (after Pierre's . . . *faut avoir les moyens d's'adapter/* [31], after Vincent's gibe on '*Creuse*' and '*Ardèche*' and towards the end of Paul's long turn);

- about Pierre, whose manner and facial expressions, like his tone, are intent, sullen, testy, and who gives the first visual sign of awkwardness in the scene, with a slight leaning forward, a raising of eyebrows and questioning look of disbelief directed at François in response to *ça dépend lesquelles*; this look also heralds the ensuing feud, and subsequent reproving looks towards François, which François provocatively ignores.

- about Paul, whose deliberateness in projecting visual signs of affability is in fact enough to arouse suspicion about the sincerity of his overtly magnanimous support of François, and to leave no doubt about his sarcasm: the overall pace of his speech and of the activities which punctuate it is, it now becomes clear, just a little too slow, too decorous; the magnitude of his actions (e.g. his cigarette stubbing) too exaggerated; the direction of his gaze too set on avoiding François, except, with great tactical intent, when he refers to him overtly (e.g. on */comme François/* [36]) or covertly (e.g. on / . . . *changez la vie/* [37]); and his smile slants too far sideways not to be sarcastic and give the game away from the start;

- about Vincent whose body behaviour can leave no doubt about the irony of his *oui dans la Creuse c'est pas mal y paraît/*... [laughs] *ou dans l'Ardèche/* [27], even if it is not grasped from his actual words: he is impassive to begin with, physically and vocally; but the way he raises his intonation on *y paraît*, looks up with a half-formed smile and then sideways to confirm his effect, gives *his* game away, even before the laughs his gibe elicits, or his beaming smile, lifting of hand from the table, palm now open, and gaze round on the by then overtly derisive *ou dans l'Ardèche.*

Not all becomes entirely clear without reference to the wider context of the film, which would set other details straight:

- the real trigger for François's hostile behaviour is in fact Marie's *en tout cas/c'était moins laid qu'ces tours/* [13]: Marie, the wife, has been unfaithful, and François's dissenting *ça dépend lesquelles/* [14] immediately after reflects his acrimony towards her; hence also his reference to */des bonnes femmes qui couchent avec n'importe quoi/* [50] at the end;
- Paul's attack on François is a way of getting his own back after an earlier row, about Jean and a forthcoming boxing match, during which François ridiculed Paul's writer's block, hence the force of the showdown; hence, too, François' references at the end to ... *un écrivain qui n'écrit rien/* [49], */un boxeur qui veut pas boxer/* [49] and */et quand on s'ra parti celui-là qui va rester avec sa danseuse . qu'a une jambe mécanique/* [50–51] (the theme of Paul's book).

But there is perhaps no need to go further with this already long account. It has made its points:

- no single source of information in the extract, whether linguistic messages, intonation patterns or visual ingredients, is sufficient, on its own, fully to make sense of it;
- exchanges are modulated not just by what individual speakers do while speaking, but also by what other people present do in response to, or independently of, what is going on verbally and non-verbally;
- the information from all sources is closely integrated and needs to be interpreted cumulatively on-line.

But this still leaves it to assess the particular relevance of paralinguistic features to fluency and learners, which entails first mapping out in greater detail the kind of functions these features fulfil, in this and other contexts.

Making sense of observations

Functions of paralinguistic features in the film extract

There is so much happening at once or in quick succession in multi-participant interactions that it is difficult to know where to start when it comes to classifying paralinguistic features and mapping out what they do. On the other hand, there were leads in the forms of behaviour already singled out in the initial part of the exercise, and in the impact they were observed to have, thus options for breaking the task down and sharing it out (with some students concentrating on particular features, others looking out for particular effects, others still focusing on a particular character, for instance). As far as non-verbal behaviour is concerned, there have been references to a range of features: facial expression, hand and arm gestures, posture, gestures relating to ongoing activities. There have been references, too, to some functions fulfilled by these features, in production and in reception.

By far the most conspicuous was the expression of emotion or attitude, magnified by the contrast between signs of geniality and signs of mounting discord (anger, sarcasm, irony, irritation, embarrassment). The way body behaviour, not least facial expression, conveys affective meaning is not a revelation; but the relevance of the signals it gives for the interpretation of messages whose illocutionary force is not necessarily what it seems, as in Paul's turn, is a reminder to students of how crucial it is to respond to non-verbal clues. The same extends to vocal characteristics. It has become clear, even without fully identifying intonation patterns, that corresponding tones of voice likewise affect the pragmatic meaning of utterances, on their own or in conjunction with non-verbal behaviour: tone of voice in some cases works as a reinforcement of what messages themselves make clear (e.g. François' outburst, or Paul's speech), yet in others is the actual key to interpretation (as in François' contrary *ça dépend lesquelles*, Julia's pleading *Pierre* and Pierre's unyielding contributions). What is important for learners to bear in mind, however, is that body behaviour and intonation give out signals to interlocutors which are bound to affect the interlocutors' response and the course of the exchange.

On the other hand, there have also been allusions to functions other than affective ones, with, for instance, the linking of head/eye movement to turn taking patterns, or of arms and hands motions to the accenting of utterance. Both François's and Paul's long turns, and everyone else's turns and behaviour for that matter, are thus punctuated by sequences of body movements which, once they are more closely correlated with utterances, point to different and complementary ways — commonly singled out in work on non-verbal communication — in which these movements link in with linguistic messages and share in the communication process (cf. for instance Kellerman (1992) for a synthesis of evidence about functions of kinesic behaviour; also Pennycook, 1985; Auer & di Luzio, 1992).

They work as visual illustration for messages — their most obvious function:

> Paul's swift sideways cutting motions of the hand thus gives disambiguating visual back-up to his reference to magic in [*pis alors/j'sais pas c'qui s'est passé là*]/*pfft/tout d'un coup coup de baguette*/ [43–44]; his sideways sweeping gesture across his body similarly backs up his *les_autres i n'ont qu'à s'installer plus loin* [46–47].

They regulate or control interaction:

- underscore turn-taking patterns, e.g. head movements and shifts in look, produced on their own or in conjunction with linguistic turn-taking markers (e.g. *ben, alors, ah hein*), whose turn-offering/turn-taking functions are made conspicuous in this sample by François's unwillingness to conform to them;
- direct or redirect messages to particular interlocutors within turns themselves, e.g. Paul's turning sideways towards Pierre on his right and nudging his arm on /*c'est 'ça s'adapter/t'as compris*/ [47], which redirects the turn at him, albeit in the disingenuous pretence that what came before was an explanation meant for him [Pierre]);
- provide information about listeners' responses, and inflect the course of exchange: cf. the raising of eyebrows (e.g. Pierre's — after François' *ça dépend lesquelles*/ [14]), averting of gaze, stiffening of posture, slowing down in the pace of activity, which, early on the extract, are instrumental in heralding and nurturing the build-up of tension between Pierre and François and, later, give the measure of Paul's sarcasm;
- sustain and coordinate the flow of utterance, by, for instance, bridging the gaps left by silent pauses: the audience's attention during Paul's long silent pauses is thus kept engaged by sequences of non-verbal activity which also tactically enhance their wilfullness, e.g. downward gaze/pouring of drink followed by upward gaze to take up where he left off in [33]; or again by pacing and monitoring intended effect — cf. Paul's looks around the table (e.g. on /*qu'est-ce que ça veut dire*/ [35], where his gaze up follows on from the offensive . . . *pas pour emmerder les_autres*/ [34] [low pitch, falling intonation visually mirrored by his putting his glass down]), or looks directed in turn at François (on /*changer la vie*/ [37]) then at people opposite him at the table to encourage acknowledgement (on *hein* [37]).

They underscore the organisation of discourse:

Paul's turn, for instance, is indexed by changes in activity and body behaviour which mark the boundaries and shifts between units of speech, e.g. /*mais pas pour emmerder les autres* [puts his glass down]/*qu'est-ce que ça veut dire* [concurrent gaze up/around the table]/. . . [picks up his cigarette, puts his elbows on the table and settles into himself in a way which anticipates the explanation to follow]/*s'adapter ça signifie quoi/ça signifie* . . . [slight sideways movement of the hand holding the cigarette in front of his mouth] *vivre avec son temps*/ [34–35] [. . .] /*ah* [head and arm emphatically up in keeping with rising intonation, heralding the shift over to contrasting information] *autrefois c'était autre chose*/[stubbing out of cigarette] *fallait pas rire avec le progrès social sinon i s'fâchait*/[37–38], etc.

François's expostulations are similarly indexed by increasingly marked arm movements: *non mais j'vais pas entendre des conneries toute ma vie* [slight up and down movements in pace with his speech] / [briefly rests his arms]/*recevoir des leçons imbéciles jusqu'à la fin des temps* [resumes up and down arms movements]/[again rests his arms briefly on the table] *écoutez/ un_écrivain qui n'écrit rien* [arms up and forward]/[arms down]*un boxeur qui veut pas boxer* [arms up and forward in Jean's direction]/[arms down]*des bonnes femmes qui couchent avec n'importe quoi* [arms up and forward in Marie's direction]/*merde* [arms down violently, drops joint and knife]/*et quand on s'ra parti celui-là qui va rester avec sa danseuse* [arms up and forward waved in Pauls' direction] [48–52], etc.

They coincide with the rhythms of speech, and link with intonation and stress; cf. for example:

Paul's arm and head raising on *ah autrefois* (see above), his sideways hand movements — matched by sideways head movements — on *s'adapter* . . . *ça signifie* as well as in between the other sequences of gestures already described.

François's up and down or forward arm movements, matched by up and down head movements, all produced in pace with his speech and with varying amplitude and speed corresponding to variations in the speed and loudness with which he utters his words.

Paralinguistic features in different contexts and relationship with fluency
What is striking about these functions is the extent to which they coincide with functions of performative and prosodic features (cf. fillers, pauses, stress, changes in speed, pitch and loudness), which were justified, when

dealing with face-to-face spontaneous interactions, by the demands of coping orally with task stress and, aurally, with the form of messages shaped by task stress (see Chapter 5). Like these features, and jointly with them, non-verbal signals interact with linguistic messages at different levels of organisation (interactional, discourse, phonological) in a way which, in spontaneous speech, was shown to sustain viability in speaking, decoding and negotiating exchange under pressure: to maintain the flow of utterance, assist syntactic and discourse segmentation, hierachise information, create speaking and decoding space, coordinate turns and provide interlocutor feedback. But the film exchange is unlike spontaneous exchange: because it is scripted and rehearsed, on-line pressure is minimised, orally, aurally and interactionally (see Exercise 10 in Chapter 5). The degree of coincidence in the functions of non-verbal and other non-linguistic signals in a sample where their strategic relevance is downplayed by the absence of task stress, nonetheless points to the roles non-verbal signals must, *a fortiori*, play in spontaneous speech, for speakers and interlocutors. Thinking back to earlier analyses and in-passing references to these roles, it becomes clear that, like performative and prosodic features, and together with them, they can work in several different and complementary ways: as time-gaining platforms and continuity devices, as syntactic markers, to make up for lapses in coherence or vagueness, to fill in the gaps of ellipsis, to maintain and regulate contact between exchange participants (cf. discussion in Chapter 5), and, also, to give iconic clues to meaning (see above). Like these features, they are help devices, in production and reception, but also fundamental ingredients in speech and exchange and, by the same token, in the projection, perception and negotiation of fluency (see Chapter 2).

The contrast with spontaneous speech, on the other hand, also magnifies the particular significance non-verbal features have in pieces, which, like the film extract, are intended for viewers/external observers, and the significance they have, too, in planned monologic speech. In both cases, planning and the absence of interactional demands minimise the effects of on-line task stress for locutors, and audiences. So that features which relieve task stress in spontaneous face-to-face interactions, including non-verbal behaviour, are freed to achieve other ends.

What makes the film extract difficult is not its linguistic content *per se*, or the form of messages, but the transactional density and interaction of the many signals it gives (linguistic and non-linguistic) so as to achieve peak expressive effectiveness in the face of constraints (length, time; see Exercise 10 in Chapter 5). Non-verbal behaviour and vocal characteristics, as we have seen, are instrumental in this process. But they are all the more important for audiences, not least audiences of FL learners, as they also, by virtue of the functions itemised above, give them precious decoding support, both in indexing utterances and exchange, and in giving clues to meaning and nuances of meaning.

In planned monologic speech (e.g. lectures, news broadcasts), what applied to performative and prosodic features (see Chapter 6) extends to non-verbal behaviour, for the same reasons. In the absence of task-stress, it is, like them and with them, freed to capitalise on its various functions to take on greater rhetorical force, pace, punctuate and illustrate discourse in a way which sustains its viability for both speaker and audience and, by the same token, its transactional efficiency (cf. for instance the use of hand movements as, or in conjunction with, discourse markers, or of pointing as a deictic gesture flagging emphases or contrasts). Body movements, by keeping audiences visually focused on the speaker, are also simply, but importantly, a means of sustaining attention, and can, for speakers, work as a release valve for nervousness.

Implications for Learners

Kinesic behaviour and voice qualities are expressive in their own right: whether they concur with the pragmatic content of messages, or alter it, they are key ingredients conveying attitudes and emotions, key ingredients in the production and comprehension of messages, and cannot be circumvented in either. Whatever non-verbal and vocal signals students may give become part of exchange, affect its course, and the interlocutor's response in reception and interaction: in the event, it makes sense for students to be proactive, to build on these signals to enhance their expressive range and control their impact, rather than leave things in the lap of gods. Likewise, whatever non-verbal and vocal signals speakers or interlocutors give modulate speech, affect the course of exchange, in a way which students must also be prepared to recognise, as a basic matter of communication.

But like performative and prosodic features discussed in previous chapters, body behaviour, in conjunction with vocal features or on its own, is, equally, a strategic resource for promoting oral and aural fluency, in ways which the foregoing discussion, backed up by earlier comments (see previous chapters), makes clear: it is, likewise, and jointly, a vehicle for sustaining continuity and fluidity in speech, decoding, and exchange.

There is a fair degree of transferability in non-verbal means of expression, at least for languages culturally as close as French and English, and, although to a lesser extent, in vocal characteristics conveying pragmatic meaning (Hurley, 1992; Kellerman, 1992). Despite differences (see Kerbrat-Orecchioni, 1994; Pennycook, 1985; also Hurley 1992 and below), they are, in this sense, a fund of ready-to-hand resources for students. On the other hand, since the process of exploiting this kind of information is mainly unconscious in one's own language (Kellerman, 1992: 250), it can hardly be assumed that students' awareness of the way it modulates responses and strategic transfer to the foreign language will take place without some forms of prompting and self-monitoring, e.g. to:

- draw attention to different categories of behaviour and their expressive or functional range (cf. analysis of the film extract; also Exercises 1, 3, and 4 in the next section);
- explore correlations between types of behaviour and speech or interactional functions (see Exercise 2);
- assess the impact of non-verbal behaviour in different contexts (see Exercise 2);

and, significantly to:

- respond to cultural differences (including proxemic, i.e. to do with interpersonal distance) (see Exercise 5).

For while cross-cultural divergences, and their impact on the viability and efficiency of speech and exchange, may not be so great between English and French or other European languages, as between them and, say, Asian languages, closeness itself can make it easier to pass over differences, bar the most obvious (Hurley, 1992). The less perceptible or the less expected the differences, the more puzzling or damaging their socio-pragmatic impact is likely to be when they come to be experienced personally, and the more likely, perhaps, they are to feed misguided perceptions of national characteristics (e.g. indiscriminatingly affiliating French people's propensity for greater physical closeness to intrusion, or their greater directness — including verbal directness — to overbearingness or rudeness). The more subtle the nature and impact of those differences, the more difficult they are to register, but the classroom setting, where face-to-face interaction with native speakers is necessarily limited, is hardly conducive to sensitisation, except through observation.

In this sense, the case for bringing students' attention to aspects and functions of paralinguistic behaviour goes beyond expanding their expressive range and communicative resources. It is also a means of equipping them to perceive cultural differences, and not only respond to them, but accept them for what they are, and foster resilience and broad-mindedness. Analyses of video-recordings, however varied, are bound to have their limits, if only because they do not necessarily strike a personal chord. What matters is to foster receptivity, and evolve a framework conducive to self-directed rationalisations.

On the other hand, the extent to which students can be expected to integrate native-like body behaviour into their own *output* is a delicate issue. There is room for practice: holding one's own in a French conversation or discussion, for instance, requires, beyond linguistic skill, a degree of physical projection which students often find difficult to emulate, but can at least try to sample as a form of briefing, if only in more or less contrived play mode. Some uses of gestures, e.g. to support language functions (concur, contradict, interrupt etc.) or punctuate discourse (in particular in planned speech) do, in any case, lend themselves quite readily to exercises (see Exercise 2). All the same, it is not easy to get a leopard to change its spots; nor is it always desirable. Hurley, while advocating a meta-cognitive approach to non-verbal communication in the classroom, is circumspect on this count:

> 'It is probably not the teacher's job to get Japanese learners to touch others more, or to get Arab learners to keep their hands still when they talk. Perhaps the most we should attempt in this sensitive domain is to highlight differences between learner and NS output and let learners decide how closely they wish to approximate TL norms (Hurley, 1992: 275).

But this 'most we should attempt' leaves no room for complacency. Students need to understand how instrumental paralinguistic features are in sustaining their fluency all round: in speech, comprehension and interaction.

Practical Applications

Examples of exercises

Exercise 1: Aural sensitisation to, and use of, voice modulations in contextualising messages.

Use (live or recorded) oral variations on basic scripts (from simple utterances on their own to more complex stretches of discourse, short poems or anecdotes, short extracts from plays, etc.), adapted to fit in different contexts, fulfill different functions, address different types of people, and/or convey different attitudes or emotions (e.g. [to take a very simple example] *'il vient demain'* as adressed to a child, to an adult friend, to a total stranger, expressed as a declarative, a question, to convey diffidence, scepticism, anger, pleasure, reassurance, etc.) and get students to:

- recognise contextual and affective parameters;
- detect corresponding intonation patterns, variations in speed, pitch, loudness (by for instance shadowing them, and inviting students to shadow them, with hand movements; or again, if using

recordings — and equipment permitting — by speeding up the tape to the point where words are no longer recognisable but the affective thrust and melodic patterns of utterances still are; this technique is also effective for sensitising students to TL vs. NL 'melodic' patterns);

- produce their own variations on the same scripts, or produce variations on samples of their own, and turn it into a guessing game (here again, speeded up recordings can be used to draw students attention to overall aspects of their performance for self-monitoring purposes).

Exercise 2: Interpretation/use of non-verbal behaviour in different contexts and functions, e.g:

In discussion and debate: Get students to view a short video sample of discussion/debate (cf. for example the debate on anti-smoking campaigns analysed in Chapter 4), in two stages: first viewing *without sound*, to observe, then discuss, how much and what kind of information is conveyed by body behaviour alone (e.g. about the role, status, attitude of participants, the function of their verbal contributions; prime the work with questions: how, including in your NL, can you tell that someone agrees, disagrees, wants to/is about to interrupt, is preventing someone else from speaking, seeks someone else's response, thinks little of someone else, etc.); subsequent viewing/s *with sound* to study and map out correlations between the types of behaviour observed and actual speech: what gestures, head or body movements (c.f. posture), facial expressions correlate, in something like the anti-smoking campaigns debate for instance, with the adversatives which initiate most of the turns? With interruptions or latchings on to someone else's turn? With hesitations? How do they compare with what native speakers of English would do in a similar set-up?

Organise micro-discussions magnifying practice of subsets of gestures and types of function, e.g. illustrate messages or replace them, punctuate messages, concur, disagree, interrupt, latch on to what other speakers say, hand over turns to others, seek a response or help from them, reject turns, give silent feedback — approval, disapproval but also interest, or withdrawal, etc. (try also shifts from a sitting to a standing position to increase freedom of movements);

In planned speech (e.g. news or documentary broadcasts, speeches):
Same procedure as in the first part of the exercise above, now with focus first on assessing what *decoding* help can be gained from speakers' body behaviour (anticipation from visual track alone), then on correlating the

features observed with topic shifts, the plotting and pacing of discourse, message illustration (cf. analysis of the lecture extract in Chapter 6 for points to consider, e.g. correlations with discourse markers, silent pausing cum stress; cf. also dubbed samples (e.g. films) to highlight, by default, the relationship between rhythm and flow of words and non-verbal rhythm and flow (Pennycook, 1985));

Same procedure as in the second part of the exercise above, with focus on indexing, accentuating, illustrating discourse, i.e. harnessing body behaviour to linguistic and performative features which promote control, for the speaker and for the audience (cf. Chapter 6, including Exercise 1 which can be adapted to focus on, or accommodate, non-verbal projection).

(See Exercise 5 for comparison with British equivalents and students' monitoring of their performance.)

Other possible applications: Situational role play (e.g. pair work involving a systematically uncooperative and physically evasive shop assistant or administrative clerk and a customer physically forcing attention and seeking a response).

Exercise 3: Paralinguistic projection through dramatisation, with back-up of NS samples

Get students in several groups to act out the same short scene from a script transcribed from a video sample (c.f. for example, the extracts from *Vincent, François, Paul . . . et les autres* and *37°2 le matin* used here, both very challenging but revealing for the transposition effort they require, or simpler passages from films or other types of samples); compare and discuss the various groups' performance, and set against the original source to refine observations and back up self-monitoring.

What matters in this kind of exercise — a 'hands-on' alternative to the work illustrated in the first part of this chapter, or indeed to the traditional scrutiny of videotapes without sound — is not so much students' performance *per se* (as should probably be stressed from the outset) as what it calls for at each stage: interpreting the script and assessing what is involved over and above linguistic messages to project the scene live; realising or recalling that, despite textual constraints, basic scripts take on distinct overtones from variations and permutations as regards voice, non-verbal projection and indeed so-called 'performative' aspects discussed in previous chapters (cf. by way of examples, different productions of the same play, or film versions of the same novel); and, like drama techniques generally, including voice training, meta-cognitively challenging students' sense of their own vocal and non-verbal behaviour.

Examples of supplementary/alternative activities

Exercise 4: Sensitisation to paralinguistic features using cartoon strips

Cartoon strips, in which all information is wholly within one's visual grasp on the page at any one time in a stable form, are handy for getting round the problems involved in using videotapes, i.e. transience, co-occurence and blending in of information from different sources. But because of the transposition effort they require to match codified graphic ingredients and corresponding 'live' ingredients of speech and exchange, they are also peculiarly conducive to reflecting on the interplay between actual messages (by and large stylised and kept to a minimum in cartoon strips) and paralinguistic clues (conversely graphically magnified, not only to make up for the cursoriness of the text, but to invite readers to construe a global dynamic and aural experience in time and space out of static, stylised images). Quite apart from the information conveyed by the actual pictures (e.g. characters' depicted facial expression, posture, gestures and what this allows one to infer about what happened before and what is to happen next in all respects), the diversity of the devices used, and the variations on the use of these devices, are an index of the range of features involved in communication beyond the strictly linguistic, and of the functions they fulfil; cf. for example what is conveyed about voice modulations (pitch, loudness, rate of speech, expressive/illocutionary intent), the locutionary and perlocutionay force of speech and events, characters' attitudes, emotions and states of mind, interactional patterns, etc. by:

- the shape, size, position, contours and colour of the speech bubbles;
- the shape, length, style, direction of the 'appendices' (i.e. the converging lines or strings of circles which link bubbles to speaking or thinking character);
- symbols (e.g. stars, lines representing movement);
- typography (e.g. lower case, capital letter, bold typeface, italics, roman characters, etc.);
- punctuation (e.g. full stops, exclamation marks, supension points, combination of exclamation marks and question marks, etc.; position in relation to text).

Possibilities for getting students more clearly to discern the various components, contrast them, and reflect on their impact: lift them out of their pictorial context (e.g. by asking students to copy them out on a sheet of paper) and compare them and their impact within or across samples; use sets of transparencies to gradually build up/recreate whole images from a core and bring out what kind of information is added at each stage; or simply contrast devices and techniques as used in different cartoon strips (e.g. *Tintin* and *Asterix*).

Exercise 5: Sensitisation to paralinguistic cross-cultural differences — comparison of French and British TV programmes
Select comparable French and British TV programmes (e.g. *Fort Boyard* and its British equivalent, other game shows, talk shows, news broadcasts, discussions) for students to watch in their own time. Give specific guidelines to give the task focus (e.g. watch small sections without sound first, look out for five differences), different tasks to different groups or students (e.g. concentrate on posture, facial expressions, types/volume/ amplitude of gesture, interpersonal distance, voice loudness, variations in pitch), and/or a different bias to the task depending on the type of programme used (e.g. focus on interpersonal distance/physical contact in *Fort Boyard* and British equivalent, neutrality/involvement in news broad- casts; host's vs. audience's physical/vocal projection in talk shows, extent of physical projection/gestures used in discussion). Discuss/compare students' reports in class, review implications as regards (a) (where applicable) the relationship between body behaviour, contextual parame- ters and viability/efficiency parameters, (b) students' own vocal/body behaviour as foreign speakers in different contexts, and (c) the perception of, and response to, so-called national characteristics; open up the discus- sion to create leads for future (live) observation (e.g. when do (French) people apologise for inadvertent physical contact? How much eye con- tact/staring is tolerated in public spaces? (see useful references in Pennycook, 1985, including Hall, 1966; also Kerbrat-Orecchioni, 1994).
Variation: Comparison of students and native speakers' paralinguistic projection. Same exercise using videorecordings of students oral work in various activities (debates, discussions, formal exposés) and comparable French TV programmes, here again to sensitise students to their own body behaviour/use of voice (in different contexts): although it is usually something of a shock to watch oneself on tape first time round, it drives home very effectively where there may be room for improvement (e.g. voice projection, mobility).
Note: Work for this exercise can be primed with a viewing of tapes in fast forward motion, which peculiarly magnifies some aspects of non- verbal behaviour (e.g. density/mobility, amplitude, diversity).

Note
1. *Vincent, François, Paul . . . et les autres* (Claude Sautet, 1974; Paris: Lira Films/Rome: President Produzioni).

Conclusion

Fluency, by virtue of its temporal dimension and of the subjectively experienced qualities that define it, has a unique potential to do justice to speech in its various performative contexts, native and non-native: it refines our awareness of its manifold forms; it alerts us to the complementary interplay and multifunctionality of its ingredients, linguistic and paralinguistic, as captured by the adjective 'fluent'; it reminds us that performance is relative and variable; it maps the parameters of negotiation in interpersonal exchange. However important accuracy is, approaching speech from a temporal perspective means, in effect, recasting our views about the traditional fluency/accuracy continuum, freeing ourselves from the one-sided decontextualised and biased notion of accuracy which prevents us from properly inhabiting speech. If, instead, we envisage a framework, embodied here in the viability/efficiency pairing, flexible enough to account for the congruences and disparities between native speakers' and FL learners' output in the unstable world of verbal exchange, we can make better comparative sense of their practice.

What gives the empirical notions of viability and efficiency credence is precisely that they are analytical tools applicable to all productions. They are methodological devices for coming to terms with native speech, in any form or context: they give students an individual observation agenda. But they are also a heuristic framework whereby students can appraise their own speech along the same lines, measure where progress has been made and is still to be made, and create an individual learning agenda.

To teach fluency is to challenge students' understanding of the workings of the spoken medium, to give them the meta-cognitive know-how and confidence to develop these agendas, and the sense of purpose to capitalise on their exposure to data. It is not a substitute for extensive practice, but it gives practice direction, and transcends the limits it has: in the classroom where it lacks scope, in quantity and variety; and in natural settings, where it has both quantity and variety, but where the proceduralisation of knowledge, and the confidence it promotes, do not necessarily equate with quality, control or discrimination. These are features, incidentally, with which students in tertiary education need to be forearmed if they are to maximise the fruitfulness of the year abroad.

To teach fluency may seem ambitious, but it is manageable. It is first and foremost the assimilation and inculcation of an attitude. It is to pay heed to what language tells us about itself in performance (and accommodate insights as seen appropriate). It is to think beyond narrow vocational concerns and measures of output in quantifiable givens. It is to bear in mind that the language students of today are the language teachers and professionals of tomorrow, those whom we trust to keep the complexities of foreign languages alive and well.

Technical approaches in recent studies augur well for the renewal of interest in fluency. Unlike them, this empirical exploration did not start with fluency. It grew out of a practical problem: disappointing in-class responses to video-recordings of oral work used as a source of feedback. While students picked on traditional *bêtes noires* (local linguistic errors and other ostensible tokens of inadequacy, including hesitations), they overlooked the interplay of features which was an index both of their weaknesses and of their strengths. The immediate needs of communication were not an issue: these students could communicate, in a range of roles and contexts. The issue was communication in all its broader ramifications. In later analyses of their interactions (see Guillot, 1989), temporal phenomena, ostensibly evidenced in 'hesitations', turned out to be the key to understanding communication as an inclusive, global complex of varied resources, and the door to recognising in fluency the one notion that could hinge students' and native speakers' performance together.

What the studies referred to and this classroom-based inductive approach share, however, is the intimation that fluency is a more fruitful and functional notion than it has been given credit for. But however much light we can throw on this neglected and under-investigated topic, certain obstinate questions are likely to keep us engaged for some time to come. What *is*, for instance the relationship between quantifiable variables and the parameters of viability and efficiency across languages? How do the defining criteria of fluency vary across languages, in relation to social and cultural correlates? And how does all this affect teaching and learning?

References

Anderson, J.R. (1983) *The Architecture of Cognition.* Cambridge, MA: Harvard University Press.

Anderson, J.R. (1985) *Cognitive Psychology and its Implications* (2nd edn). New York: Freeman.

Auer, P. and Di Luzio, A. (eds) (1992) *The Contextualization of Language.* Amsterdam, PA: John Benjamins.

Beattie, G. (1977) The dynamics of interruption and the filled pause. *British Journal of Social and Clinical Psychology* 16, 283–4.

Beattie, G. (1983) *Talk: An Analysis of Speech and Non-verbal Behaviour in Communication.* Oxford: Oxford University Press.

Benson, P. and Voller, P. (eds) (1997) *Autonomy and Independence in Language Learning.* London: Longman.

Bergson, H. (1959) *Oeuvres.* Editions du Centenaire. Paris: Presses Universitaires de France.

Bialystok, H. (1990) *Communication Strategies.* Cambridge, MA: Blackwell.

Blanche-Benveniste, C. (1995) De la rareté de certains phénomènes syntaxiques en français parlé. *Journal of French Language Studies* 5 (1), 17–29.

Blanche-Benveniste, C. (1997) *Approches de la Langue Parlée en Français.* Paris: Ophrys.

Blanche-Benveniste, C. and Jeanjean, C. (1987) *Le Français Parlé.* Paris: Didier Erudition.

Brazil, D. (1995) *A Grammar of Speech.* Oxford: Oxford University Press.

Brown, G. and Yule, G. (1983) *Teaching the Spoken Language.* Cambridge: Cambridge University Press.

Brown, G., Malmkjaer, K., Pollitt, A. and Williams, J. (eds) (1994) *Language and Understanding.* Oxford: Oxford University Press.

Brumfit, C.J. (1984) *Communicative Methodology in Language Teaching.* Cambridge: Cambridge University Press.

Burt, M.K. and Kiparsky, C. (1972) *The Gooficon: A Repair Manual for English.* Rowley: Newbury House.

Callamand, M. (1987) Analyse des marques prosodiques de discours. *Etudes de Linguistique Appliquée* 66, 49–70.

Canale, M. (1983) From communicative competence to communicative language pedagogy. In J.C. Richards and R.W. Schmidt (eds) *Language and Communication* (pp. 2–27). London: Longman.

Canale, M. and Swain, M. (1980) Theoretical bases of communicative approaches to second language teaching and testing. *Applied Linguistics* 1 (1), 1–39.

Caron, J. (1989) *Précis de Psycholinguistique.* Paris: Presses Universitaires de France.

Carter, R. and McCarthy, M. (1997) *Exploring Spoken English*. Cambridge: Cambridge University Press.

Chafe, W. (1980) *The Pear Stories: Cognitive, Cultural and Linguistic Aspects of Narrative Production*. Norwood, NJ: Ablex.

Chafe, W.L. (1982) Integration and involvement in speaking writing and oral literature. In D. Tannen (ed.) *Spoken and Written Language: Exploring Orality and Literacy — Advances in Discourse Processes* 9, (35–54). Norwood, NJ: Abex.

Chafe, W.L. and Danielewicz, J. (1987) Properties of spoken and written language. In R. Horowitz and S.J. Samuels (eds) *Comprehending Oral and Written Language* (pp. 83–113). London: Academic Press.

Chambers, F. (1997) What do we mean by fluency? *System* 25 (4), 535–44.

Chaudron, C. (1988) *Second Language Classrooms*. Cambridge: Cambridge University Press.

Chomsky, N. (1965) *Aspects of the Theory of Syntax*. Cambridge, MA: MIT Press.

Clifton, C. Jr, Frazier, L. and Rayner, K. (eds) (1994) *Perspectives on Sentence Processing*. Hillsdale, NJ: Lawrence Erlbaum Associates.

Cole, R.A. (ed.) (1980) *Perception and Production of Fluent Speech*. Hillsdale, NJ: Lawrence Erlbaum Associates.

Collins Cobuild English Language Dictionary (1987). London: Collins.

Collins English Dictionary (1994) (first edition 1979). London: Collins.

Corder, S.P. (1981) *Error Analysis and Interlanguage*. Oxford: Oxford University Press.

Couper-Kuhlen, E. (1992) Contextualizing discourse: The prosody of interactive repair. In P. Auer and A. Di Luzio (eds) *The Contextualization of Language* (pp. 337–64). Amsterdam, PA: John Benjamins.

Crystal, D. (1971) Stylistics, fluency, and language teaching. *CILT Reports and Papers* 6, 34–52.

Crystal, D. (1981) *Directions in Applied Linguistics*. London: Academic Press.

Crystal, D. and Davy, D. (1975) *Advanced Conversational English*. London: Longman.

Crystal, D. and Quirk, R. (1964) *Systems of Prosodic and Paralinguistic Features in English*. The Hague: Mouton.

Dalton, P. and Hardcastle, W.J. (1977) *Disorders of Fluency and their Effects on Communication*. London: Edward Arnold.

Darot, M. and Lebre-Peytard, M. (1983) Oral: les hésitations. *Le Français dans le Monde* 180, 102–4.

De Beaugrande, R. (1985) General constraints on process models of language comprehension. In A.M. Aitkenhead and J.M. Slock (eds) *Issues in Cognitive Modelling* (pp. 161–174). London: Lawrence Erlbaum.

Dechert, H.W. (1980) Pause and intonation as indicators of verbal planning in second-language speech productions: Two examples from a case study. In H.W. Dechert and M. Raupach (eds) *Temporal Variables in Speech* (pp. 271–85). The Hague: Mouton.

Dechert, H.W. (1984) Second language productions: Six hypotheses. In H.W. Dechert, D. Möhle and M. Raupach (eds), *Second Language Productions* (pp. 211–30). Tübingen: Gunter Narr.

Dechert H.W., Möhle, D. and Raupach M. (eds) (1984) *Second Language Productions*. Tübingen: Gunter Narr.

Dechert, H.W. and Raupach M. (eds) (1980) *Temporal Variables in Speech*. The Hague: Mouton.

Dechert, H.W. and Raupach, M. (eds) (1989) *Interlingual Processes*. Tübingen: Gunter Narr.

Djian, P. (1985) *37°2 le matin*. Paris: J'ai lu.

Duez, D. (1982) Silent and non-silent pauses in three speech styles. *Language and Speech* 25 (1), 11–28.

Ellis, R. (1985) *Understanding Language Acquisition*. Oxford: Oxford University Press.

Ellis, R. (1990) *Instructed Second Language Acquisition*. Oxford: Blackwell.

Faerch, C. and Kasper, G. (eds) (1983) *Strategies in Interlanguage Communication*. London: Longman.

Ferguson, C.A. (1971) Absence of copula and the notion of simplicity: A study of normal speech, baby talk, foreigner talk, and pidgins. In D. Hymes (ed.) *Pidginization and Creolization of Languages* (pp. 141–50). Cambridge: Cambridge University Press.

Ferguson, C.A. (1977) Baby talk as simplified register. In C.E. Snow and C.A. Ferguson (eds) *Talking to Children: Language Input and Acquisition* (pp. 209–35). Cambridge: Cambridge University Press.

Fillmore, C.J. (1979) On fluency. In C.J. Fillmore, D. Kempler and W.S.-Y. Wang (eds) *Individual Differences in Language Ability and Language Behavior* (pp. 85–101). New York: Academic Press.

Flores D'Arcais, G.B. and Schreuder, R. (1983) The process of language understanding: A few issues in contemporary psycholinguistics. In G.B. Flores d'Arcais and R.J. Jarvella (eds) *The Process of Language Understanding* (pp. 1–41). New York. John Wiley & Sons.

Fluharty, G.W. and Ross H.R. (1981) *Public Speaking and Other Forms of Speech Communication*. New York: Barnes and Noble.

Frauenfelder, U.H. and Tyler, L.K. (1987) *Spoken Word Recognition*. Cambridge, MA: MIT Press.

Garman, M. (1990) *Psycholinguistics*. Cambridge: Cambridge University Press.

Goldman-Eisler, F. (1964) Language and the science of man (discussion and further comments). In E.H. Lenneberg (ed.) *New Directions in the Study of Language* (pp. 109–30). Cambridge, MA: MIT Press.

Goldman-Eisler, F. (1968) *Psycholinguistic Experiments in Spontaneous Speech*. New York: Academic Press.

Gregg, K.R. (1984) Krashen's Monitor and Occam's razor. *Applied Linguistics* 5 (2), 79–100.

Grenfell, M. and Harris, V. (1993) How do pupils learn? (Part 1). *Language Learning Journal* 8, 22–5.

Grice, H.P. (1975) Logic and conversation. In P. Cole and J.L. Morgan (eds) *Syntax and Semantics*. Vol. 3 (Speech Acts) (pp. 41–58). London: Academic Press.

Griffith, R. (1991) Pausological Research in an L2 context: A rationale, and review of selected studies. *Applied Linguistics*, 12 (4), 345–64.

Grosjean, F. and Deschamps, A. (1975) Analyse contrastive des variables temporelles de l'anglais et du français: vitesse de parole et variables composantes, phénomèmes d'hésitations. *Phonetica* 31, 144–84.

Guillot, M-N. (1989) The concept of fluency: Its nature and applications in French oral classes at university level (unpublished doctoral dissertation).

Hall, E.T. (1966) *The Hidden Dimension*. New York: Doubleday.

Halliday, M.A.K. (1987) Spoken and written modes of meaning. In R. Horowitz and S.J. Samuels (eds) *Comprehending Oral and Written Language* (pp. 55–82). London: Academic Press.

Hammerly, H. (1991) *Fluency and Accuracy*. Clevedon: Multilingual Matters.
Handel, S. (1989) *Listening: An Introduction to the Perception of Auditory Events*. Cambridge, MA: MIT Press.
Harder, P. (1980) Discourse as self-expression — on the reduced personality of the second-language learner. *Applied Linguistics* I, 262–70.
Hatch, E. (1983) Simplified input and second language acquisition. In R.W. Andersen (ed.) *Pidginization and Creolization as Language Acquisition* (pp. 64–86). Rowley, MA: Newbury House Publishers.
Hieke, A.E. (1981) A content-processing view of hesitation phenomena. *Language and Speech* 24 (2), 147–60.
Horowitz, R. and Samuels, S.J. (eds) (1987) *Comprehending Oral and Written Language*. London: Academic Press.
Hurley, D.S. (1992) Issues in teaching pragmatics, prosody, and non-verbal communication. *Applied Linguistics* 13 (3), 259–80.
Hymes, D. (1972) On communicative competence. In J.B. Pride and J. Holmes (eds) *Sociolinguistics* (pp. 269–93). Harmondsworth: Penguin Books.
Jackson, H.J. (1988) *Words and their Meaning*. London: Longman.
Johnson, K. (1996) *Language and Skill Learning*. Oxford: Blackwell.
Kellerman, S. (1992) 'I see what you mean': The role of kinesic behaviour in listening and implications for foreign and second language learning. *Applied Linguistics* 13 (3), 239–58.
Kerbrat-Orecchioni, C. (1990) *Les Interactions Verbales (Tome I)*. Paris: Armand Colin.
Kerbrat-Orecchioni, C. (1994) *Les Interactions Verbales (Tome 3)*. Paris: Armand Colin.
Kess, J.F. (1992) *Psycholinguistics*. Amsterdam, PA: John Benjamins.
Krashen, S.D. (1977) The monitor model for adult second language performance. In M. Burt, H. Dulay and M. Finocchiario (eds) (1977) *Viewpoints on English as a Second Language* (pp. 152–61). New York: Regents.
Krashen, S.D. (1981) *Second Language Acquisition and Second Language Learning*. Oxford: Pergamon Press.
Krashen, S.D. (1982) *Principles and Practice in Second Language Acquisition*. Oxford: Pergamon Press.
Krashen, S.D. (1985) *The Input Hypothesis: Issues and Implications*. London: Longman.
Langford, D. (1994) *Analysing Talk*. London: Macmillan.
Languages Lead Body (1993) *National Language Standards*. London: Crown.
Languages Lead Body (1996) *The Revised National Language Standards*. London: Crown.
Larsen-Freeman, D. and Long, M.H. (1991) *An Introduction to Second Language Acquisition Research*. London: Longman.
Leeson, R. (1975) *Fluency and Language Teaching*. London: Longman.
Lennon, P. (1984) Retelling a story in English as a second language. In H.W. Dechert, D. Möhle and M. Raupach (eds) *Second Language Productions* (pp. 50–68). Tübingen: Gunter Narr.
Lennon, P. (1990) Investigating fluency in EFL: A quantitative approach. *Language Learning* 40 (3), 387–417.
Lennon, P. (1991) Error: Some problems of definition, identification, and distinction. *Applied Linguistics* 12 (2), 180–96.
Lhote, E. (1995) *Enseigner l'Oral en Interaction*. Paris: Hachette.
Local, J. (1992) Continuing and restarting. In P. Auer and A. Di Luzio (eds) *The Contextualization of Language* (pp. 273–96). Amsterdam, PA: John Benjamins.
Long, M.H. (1983a) Native speaker/non-native speaker conversation and the negotiation of comprehensible input. *Applied Linguistics* 4 (2), 126–41.

Long, M.H. (1983b) Native speaker/non-native speaker conversation in the second language classroom. In M. A. Clarke and J. Handscombe (eds) 1983. *On TESOL '82: Pacific Perspectives on Language Learning and Teaching* (pp. 207–25). Washington DC: TESOL.

Longman Dictionary of Contemporary English (1987) (first edition 1978). Harlow: Longman.

MacKay, D.G. (1987) Constraints on theories of sequencing and timing in language perception and production. In A. Allport, D. MacKay, W. Prinz and E. Scheerer (eds) *Language Perception and Production* (pp. 407–29). London: Academic Press.

Maclay, H. and Osgood C.E. (1959) Hesitation phenomena in spontaneous English speech. *Words* 15, 19–44.

Malim, T. (1994) *Cognitive Processes*. London: Macmillan.

Manser, M.H. and Turton, N.D. (1987) *The Penguin Wordmaster Dictionary*. Harmondsworth: Penguin Books.

Matasci-Galazzi, E. and Pedoya-Guimbretière, E. (1987) A l'écoute de Bernard Pivot: Une stratégie de hiérarchisation des informations par la prosodie. *Etudes de Linguistique Appliquée* 66, 106–17.

Matter, J. (1989) Some fundamental problems in understanding French as a foreign language. In H.W. Dechert and M. Raupach (eds) *Interlingual Processes* (pp. 105–19). Tübingen: Gunter Narr.

McCarthy, M. and Carter, R. (1994) *Language as Discourse*. London: Longman.

McLaughlin, B. (1978) The monitor model: Some methodological considerations. *Language Learning* 28 (2), 309–32

McLaughlin, B. (1987) *Theories of Second-Language Learning*. London: Edward Arnold.

McLaughlin, B., Rossman, T. and McLeod, B. (1983) Second language learning: An information processing perspective. *Language Learning* 33, 135–58.

McLaughlin, M.L. (1984) *Conversation: How Talk is Organized*. London: Sage.

Meikle, J. (1997) Smoothing the journey. *The Guardian Higher Education* July 15, iv.

Mermet, G. (1996) *Francoscopie 1997*. Paris: Larousse-Bordas.

Möhle, D. (1984) A comparison of the second language speech production of different native speakers. In H.W. Dechert, D. Möhle and M. Raupach (eds) *Second Language Productions* (pp. 26–49). Tübingen: Gunter Narr.

Möhle, D. and Raupach, H.W. (1989) Language transfer of procedural knowledge. In H.W. Dechert and M. Raupach (eds) *Transfer in Language Production* (pp. 195–216). Norwood NJ: Ablex.

Moore, B. (1982) *Introduction to the Psychology of Hearing*. London: Academic Press.

Morrison, D.M. and Low, G. (1983) Monitoring and the second language learner. In J.C. Richards and R. Schmidt (eds) *Language and Communication* (pp. 228–50). London: Longman.

Nation, P. (1989) Improving speaking fluency. *System* 17 (3), 377–84.

Nolasco, R. and Arthur, L. (1987) *Conversation*. Oxford: Oxford University Press.

O'Malley, J.M. and Uhl-Chamot, A. (1990) *Learning Strategies in Second Language Acquisition*. Cambridge: Cambridge University Press.

Oxford, R.L. (1989) Use of language learning strategies: A synthesis of studies with implications for strategy training. *System* 17 (2), 235–247.

Oxford English Dictionary (1961) (first published 1933). London: Oxford Clarendon Press.

Pawley, A. and Hodgetts Syder, F. (1983) Two puzzles for linguistic theory: Native-like selection and native-like fluency. In J.C. Richards and R. Schmidt (eds) *Language and Communication* (pp. 191–226). London: Longman.

Pennycook, A. (1985) Actions speak louder than words: Paralanguage, communication and education. *TESOL Quarterly* 19 (2), 259–82.

Pica, T. (1994) Research on negotiation: What does it reveal about second-language learning conditions, processes and outcomes? *Language Learning* 44 (3), 493–527.

Raupach, M. (1983) Analysis and evaluation of communication strategies. In C. Faerch and G. Kasper (eds) *Strategies in Interlanguage Communication* (pp. 199–209). London: Longman.

Richards J.C., Platt, J. and Weber, H. (1985) *Longman Dictionary of Applied Linguistics*. London: Longman.

Richards, J.C. and Schmidt, R.W. (eds) (1983) *Language and Communication*. London: Longman.

Riggenbach, H. (1991) Toward an understanding of fluency: A microanalysis of non-native speaker conversations. *Discourse Processes* 14, 423–41.

Rumelhart, D.E. and Norman, D.A. (1978) Accretion, tuning, and restructuring: Three modes of learning. In J. Cotton and R. Klatzky (eds) *Semantic Factors in Cognition* (pp. 37–53). Hillsdale NJ: Erlbaum.

Savignon, S. (1972) *Communicative Competence: An Experiment in Foreign Language Teaching*. Philadelphia: Center for Curriculum Development.

Schmidt, R. (1992) Psychological mechanisms underlying second language fluency. *SSLA* 14, 357–385.

Schuman, J.H. (1976) Second language acquisition: The pidginization hypothesis. *Language Learning* 26 (2), 391–408.

Schwitalla, J. (1992) Comments on Margret Selting: Intonation as a contextualisation device. In P. Auer and A. di Luzio (eds) *The Contextualization of Language* (pp. 259–71). Amsterdam, PA: John Benjamins.

Selting, M. (1992) Intonation as a contextualizing device: Case studies on the role of prosody, especially intonation, in contextualizing story telling in conversation. In P. Auer and A. Di Luzio (eds) *The Contextualization of Language* (pp. 233–58). Amsterdam, PA: John Benjamins.

Skehan, P. (1989) *Individual Differences in Second-Language Learning*. London: Edward Arnold.

Smith, A.H. and O'Loughlin, J.L.N. (1946) *Odhams Dictionary of the English Language*.

Spolsky, B. (1989) Communicative competence, language proficiency, and beyond. *Applied Linguistics* 10 (2), 138–54.

Stenström, A.-B. (1994) *An Introduction to Spoken Interaction*. London: Longman.

Swain, M. (1985) Communicative competence: Some roles of comprehensible input and comprehensible output in its development. In S.M. Gass and C.G. Madden (eds) *Input in Second Language Acquisition* (pp. 235–53). Rowley, MA: Newbury House Publishers.

Swain, M. (1995) Three functions of output in second language learning. In G. Cook and B. Seidelhofer (eds) *Principles and Practice in Applied Linguistics* (pp. 125–44). Oxford: Oxford University Press.

Tannen, D. (1989) *Talking Voices*. Cambridge: Cambridge University Press.

Tarone, E. (1980) Communication strategies, foreigner talk and repair in interlanguage. *Language Learning* 30 (1), 417–31.

Tarone, E. (1983) Some thoughts on the notion of communicative strategies. In C. Faerch and G. Kasper (eds) *Strategies in Interlanguage Communication* (pp. 61–74). London: Longman. First published in *TESOL Quarterly* (1981) 15, 285–95.

Taylor, T.J. and Cameron D. (1987) *Analysing Conversation: Rules and Units in the Structure of Talk*. Oxford: Pergamon Press.

Temple, L. (1985) He who hesitates is not lost: Fluency and the language learner. *Revue de Phonétique Appliquée* 73/75, 299–302.

Towell, R. (1987) Variability and progress in the language development of advanced learners of a foreign language. In R. Ellis (ed.) *Second Language Acquisition in Context* (pp. 113–127). London: Prentice-Hall International.

Towell, R. and Hawkins, R. (1994) *Approaches to Second Language Acquisition*. Clevedon: Multilingual Matters.

Towell, R., Hawkins, R. and Bazergui, N. (1996) The development of fluency in advanced learners of French. *Applied Linguistics* 17 (1), 84–119.

Traverso, V. (1996) *La Conversation Familière*. Lyon: Presses Universitaires de Lyon.

Uhmann, S. (1992) Contextualizing relevance: On some forms and functions of speech rate changes in everyday conversation. In P. Auer and A. Di Luzio (eds) *The Contextualization of Language* (pp. 297–336). Amsterdam, PA: John Benjamins.

Van Dijk, T.A. (1987) Episodic models in discourse processing. In R. Horowitz and S.J. Samuels (eds) *Comprehending Oral and Written Language* (pp. 161–96). London: Academic Press.

Van Dijk, T.A. and Kintsch, W. (1983) *Strategies of Discourse Comprehension*. New York: Academic Press.

Wagner, J. (1983) Dann du tagen eineeeee — weisse Platte — an analysis of interlanguage communication in instructions. In C. Faerch and G. Kasper (eds) *Strategies in Interlanguage Communication* (pp. 159–74). London: Longman.

Widdowson, H.G. (1983) *Learning Purpose and Language Use*. Oxford: Oxford University Press.

Widdowson, H.G. (1989) Knowledge of language and ability for use. *Applied Linguistics* 10(2), 128–137.

Widdowson, H.G. (1990) *Aspects of Language Teaching*. Oxford: Oxford University Press.

Wiese, R. (1984) Language production in foreign and native languages: Same or different? In W. Dechert, D. Möhle and M. Raupach (eds) *Second Language Productions* (pp. 11–25). Tübingen: Gunter Narr.

Wilson, D. (1994) Relevance and understanding. In G. Brown, K. Malmkjaer, A. Pollitt and J. Williams (eds) *Language and Understanding* (pp. 35–58). Oxford: Oxford University Press.

Wioland, F. (1991) *Prononcer les Mots du Français*. Paris: Hachette.

Wioland, F. and B.J. Wenk (1983) Prenez le temps. Pour faire "Français", pensez au rythme! *Le Français dans le Monde* 172, 79–83.

Index

Note: Highly recurrent terms (e.g. [oral] fluency, production) are not included in this index.

178